THE 100 GREATEST AMERICAN CARS

BY JAN P. NORBYE

TAB TAB BOOKS Inc.
BLUE RIDGE SUMMIT, PA. 17214

FIRST EDITION

SECOND PRINTING

Printed in the United States of America

Library of Congress Cataloging in Publication Data

Norbye, Jan P
    The 100 greatest American cars.

    Includes index.
    1. Automobiles—United States—History.
I. Title.
TL23.N67   629.2′222′0973   80-28860
ISBN 0-8306-9623-7
ISBN 0-8306-2071-0 (pbk.)

Cover courtesy of Siskin Enterprises, Inc.
1979 South 700 West
Salt Lake City, Utah 84104

Acknowledgements

While the opinions expressed in this book are entirely my own, and I am solely responsible for the selection of the cars, it would not have been possible to illustrate the book without the invaluable help of many friends and supporters.

Infinite thanks are due to James J. Bradley, Curator of the National Automotive History Collection, Detroit Public Library, for his valiant efforts, fruitful beyond expectation, to dig out photos of many rare vehicles.

I wish to express particular gratitude to Richard A. Teague, director of design, American Motors Corporation, for sending me pictures of the cars in his private collection, and to Al Rothenberg of the Motor Vehicle Manufacturers Association for supplying photographs from the association's archives.

I am greatly indebted to L. Scott Bailey, president of Automobile Quarterly Publications, Princeton, New Jersey, for his kind permission to reprint photos used on Automobile Quarterly calendars.

Many thanks to William S. Jackson of Hummelstown, Pennsylvania, and Kenneth H. Stauffer of Pottstown, Pennsylvania, for their kindness in letting me use some of their photos which originally appeared in The Antique Automobile.

A special word of thanks to John A. Conde, Curator, Henry Ford Museum, Dearborn, Michigan, for making pictures from the museum's files available for this book.

I am extremely grateful to the following public relations officials who took great pains in supplying me with photographs of past products of their companies or ancestor firms:

Gene Swaim of American Motors for Hudson and Nash pictures;

Tom Jacobowski of Chrysler Corporation for Chrysler and Imperial pictures; John N. Woodford and Robert H. Harnar of the Ford Motor Company for Ford and Lincoln pictures;

Miss P. Montgomery of Cadillac Motor Car Division for Cadillac and La Salle pictures;

Thomas A. Pond of Buick Motor Division for Buick pictures;

Fritz B. Bennetts of Oldsmobile Division for Oldsmobile pictures; and Stanley C. Richards of Pontiac Motor Division for Pontiac pictures.

To all, I wish to say that without their help, this book would not be what it is, and I express my hope that they will approve of the manner in which their material has been used. It is also my wish that they will find something of interest in the text.

Jan P. Norbye

Contents

Foreword

Going down memory lane with fellow car enthusiasts is one of my favorite pastimes, and though it sometimes leads to argument over the relative merits of one car as measured against another, these discussions are often enlightening and advance one's knowledge of the subject.

Talks of this kind rarely lead to a unanimous conclusion: most participants go away holding the same opinions they came in with. And perhaps that is as it should be. We do not get together and talk about cars with the aim of achieving anything but sharing an interest, trading observations, and developing a genial companionship. Rarely do we argue to convince others to change their minds. It may be true if one man says, "My Blooper Bluebell Breezeway is superior to your Bleeper Boggledoon B-7 in every way." And if it's true—on the basis of the facts, (i.e.) specifications, performance, etc.—then it's usually accepted without argument.

Retrospect tends to make all cars shine a little brighter. We are more tolerant of their shortcomings when they are not used for our daily transport. Our minds are then free to concentrate on their good points and build up the reputations of our favorite cars, hopefully winning them a place of respect in the community of car lovers.

This is a book for people who love cars. I have always loved cars—big cars, small cars, sports cars, family cars, luxury cars, long cars and short cars, low cars, and tall cars, open cars and closed cars, fast cars and slow cars, gorgeous-looking cars and plain-looking cars.

Cars, like men, are not created equal. Two cars, designed by different men and built in different places, with different materials and methods, are by nature different. These differences are fascinating to auto enthusiasts and we go to extreme lengths to acquire knowledge and understanding of them.

And we talk about them. Mention some old name that has been forgotten by all but the most hard-bitten core of auto historians, and someone, probably with an imperfect memory of what it was, will say something like, "Now there was a great car."

Whether their greatness is real or imagined, great cars get talked about more than ordinary cars. You never hear a conversation at an old car meet, or anywhere else for that matter, where one guy recalls "My Dad used to own a 1933 Hartley Hotspur," only to have his interlocutor retort "Yeah, now there was an ordinary car."

The ordinary tends to be boring, while the unusual and outstanding attracts our attention and perhaps elicits our admiration. Greatness in cars of all ages is much admired by car lovers of all ages. However, greatness is not perceived in the same manner by all of us, and that is why it is necesaary for me to explain how I see greatenss and try to reach some sort of definition. It is also necessary to keep in mind that not all cars were built in pursuit of greatness. In fact, most cars were not. Most cars have been built to provide transportation their buyers could afford, and do it will enough to keep its maker in business.

From this fact we see there is a note of exclusivity implied in the term "greatness" as applied to cars. The great car is not likely to be one that a large number of customers can afford. On the other hand, I have absolutely ruled out a high price as a qualification for greatness. A car selling at a relatively low price can be a greater masterpiece than all the expensive ones of its period. A low price must not stop us from recognizing greatness in the intelligence of its concept, trendsetting engineering, or influence on the evolution of design and public taste.

But those criteria are not enough to qualify a car as being great. And the reflection that cars must be compared with others of their period leads to the realization that the definition of greatness may vary from one epoch to another. The ingredients of automotive greatness are certainly not the same in 1980 as they were in 1930. They have changed several times in that 50-year time span. In earlier times, people had other priorities and other preoccupations, and the qualities that made a car great changed in an evolutionary pattern from the birth of the industry until the car had been accepted throughout the nation as every man's means of personal mobility.

Emphasis on sales success and mass production have colored all written accounts of America's automobile history. The fascinating story of the American auto industry's production race is in some respects the history of the automobile in the western hemisphere. Yet it is not the complete history, for there were important car manufacturers who stayed out of the production race by choice. This must not be taken as a statement to the effect that they were unable to compete.

They were indeed competing—and competitive. It's just that their mode of competition differed fundamentally in its nature and expression. Every car offered for sale is a compromise, and any hard-boiled observer will say it's a compromise between quality and price. The leaders in the production race were forced to compromise quality. Other auto makers were content to sacrifice quantity and strive for a maximum of quality.

The quality of an automobile is a complex subject. One car can contain elements of both very low and very high quality. But the overall quality of a car? Can it be identified? Can it be measured? There are no standards, and there never were, except in the minds of the responsible engineers. Every chief engineer of an automobile company competing in the quality car market must have set certain standards for what was acceptable, and what was not. The precise levels would be determined by his own ideals (and those of the company's management) plus their perception of the quality levels generally maintained by their competitors.

The necessity to prosper, which means the company's need to make a profit, worked as a regulator with regard to ideals, and kept them from getting too far removed from realities of the market place.

Even in the quality car market, manufacturers felt the need to maintain a certain volume of production to control unit cost. In no case were cars truly built "regardless of cost." Quality was always balanced against price. The price had to be low enough to attract a sufficient number of customers to enable the factory to operate with an output high enough to bring a profit.

Several American automobile engineers with high ideals were fortunate enough to serve under, or as members of, managements that were sympathetic to those ideals. Some even had enough power within their corporations to assert their ideals in the face of opposition from directors whose outlook centered on profitability to the exclusion of all other facets of other operations.

High ideals imply greatness in work. What does that mean, in terms of product? First of all it means a basic design of a certain size, weight and appearance. It means high standards for quality of raw materials, purchased components, workmanship, and inspection. It means a presence of quality in areas that are meaningful to the customer. The buyer may not understand engineering, or aerodynamics, but knows about ride comfort, ease of driving, noise and vibration, and all aspects of performance (acceleration, top speed, fuel consumption). To produce a successful quality car, something more was needed than just the motivation to build such a vehicle. At all stages of creating a car it involved a set of characteristics that can be summed up in a word: *skill.*

Skill is an important ingredient in every field of human endeavor. Skill is not acquired with ease, or quickly, but comes to an individual as a by-product of industry, perseverence, ambition, and the application of intelligence. You cannot become skilled by merely deciding to be skilled; it takes time and effort. You become a skilled swimmer not just by swimming a lot, but by consciously working to improve your swimming techniques. The same applies to skiing, skating, and riding a bicycle.

There is no difference between skills used in spare time activities and skills used in professions. The point I wish to make is that skill comes essentially with experience. The blacksmith with twenty years' experience is on the average a better blacksmith than the one who has five years' experience. Parallel situations existed in the areas of tinkers and wheelwrights, cobblers and armorers.

The medieval guilds made it a major part of their functions to reward seniority in the trade, because seniority, by their definition, was synonymous with higher skill. The industrial revolution changed nothing as far as the value of skill was concerned. Skills changed, and new professions were created. The typical machinist of the 1850's, in fact, improved his skill at an accelerated pace, due to the arrival of higher-precision tools.

Skill in automotive engineering and design did not exist at the birth of the industry. When the automobile was invented, there were no automobile engineers around. Many of the auto pioneers were self-taught, others came from the technological institutes that had traditionally formed the engineering minds of America's armaments, railroad, shipbuilding and construction industries. Automotive engineering was not made a specific subject until several generations of car designers had graduated, usually as mechanical or electrical engineers.

The design engineer's tools are grouped around his drawing board, and his skills are far more abstract than the artisan's with imagination playing a great part. He is working at a higher intellectual level. But the men who built America's earliest cars had little or no experience in actually working at the job of designing cars.

A long time went by from the day the first automobile took to the road until the day when the first *good* automobile was built. It was a longer way still to the day when the first GREAT automobile was created.

The difficulties of building cars loomed so large in the early days of the industry that I still find it surprising that truly great cars came into being as early as they did, despite the hopes, ambitions and aspirations of the pioneering auto engineers. They had no higher wish than to build great cars. When automotive engineering was still practically uncharted territory, there was quality competition in all price classes.

High-priced cars made faster advances in quality than lower-priced cars, however. There are many reasons for this. Makers of high-priced cars could afford more expensive materials. They could be lavish with special steels, light alloys, fine wood, leather, and so on. They could use ball and roller bearings where plain bearings were usually considered good enough. They spent more money on research, testing, development, redesign. This in turn would affect the engineer working under the privileged conditions that a bigger budget assured. His sense of accomplishment would be gratified. Demonstrably, performing quality work heightened job satisfaction, and spurred him on to new feats in the quest for quality.

It's useless to pretend, in view of the foregoing, that the first American cars were "great." The poineers, regardless of chronology, such as Duryea, Haynes, Nadig, and Lambert were just searching for a workable automobile, but not a great one.

The same goes for Henry Ford and most of his contemporaries, even though some made a closer approach to the concept of the GREAT car than others. The pioneers of the great cars were progressive thinkers, always exploring new ideas to endow their next automobiles with greater quality, speed, comfort, luxury and safety than existing examples. The great American car was born out of the desire of such men to build the absolute best in automobiles.

Quality and reliability were the paramount considerations, taking precedence over all others, but not to the exclusion of others mentioned above. Quality and reliability are still indispensable priorities. Of course, over the years customers' demands have grown exponentially with the accomplishments achieved by the car makers. Lack of quality and reliability was a principal cause of the high failure rate among auto manufacturers prior to 1915. Cars that excelled in the area of quality and reliability acquired a reputation for greatness.

As the car-buying clientele became more discerning and critical of cars, their demands for space and comfort, power and speed increased. Their concept of safety was still quite primitive, centering on concern for brakes that worked, steering linkages that did not break, wheels that did not fall off, and so on. Safety was not separated in people's minds from basic quality and reliability.

Requirements in the way of comfort were often confused with the spaciousness of the seating. Luxury entered the picture with the arrival of closed bodywork, judged by the standards of fine furniture and the art and decoration of private houses at the time. Space and luxury soon became essential requirements for a car's chances of being recognized as possessing greatness.

Without power and speed, few people would consider a car as being great. Increasingly, the demand for brute power was modified by the public's desire for silent, odorless, and vibration-free power. These considerations surfaced as early as 1910 and by 1940 had become as important as the power itself.

Ease of driving was not required of the great cars for many years. Simplifying the driving task was a major concern among builders of low-priced, mass-produced cars, and Oldsmobile advertised its Curved Dash model with the slogan "Nothing to Watch but the Road," in an attempt to appeal to inexperienced drivers.

But the men who bought great cars were sportsmen, and proud of their skill in driving these cars. Many of the pioneering great cars were chauffeur-driven, by paid servants who had no business complaining about the complicated controls and the frequent need for adjustments and maintenance.

Improvements in ease of driving flowed from the low end of the market to the high until the mid-1920's, and then the situation was slowly reversed, as more women began taking the wheel themselves. After automatic spark advance came the automatic choke; power brakes were followed by power steering, and automatic transmissions came in to render skill with clutch and gearshift unnecessary. Thus the social evolution affected the concept and makeup of the great car.

Throughout the era of cheap gasoline, fuel mileage was not a matter of concern for buyers of great American automobiles. Many lived in a total unawareness of how many miles their cars could run on a gallon of fuel.

In the light of our present objectives, with the efficient use of energy at the head of the list, it is not only justifiable but logical to award progress in fuel economy by introducing it as a consideration for qualifying as a great car. Not as miles-per-gallon per se, or as a percentage gain over a preceding model, instead, I propose to give an edge to great cars that anticipated fuel-saving ways in one way or another, from better engines to weight-saving design and better aerodynamics.

No attempt will be made here to identify THE greatest American car of all time. My readers will no doubt have their own candidates for that title.

Since I have ventured to select the 100 greatest, however, I should explain some of the restrictions imposed on the entries. Some restriction was felt to be necessary in order to avoid comparisons between cars of widely different types, built for widely different purposes. Consequently, eligibility was reduced to cars built for four to six passengers (or having chassis capable of being fitted with such bodywork). Open cars are admissible for the 1905-1915 period, in keeping with the practice of the time, but later models must have been available with closed bodies.

Above all, we are dealing strictly with production cars, manufactured for sale to the public. Experimental cars, prototypes, and privately built "one-of" specials are excluded.

As a leading criterion for selection as one of the 100 greatest cars, I have adhered to a rule which states that the car's creators must have had aspirations of greatness. That rule implies a deliberate striving for perfection within the limits of the possible—possibilities varying from company to company and from year to year. And it must have succeeded in reaching greatness to the extent of surpassing the average by a wide margin, as measured against the priorities of its time. Perhaps this rule does eliminate many good, interesting, and worthy cars, but at least my reasons have now been made clear.

Ford's Model T had greatness of a kind but that's not the greatness that has guided the selection of these 100 cars. The T-head Mercer and the Stutz Bearcat were great cars, but they were great only as sports cars, and therefore outside the scope of this book. Ford's first V-8 was sensational rather than great mostly because of the engine. Great cars must have a balanced, general greatness; not just one or two elements of greatness. For the same reason, cars like the 1953 Studebaker, whose excellence lay in one single area (body design) have been eliminated. And why isn't the Chrysler Airflow one of the 100 Greatest? For all its innovations, it failed in the one area in which it was designed to excel; it didn't have a much lower air drag than the standard Chrysler body.

As a final word of apology to those readers who may wish to dispute my selection, I must say that I do not expect my tentative definition of greatness to withstand the test of time any better than the list of cars I have chosen. There is an element of personal preference in my selections. Like other car enthusiasts, I have my favorites. On the other hand, I have acted in the interest of obtaining greater variety by choosing a number of lesser known cars when Packard, for instance, year for year, would have had a perfectly palatable contender, perhaps even a preferable choice, but a car too similar to another Packard already described or coming up later in the chronology. With that, I leave the reader to start his examination of the cars, appropriately, with a Packard.

Chapter 1
The Birth of the Great
American Car: 1904 to 1910

The Packard model L is undoubtedly America's first great car (Fig. 1-1). It was made in Detroit, giving that city a claim to the title of home of cars of quality, besides being the center of the nation's auto industry. It was a product of the Packard Motor Car Company, which moved the business from Warren, Ohio, where James Ward Packard had operated as the Ohio Automobile Company.

1. PACKARD MODEL L, 1904

J. W. Packard was 36 years old when he built his first car. Together with his brother, William Doud Packard, he was at that time running a small electrical-equipment shop in Warren, and according to legend, he was determined to build his own car in order to have more reliable and satisfactory transportation than his Winton offered. Thus, it can be seen that he did not start out with the idea of building cars on an industrial scale.

Among his qualifications, J. W. Packard had a degree in mechanical engineering from Lehigh University from which he was graduated in 1884. But that was not enough. He needed help in the form of skill at this new, unknown task of automaking. Leaving pride and idealism aside, he lured two experienced engineers, George L. Weiss and W. A. Hatcher, away from Winton. With these men, the Packard brothers built the first Packard car. It was a spindly machine—a wire-wheeled, tiller-steered, single seater powered by a single-clyinder engine delivering 9 hp at 800 rpm.

Not the sort of stuff of which greatness is made, one might think. And yet it was the start of Packard's climb to greatness. For

Fig. 1-1. The 1904 Packard Model L Roadster.

his little car was noticed for its dependability, and customers traced it to the electric shop, entered Packard's office, and demanded that he build cars just like it for them. Packard agreed, and formed the Ohio Automobile Company.

By 1902 the Packard car left its birthplace in Warren, Ohio and moved to Detroit. That happened because a leading Detroit businessman, Henry B. Joy, became impressed with the Packard car in 1901 and not only bought Packard cars but also invested in the Packard Electrical Company. He saw the Packard car as an excellent business proposition in view of its appeal and the ever-growing demand for it, and determined to get the Packard into series production. The Packard factory in Detroit was much larger than the shop in Warren with two acres of floor space and a work force of 247 men.

From the moment operations began in Detroit, Joy dominated the scene, though J. W. Packard held the title of president. Joy chose the position of factory manager for himself, and hired Joseph Boyer to handle the company's business affairs.

Joy also understood that the market for single-cylinder cars, while still expanding, was not likely to assure long-term prosperity for Packard. Not content with the idea of a two-cylinder engine, he wanted to jump right to the four-cylinder car. But J. W. Packard disagreed. He saw the single-cylinder engine, with all its simplicity, as the main reason for the reliability of the Packard car, and was loathe to change the formula. Naturally, it was Joy's will that prevailed, and he engaged a European engineer with experience in automobile design for the specific purpose of creating a new four-cylinder model.

It's undeniable that in the early days, there was profound European influence in the evolution of the great American car. Some fine cars from this side of the Atlantic were even built under license from European builders, others were unauthorized copies drawn up by American engineers, and some were designed by European engineers for American manufacturers.

The Packard belongs in the latter category, with its own "in-house" French designer. This was Charles Schmidt, who had worked under Henri Brasier as an engineer with Automobiles Mors in Paris.

Schmidt's first design for Packard was the four-cylinder Model K of 1903. Very few were made. The prototype was not fully satisfactory to Henry B. Joy, and J. W. Packard also had his say in the matter. By dint of steady work, it was transformed into a highly refined car which became the Model L.

Every European auto engineer of the time had been entranced by the 1901 Mercedes, which effectively set the pattern for car design and architecture for more than a decade. The Model L Packard followed its general layout, with a low-slung, pressed-steel frame supported by well-spaced front and rear axles. Longitudinal, semi-elliptic leaf springs were used at the rear end, while the front axle had a transverse leaf spring.

The engine sat in front, under a fashionably long hood. In contrast with Mercedes and Mors practice, Schmidt rejected the chain-driven rear axle in favor of a shaft-drive system.

The transmission was of the sliding gear type with three forward speeds and reverse, having direct drive on top gear. The driver worked a quadrant shift with a separate lever for reverse gear.

Along with Apperson, Packard was first to adopt the internal-expanding cone clutch, in 1904. The clutch was attached to the engine flywheel, and a propeller shaft took the drive to the three-speed transmission, which was combined with the final drive and differential gears in an extension of the rear axle casing. It could well be said that with this design Schmidt had invented the ancestor of the modern transaxle.

The driving thrust was taken up by a radius rod from the transmission to a cross member on the frame. Brake drums were mounted in rear wheels, with internal-expanding shoes worked by the brake pedal, and an external-contracting band acting on the same drum, operated from the emergency brake lever.

Schmidt showed less originality in his engine design, preferring not to stray from the known and successful principles of leading European makes.

The Packard four-cylinder engine had cylinders cast in pairs with integral L-heads and water jackets. All valves were mechanically operated from a gear-driven camshaft. At this time, suction-operated inlet valves were still quite common on both sides of the Atlantic. The crankshaft ran in three main bearings and had no counterweights. Engine balance was evidently not one of Schmidt's foremost areas of expertise. For its time, however, the Packard engine, bolted rigidly to the frame, was considered smooth.

With its 3.875-inch bore and a stroke of 5.125 inches, it had a displacement of 242 cubic inches. It delivered 20 hp at 750 rpm. These figures are quite modest, and show that Schmidt sought to satisfy J. W. Packard on the question of reliability by keeping the engine running at stress levels well below safe limits. The driver controlled the speed by something closely akin to a modern accelerator.

Packard used a pedal-operated inlet-valve governor to control engine speed up to its maximum of 850 rpm. It also had an ignition governor which automatically advanced or retarded the spark in accordance with the motion of a cam guided by a sliding sleeve on the camshaft, actuated by a centrifugal governor. This device was based on a J. W. Packard patent from 1901.

Packard's Model L had a radiator grille with the beginnings of a fluted pattern, which stretched back along the full length of the hood—a sculptured design that came to be regarded as a Packard trademark (Fig. 1-2).

The car had right-hand drive, with handbrake and gearshift levers mounted outside. Hand throttle and spark advance were carried on the steering wheel, and a bulb horn was attached to the side of the driver's seat. Acetylene headlamps were mounted on either side of the cowl.

The usual body was an open four-seater, with entrance to the back seat from the curb side only. Instead of a running board, which filled the space between front and rear fenders on the right, the left side had a toolbox and exhaust muffler. No front doors were fitted, the cockpit being open down to the floorboards.

Charles Schmidt was a keen driver, and made headlines in Detroit by setting a world's non-stop record by driving a Model L for 1,000 miles in 29 hours 53 minutes and 37.6 seconds on the Grosse Pointe track on August 6-8, 1904. That comes out to an average of almost 34 mph.

As a demonstration of its reliability, in September 1904 a Model L Packard was driven 506 miles from Los Angeles to San Francisco, crossing the coastal mountains several times and fording a number of rivers, carrying four persons and 150 pounds of baggage, in a running time of 38 hours 42 minutes.

Packard produced 200 cars during 1904, but the company reputedly lost $200,000 on the Model L, which was replaced by the Model N in 1905, a car which resembled it closely, and also failed to bring a profit, despite a rise in production to 700 cars.

2. COLUMBIA, 1904

America's second great car was also built in 1904, by the Electric Vehicle Company of Hartford, Connecticut. Despite the name of the company, it was not a battery-driven car, but one which had a four-cylinder gasoline engine (Fig. 1-3).

This company was one of the many industrial subsidiaries held directly or indirectly by Colonel Albert A. Pope of the Pope Manufacturing Company.

Fig. 1-2. Another 1904 Packard Model L, this one a sedan.

For some years, Albert A. Pope was king of the American bicycle industry. A Bostonian by birth, he fought on the Union side in the Civil War, and built his industrial enterprises with three thousand dollars he had saved from his soldier's pay. In the 1890's he branched out into steel-making, rubber and tires, and electric vehicles. By the turn of the century, Pope companies were producing an impressive line of electrically driven vehicles under the Columbia trademark.

The gasoline-powered Columbia was the creation of a brilliant young man, Hiram Percy Maxim. In 1892, at the age of 23, he turned his attention from weaponry to automobiles. He was the son of Hiram Stevens Maxim, inventor of the Maxim rapid-firing gun, and a nephew of Hudson Maxim, the inventor of smokeless gunpowder. After graduating from the Massachusetts Institute of Technology, he went to work for the American Projectile Company in Lynn, Massachusetts.

In 1895, after three years of studies and experimentation, he installed a gasoline engine in a Columbia tricycle. In July of that year he was invited to join the Motor Carriage Department of the Pope group in Hartford, Connecticut, where the first Columbia electric vehicles were being produced. That same year Colonel Pope ordered Maxim to develop a gasoline-powered automobile.

A prototype was built in 1903, with a two-cylinder engine and chain drive. While it was not a copy of any existing vehicle, American or European, it did not show much originality. It resembled other, typical cars of its day, as if Maxim had derived a synthesis of current practice. This model went into production early in 1904, while Maxim was busy on a more ambitious design. It was to be a four-cylinder touring car incorporating the most modern features then coming into use.

The result was a magnificent car that looked not unlike the Decauville, a French machine built in Corbeil, a few miles from Paris, and was recognized as being of advanced concept and construction without slavishly following the Mercedes layout. (Before Henry Royce built his first car, he bought, tested and examined a Decauville.)

Maxim placed the engine in the front end of the frame, but set it well back from the front axle, leaving room for a coil-type radiator low down between the dumb-irons. A cone clutch was coupled to the flywheel, and a shaft took the drive to a centrally located four-speed transmission of the sliding-gear type. It had a

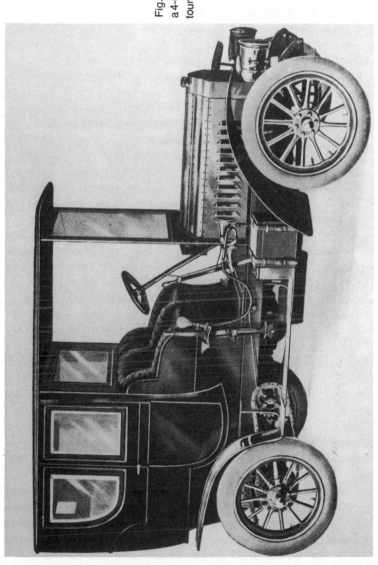

Fig. 1-3. The 1904 Columbia a 4-cylinder, gasoline powered touring car.

quadrant shift and drove a jackshaft mounted transversely in the chassis and carrying sprockets for chain drive to the rear wheels.

The rear wheels were free-wheeling on the axle, with their hubs anchored to the drive sprockets. This system allowed the engine to return to idle when the car was coasting, which reduced wear and tear on the engine and drive line, and made a contribution to saving fuel (although that was not considered important by either Maxim or Columbia's customers).

No doubt it threw a heavier burden on the brakes, but Maxim had taken that into account. The drive sprockets carried big service-brake drums, and auxiliary brakes worked on separate drums mounted in the rear wheel hubs.

Roads were generally poor, even in New England, and Maxim paid due attention to assuring mobility even in case of partial drive-line failure. The final drive unit was designed so that the differential gears could be locked, enabling the car to be driven by one wheel in case one of the chains should break.

The four-cylinder Columbia engine delivered 24 hp at 900 rpm from a displacement of 393 cubic inches. It had "square" cylinder dimensions, with 5-inch bore and stroke. Interestingly, Columbia's twin actually had oversquare cylinders, with a shorter (4½-inch) stroke and the same 5-inch bore. The makers claimed 14 hp for the twin.

For 1905, Maxim designed an enlarged version of the same engine, rated at 36 hp, and led the gasoline-driven car engineering department through its most successful years. But Maxim left Columbia in 1907, and went into partnership with T. W. Goodridge (former general manger of Studebaker Automobile Company) to manufacture electric vehicles in Hartford under the trade name Lenox. After about two years, this business folded.

Maxim drifted out of the auto industry after the Maxim-Goodridge failure. For many years he worked as a motor engineer with Westinghouse Electric & Manufacturing Company. Later, he turned his mind to acoustical inventions. He perfected a silencer for aircraft engines in 1928 and was also the inventor of the Maxim silencer for small firearms. Maxim died at the age of 67 in 1936.

As for the fate of the Columbia car, it upheld its reputation as a high-quality product long after Maxim's departure. But in 1909, Colonel Pope died and his industrial empire split up. The Electric Vehicle Company was swallowed up by Benjamin Briscoe's United States Motor Compnay in 1910, incorporating Columbia, Maxwell, Stoddard-Dayton, Alden Sampson, and Brush. After the collapse of U. S. Motor Co. in 1913, the only survivor was the Maxwell.

3. LOCOMOBILE TYPE D, 1904

Curiously, the third of America's great cars also came from New England and has indirect links with Pope and the Columbia. It was built at Chicopee, Massachusetts, by the Locomobile Company of America (Fig. 1-4).

The 1904 Locomobile was designed by Andrew L. Riker, a 35-year-old engineer educated at Columbia University, New York City. He had come to Locomobile as vice president and chief engineer in 1902 after four years with Pope's Electric Vehicle Company, producer of Columbia cars.

It was his electrical engineering background that first brought him into the auto industry. As early as 1884 he had built an electric tricycle, and during his years as proprietor of the independent Riker Electric Motor Company, the dream of building cars never left him. He produced his first four-wheeled vehicle in 1895, and three years later formed the Riker Motor Vehicle Company, which he sold to Pope's organization in 1900 for two million dollars. Pope hired Riker as superintendent of the Electric Vehicle Company in Hartford, but Riker left in 1901 after a disagreement with the president, George H. Day, and Hiram Percy Maxim.

The Locomobile Company was then making steam cars in the former Stanley plant at Newton, Massachusetts, to designs by F. E. and F. O. Stanley (who had sold their Stanley Steamer patents and signed a contract to keep out of the auto industry for a 10-year period). The Locomobile Company was owned by Amzi L. Barber, who installed Samuel T. Davis, Jr. as general manager. It was Davis who saw the coming demise of the steam car and took steps to add a line of gasoline-powered models to the product range. Locomobile had completed about 5,000 steam cars over a four-year period, when the gasoline models were added.

Davis, son-in-law of Amzi Barber, became president of Locomobile in 1902. He had a degree in civil engineering from Rensselaer Polytechnic Institute, and was a leader in America's auto industry until his death in 1915 at the age of 42.

It was Davis who hired Riker to direct the design and construction of the gasoline-powered Locomobile at the beginning of 1902. In 1903 Locomobile had taken over a plant at Chicopee, Massachusetts from the defunct Victor Automobile Company and Riker retooled it for his new car.

The Type D engine delivered 16 hp at 900 rpm in its original form. Bore and stroke were 4 × 5 inches, giving 251 cubic inch displacement.

Fig. 1-4. Locomobile Type D, 1904, designed by Andrew Riker.

Riker's four-cylinder engine for the Locomobile Type D was cast in pairs, with integral heads, valve chambers, and water jackets. It was an F-head design with automatic inlet valves positioned face to face with side exhaust valves operated from a camshaft running below the valve chambers.

This valve gear may seem like a retrograde step, since mechanically operated inlet valves were coming into use but Riker probably chose this setup because the Type D was created as a pair of existing two-cylinder engines on a common crankcase. Later in 1904, Riker redesigned the engine with pushrod and rocker arm actuation of the inlet valves, and power output increased to 20 hp.

The engine had a two-piece crankcase, with its upper part (from the lower edge of the cylinder to the crankshaft center line) made of bronze. The lower crankcase, serving as oil sump, was made of aluminum.

A one-piece crankshaft was used, running in three main bearings. A gear on the camshaft drove the water pump and electric generator. Coil and battery ignition was used, with a separate trembler coil for each cylinder. There was an oil reservoir outside the crankcase, and a centrifugal oil pump. The lubrication system was intended to provide a steady flow of oil, with splash lubrication of the cylinder walls, which had an overflow groove leading to vertical return lines. An air-heater connection from the exhaust pipe to the carburetor base provided a hot-spot for warming the

24

mixture. This was a very forward-looking device which did not come into general use until many years later.

Riker also invented a centrifugal governor which automatically throttled the air intake and retarded the spark. It was mechanically driven from the water-pump and generator shaft, and had a simple linkage to the carburetor. A manual throttle control was operated from a lever on the steering wheel.

The gearshift was sequential, working in a quadrant. The driver's right hand had to work both gearshift and emergency brake levers. The car had a modern pedal arrangement with a clutch pedal to the left of the steering column and a brake pedal to the right, with a throttle-control pedal to the right of the brake. The dashboard held a coil box and an oil-circulation gauge.

Riker placed the gearbox in the middle of the chassis, separated from the engine flywheel by a short shaft. The transmission included the final drive and differential gears, with a jackshaft carrying pulleys for chain drive on each side to the rear wheels.

The chassis was based on a channel-steel frame with side members tapering towards the ends, and a sub-frame carrying the engine and transmission.

The prototype had a Panhard-type tubular radiator, but in 1904 Riker adopted the honeycomb radiator first introduced by Mercedes in 1901. The 1903 prototype also had a three-speed transmission, but for the 1904 model, Riker adopted a four-speed transmission. At the same time, the engine received high-tension magneto ignition instead of make-and-break ignition.

The Type D was built on an 84-inch wheelbase, which seems short for a luxury car, but quite spacious bodywork could be fitted on its chassis. Everything on the car was machined to the highest precision, and it was both strong and durable.

The original prototype was still running in 1912, having accumulated an estimated mileage of between 150,000 and 175,000 miles. According to a 1912 report in *The Horseless Age*, "This car inaugurated many of the features which gained the Locomobile its reputation for strength and safety. Mr. Riker used on this car a manganese bronze engine bed, a manganese bronze transmission, and many other features which the Locomobile has retained to this day."

We will meet Mr. Riker again in a chapter dealing with a later model Locomobile. Locomobiles were great cars for as long as the make was alive.

4. PEERLESS MODEL 9, 1905

For many years Cleveland, Ohio, was a hotbed of automaking activity, and its factories have indeed turned out many great cars over the years. The first was a product of the Peerless Motor Car Company, built to the designs of Louis Phillip Mooers who had served as its chief engineer since 1901.

Despite his youth, Louis P. Mooers was no newcomer to car design and construction. He had two years experience as a mechanic on Panhard-Levassor cars in France. In 1897 while living and working in Watertown, Massachusetts, he began to build a single-cylinder car of his own design, and had it ready for the road in 1898. Two years later, now in New Haven, Connecticut, he built a second experimental car, which brought him into contact with Peerless and led him to Cleveland.

His first job, the 1901 Peerless, was a copy of the de Dion Bouton Motorette, with its horizontal single-cylinder engine bolted to the rear end of the frame. The first original Peerless was completed in the summer of 1901 and was an 8 hp single-cylinder model with a front-mounted engine and chain drive to the rear axle.

The following year Mooers prepared a more advanced car, with vertical-twins of 12 and 16 hp, mounted in the nose of the chassis. Peerless built 90 of these machines, while Motorette production was discontinued.

The 1902 Peerless twin had a three-speed countershaft transmission and shaft drive with a spiral-bevel rear axle. Thus Mooers was one of the first American engineers to adopt shaft drive as pioneered by Louis Renault in 1898. He was preceded by a slight margin of time by the Autocar designed by Louis S. Clarke. Mooers used Hotchkiss drive before Hotchkiss did, and invented an arched rear axle that made the wheels run with permanent positive camber—but had full-floating hubs before anyone else.

The 1902 vertical-twin engine featured jump-spark ignition with trembler coils and dry batteries; and cooling by a tubular radiator fed by a water pump, friction-driven from the flywheel.

The frames were constructed of channel-iron sections, at a time when most American cars used tubular steel or wooden frames with iron reinforcements. Mooers was instrumental in getting A. O. Smith out of the bicycle-frame business and into the auto-frame industry.

The 1902 16 hp Model F weighed about 1,800 pounds and had relatively good performance.

L. H. Kittridge, the general manager, realized the publicity value of racing, as demonstrated by Winton, Ford, and others. But the Peerless twin was not fast enough to be a racing car, and Mooers was directed to draw up a four-cylinder model.

The result was a car that became nationally famous as the Green Dragon. In the hands of Barney Oldfield, the Green Dragon ran away from all rivals on race tracks all over the country, breaking every official record for distances between one and 50 miles. At Los Angeles in October, 1904, Oldfield covered 9 miles in 8 minutes 4 seconds, an average of 66.9 mph.

Designed in 1903, the Green Dragon was powered by a 60-hp four-cylinder engine with 6-inch bore and stroke and a displacement of 679 cubic inches. It was a T-head design with the cylinders cast en bloc, using steel liners. The racing car design was modified for a production model, with several sizes of the same basic four-cylinder engine. By the end of 1903, the two-cylinder models were discontinued.

The 1903 four-cylinder models were continued in 1904, with some improvements. Type 8 had a 24-hp engine with cylinders cast singly and Type 7, with cylinders cast in pairs, was rated at 35 hp. The latter was equipped with a four-speed transmission.

A descendant of the Green Dragon, Type 12, was a giant 60-hp model on a 107-inch wheelbase, selling for $6,000; the lowest-priced 1904 Peerless listed at $3,700. It was the smaller models that showed the most of Mooers's capacity to innovate and refine his original ideas.

The Type 7 and 8 engines had fly-ball speed governors, a mechanical oiler system for the bearings, and jump-spark ignition. The chassis featured cam and lever steering gear, artillery wheels and clincher tires, and two brake systems, one acting on the drive shaft and another on drums in the rear wheels.

Lewis Harris Kittridge was the moving power in the Peerless organization, in spite of the fact that his title of general manager made him nominally subordinate to the president, I. M. Blanchard. When Blanchard retired in 1906, Kittridge succeeded to the presidency.

In 1905-06 Peerless built a new plant in Cleveland with floor space of 90,000 square feet, and production capacity grew to 700 cars a year. Actual output in 1907 was 689 cars. That's not mass production. Peerless cars were built by craftsmen, whose methods would bring an efficiency expert to tears, but whose work bore the mark of superior quality.

"To restate a cardinal point," wrote Dr. Robert F. Croll in the *Gazette of the Society of Automotive Historians* "during this experimental period the firm was more interested .in designing and building a quality car than in producing vehicles in quantity."

The point is amply illustrated by the Models 9 and 11 from 1905. They had new overhead-valve engines designed by Charles Schmidt, who had left Packard, and replaced Mooers as chief engineer of Peerless. Model 9 was 24-hp four-cylinder engine with 4.25-inch bore and 5-inch stroke, giving 284 cubic-inch displacement. Model 11 had somewhat larger cylinders and a displacement of 369 cubic inches, for a rated output of 34 hp at 1,100 rpm.

But Schmidt had not had time to redesign the chassis, which showed Mooers's latest advances. The frame was made of cold-rolled, pressed, channel-section steel, reinforced by trussing. There was a new expanding cone clutch, springloaded in the radial plane, pressing outward and backward, instead of inward and forward, as in the older type.

Four-speed transmissions were mounted separately in the middle supported by an extension of the engine subframe. Shaft drive to the rear axle was retained, with universal joints at both ends of the propeller shaft. External contracting drum brakes were fitted on the rear wheels, with a third drum on the transmission output shaft, one set worked by pedal and the other by lever.

"Engine balance and silence, luxury of ride, etc. was as good as could be obtained," wrote E. Stanley Cope about the Peerless in *The Antique Automobile* (March 1962). He went on: "The bodies were of the best, with 18 coats of hand brushed varnish, and in some, fittings of silver."

After Mooers left Peerless he worked successively for Moon, Geneva, Excelsior, Palmer-Singer and Keeton. In 1911 he incorporated the Mooers Automobile Company in New York for the purpose of building his own cars, but the enterprise never got into actual production. For a year, Mooers was an engine designer with Herschell-Spillman in North Tonawanda, New York and then worked five years as a fire-engine engineer with Ahrens-Fox. From 1920 to 1929 he acted as an engineering consultant to various clients in the auto industry, designed the Balboa car in 1924-25, and then retired to Miami, Florida, where he lived quietly until his death in 1962.

As for Schmidt and his achievements at Peerless, we'll look at that later, in its proper, chronological place.

5. FORD MODEL K, 1906

Now, back to Detroit, for a look at a remarkable machine produced by the Ford Motor Company, then still located in the heart of the city: the Model K was built in Ford's plant on Piquette Avenue (Fig. 1-5).

It was Henry Ford's first attempt to produce a high-grade, powerful touring car. It was not the kind of automobile Henry Ford personally cared most about, and it was somewhat lacking in reliability, perhaps because it was placed in production without adequate testing and development. But it is significant, as the first attempt of one of the nation's largest auto manufacturers to produce a prestige car.

It can be regarded as a precocious Lincoln, if you will. It certainly was out of character for Ford to produce such a vehicle, having his market base in the low-priced two-cylinder type of car. Though Henry Ford must have given his approval for the Model K project, he is not believed to have shared in its design. The idea for it probably came from Alexander Malcomson, a coal merchant who was Ford's majority stockholder, perhaps with the support of James Cousins, Ford's chief accountant. The man who did the actual engineering for it was C. Harold Wills, Ford's top technical expert.

C. Harold Wills had joined Ford Motor Co. at its foundation in 1903 and was named technical assistant to Henry Ford. His title changed to shop superintendent in 1904, but he was really Ford's chief engineer.

Wills had known Ford since 1899, when, while working for the Boyer Machine Company, he used his spare time to help build Ford's racing prototypes, the "999" and the "Arrow". Trained as a toolmaker, Wills did not hold an engineering degree, but had studied engineering, chemistry and metallurgy in evening classes. His principal assistant at Ford was Joseph Galamb, an Hungarian-born technician with some experience in design engineering, whom Wills had hired as a draftsman.

The Model K Ford stood on a 114-inch wheelbase with a 56-inch track and weighed 2,400 pounds. Thus, it is not an overgrown giant, but rather represents an attempt to build a powerful luxury car in a rational package (Fig. 1-6).

The frame was made of cold-pressed, chrome-nickel steel, with long, straight channel-section side members. Springs were full-elliptical at the rear and semi-elliptical on the front axle. Its

Fig. 1-5. The 1906 Ford Model K, Ford's first high-grade touring car.

artillery wheels were shod with 34×4-inch tires of the double-tube clincher type.

In basic construction, therefore, Wills demonstrated full understanding of the demands of the clientele in the high-priced market, above all in terms of comfort. How about strength,

Fig. 1-6. Henry Ford seated at the wheel of a 1906 Model K.

stamina, and safety? Wills had thought of it all, and came up with some interesting solutions.

For example, the rear axle had roller bearings, with ball-type thrust bearings. The driving thrust was taken by a torque tube assisted by diagonal stays—a remarkably advanced design which relieved the leaf springs of the burden of pushing the car. The diagonal stays located the axle laterally and carried the weight.

The front axle was one-piece, chrome-nickel steel forging of 1-beam section, and front wheel hubs had large-size ball bearings. Ford made its own irreversible steering gear.

The K had the most modern brakes available at the time, with drums of the internal-expanding type on the rear wheels, worked by a hand lever, plus a pedal-operated external-contracting brake on the propeller shaft.

What about power and speed? It would do 50 mph with ease. The engine was an L-head, in-line six with individually cast cylinders. With its 4.5-inch bore and 4.25-inch stroke, it had a total displacement of 405.5 cubic inches and was rated at 40 hp.

The cylinders were cast with integral heads, valve chambers, and coolant jackets. Its crankshaft was a solid steel drop-forging with seven main bearings of unusually generous width and diameter.

Wills took advantage of the overlapping power pulses of the six to lighten the flywheel—it weighed only 65 pounds and was 14 inches in diameter at a time when 100 pound flywheels of 18-20 inches diameter were common on four-cylinder engines.

It had positive oil feed to all engine parts, by a mechanical oiler. Magneto ignition was used, with one spark plug per cylinder. The firing order was 1-2-3-6-5-4 rather than the usual 1-5-3-6-2-4.

Its transmission, however, was something of an anomaly. A two-speed, pedal-controlled planetary transmission was used, with shaft drive to the rear axle. This was the same type of transmission used on Ford's light cars, with one-third the power and half the speed of the Model K. Probably Wills and Galamb felt that the extra power reduced the need for additional steps of gearing, as was common in other high-speed cars. But the engine's limited speed range diminished the car's driveability, and the existence of only one indirect gear rather than two or three upset the general smoothness of the car's motion.

Some of the car's shortcomings were cured in 1907. A dual ignition system was adopted, with two plugs per cylinder, one fired by the high-tension magneto, and the other by a coil-and-battery system. The artillery wheels were reinforced, and even the frame was beefed up to resist twisting.

Originally, Model K prices started at $2,500 fob Detroit, at a time when the Model N was listed at $550. The base price went up to $2,800 in 1907, and buyers who wanted gas lamps and a cape top were asked to hand over an even $3,000.

Model K was not well-received in the market place. Less than 1,000 units were sold in three years' production. The K was dropped late in 1908, along with the smaller S and N four-clyinder cars to make room for the Model T in a sweeping one-model-only program that was to last for 19 years.

But its demise was not the end of either Henry Ford's or C. Harold Wills's involvement with great cars. We'll meet them again in the Twenties.

6. WINTON MODEL K, 1906

While Ford's Model K was one of America's first six-cylinder cars to reach production, Winton's Model K was one of his last four-cylinder models before switching to the six. The Winton car was built in Cleveland, Ohio, sharing the local limelight with Peerless, while the biggest auto maker there was White, then getting ready to switch from steam to gasoline power (Fig. 1-7).

The Winton Motor Carriage Company had a smaller factory than Ford, and because the Winton Model K was not intended for big production run, the price was set fairly high. The chassis alone was listed at $2,500. With limousine body it cost $3,500 or about half the price of a contemporary Peerless.

The man who built this car, Alexander Winton, was a naval engineer from Scotland, who got his mechanical experience in his father's farm implement shop, shipyards, and in the engine room of steamships.

Winton came to America at the age of 24, having worked his way over as a ship's machinist, and found a job with the Phoenix Iron Works in Cleveland, Ohio. After four years he had saved enough money to start his own business, and in 1888 he formed the Winton Bicycle Company. He designed and built a motorcycle in 1895, and made his first car in 1896.

It ran so well that he decided to step seriously into the world of automobiles, and in 1897 drove one of his cars from Cleveland to New York in ten days. He built 21 cars that year. He hired Leo Melanowski as chief engineer, and together the two evolved the concept of a two-cylinder model with vertical engine and friction-disc drive, wire wheels and 40 × 4-inch pneumatic tires.

Winton's first cars had a single-cylinder engine under the seat, with chain drive to the rear axle. Instead of throttled carburetor, Winton controlled engine speed by regulating the inlet valve, to give a useful speed range from 200 to 700 rpm, useful at such low speed mainly because of the enormous flywheel. Winton's engine lubrication system was a primitive drip-wick type. The inlet valve control was pneumatic, with an air cylinder under the accelerator pedal linked to a similar unit that was arranged to limit valve lift.

Winton also experimented with a compressed-air starter as early as 1896, and it became a standard production item on his cars.

Thus we can see in Winton's imaginative engineering the embryo of greatness to come. But there were many steps along the way.

Winton went to a 15-hp two-cylinder engine for his 1902 production models and the laminated wood frame was replaced by a steel-girder structure. A larger twin for 1903 delivered a full 20 hp. These were cars of simple concept but built by craftsmen to high standards of workmanship, and the prices reflected that. A standard Winton was listed at $2,500 in 1904, including windshield, canopy top and headlamps.

Winton's reputation was built mainly on the success of his Bullet racing models which set a great number of track records in 1902 and 1903. On March 28th, 1903, Alexander Winton himself drove his four-cylinder Bullet on Ormond Beach, Florida, at 69 mph over a one-mile stretch.

The second Bullet was built for the 1903 Gordon Bennett Cup race, and was powered by two four-cylinder engines coupled together to make a horizontal straight-eight of no less than 1,029 cubic inches. Its 80 hp enabled it to capture a one-mile record in 55 seconds (65.45 mph) and a 15-mile record in 14 minutes 31 seconds (60.6 mph). With Barney Oldfield at the wheel it set two world records at Empire City track in 1903, with a 5-mile run in 5 minutes 1 second (59.8 mph) and a 10-mile run in 9 minutes 43 seconds (61.75 mph). The racing experience did much to speed up development of improved and more advanced Winton production cars.

All two-cylinder engines were replaced by four-cylinder units for 1905, and Winton cars grew in size and were given more elaborate coachwork. The Winton four was built in three engine sizes, matched by three sizes of chassis. The larger two were available with closed bodies, the smaller one was built only as an open touring car with side entrance.

For 1906, the model range was simplified, and only one chassis, one engine, were offered. Winton Model K: the first truly great Winton.

The engine had its cylinders cast in pairs, with integral heads. With a bore of 4.75 inches and a 5.00-inch stroke, it had 354.4 cubic inch displacement and was rated at 40-50 hp. It was coupled to a two-speed planetary transmission with two individual clutches, which imposed certain limits on driveability, comfort and fuel economy.

In addition to the compressed-air starter, Winton included three new pneumatic devices on this car. The Hill automatic lubricator was air-operated. It had a vacuum-tank type of fuel feed, and retained the air-controlled inlet-valve lift governor. Winton made his own carburetor, which was not uncommon at that time, before Carter, Stromberg, Holley and other famous makes were available in a variety of standard types.

In order to give easy access to the crankshaft bearings, Winton split the crankcase vertically, one half being easily removable. And in an unusual quest for silent running, Winton equipped the engine with rawhide timing gears.

Model K was an impressively large touring car, yet with lightness and litheness apparent in its overall design. It was built on a 106-inch wheelbase and weighed about 2,200 pounds with side-entrance tonneau body and canopy top.

For 1907 the Model K was replaced by a Model XIV, an enlarged vehicle powered by the same engine. A new Model M, added in 1907, featured a four-speed countershaft transmission with direct drive on third and overdrive on top gear. Winton had acted to remedy the main drawback in the Model K.

At midsummer, 1907, Winton produced his first six, the Model XVI, and the fours were phased out. Cylinders were cast in pairs, and the vertically split crankcase was retained. The crankshaft ran in four main bearings. The car had a wet clutch, made of 65 steel discs running in oil, and used a three-speed transmission.

The Winton Six was undoubtedly endowed with elements of greatness, even in its first edition. But it was the four-cylinder Model K that put Winton in the select class of master-builders of automobiles. The six also evolved into a great car, as we shall see at our next meeting with Alexander Winton.

Fig. 1-7. Winton Model K of 1906.

7. ROYAL TOURIST 4-40, 1906

What made the Royal Tourist great was above all its speed and acceleration. It was relatively light, with a curb weight of about 2,400 pounds, so that its 40 hp was sufficient to give it remarkable performance. With its 114-inch wheelbase and 56-inch track, front and rear, it was extremely stable on the road. It was not built with a particularly low frame, but had ample ground clearance to keep it from getting stuck on bad roads.

It was a tough car, intelligently designed and built with great care and attention (Fig. 1-8). It had a businesslike air about it, with nothing pompous or grandiose, looking proud to be what it was, and free of any pretense to be anything else.

With a list price of $3,500 it was a serious competitor in the lower range of the prestige market, competing head-on with the Thomas Flyer 4-60, the 50 hp Haynes Model R, the Peerless Model 14, Winton Model K, National Model D, and the 50-hp Wayne.

This was a particularly difficult market segment to operate in, for cars that pretended to do the same job—or almost—were offered at considerably lower prices by companies such as Oldsmobile, Franklin, Rambler, Premier and St. Louis. But the Royal Tourist was clearly their superior in concept, engineering and quality. It was a product of the Royal Motor Car Company, of Cleveland, Ohio, and manufactured from designs by Robert Jardine.

The business can be traced back to the Hoffman Bicycle Company which prospered in the Nineties but entered the twentieth century with its market, like Pope's, showing signs of severe contraction. The Hoffman executives did not sit idly by and watch other bicycle manufacturers develop cars and begin auto production. In 1902 it began producing a light steam car, powered by a two-cylinder 6 hp engine, with chain drive. It hit the market just at the time steam power and battery-electric cars lost out to the gasoline-driven automobile.

The situation called for drastic measures, and the Hoffman Bicycle Company was dissolved to make room for a new organization, the Royal Motor Car Company, formed to manufacture gasoline-powered automobiles. Hoffman backers looked with interest at the success of the Berg Automobile Company, a business belonging to Hart O. Berg, who had been associated with the Electric Vehicle Company (Columbia) in New York as early as 1897.

But the Berg was not copied from the Columbia. It was an original design, made in two- and four-cylinder versions, by an experienced engineer named Robert Jardine. The solution was evident. Royal, that is, the ex-Hoffman backers, persuaded Jardine to leave Berg and accept the position of chief engineer of the Royal Motor Car Company. Berg cars were discontinued in 1905, as the company disappeared in a merger with Meteor and Worthington.

Robert Jardine was born and educated in Cleveland, and had been working as an engineer with the local firm that produced de Dion-Bouton tricycles under license from Paris. Inspired by these machines, he went to France in 1899 and was able to find a place on the Clement engineering staff (a company to become famous for the Gladiator and Clement-Bayard automobiles).

After a year's time, he left Clement to serve as works manager for the European Electric Vehicle Company in Paris, returning to Cleveland in 1903, where he linked up with Hart O. Berg. Robert Jardine was then 27 years old.

The first Royal Tourist of 1904 was a direct development of his original design for Berg, a light car with a rear-entrance tonneau body, powered by an 18/20 hp two-cylinder engine. A four-cylinder model was added before the end of 1904, and in 1905 the two-cylinder models were phased out.

The Cleveland environment stimulated Jardine to build more powerful, faster cars, surrounded as he was by Peerless, White, F.

Fig. 1-8. The Royal Tourist 4-40 of 1906, noted for its speed and acceleration.

B. Stearns, and Winton. The 1906 model 4-40 was as modern as anything produced by the older, established Cleveland car makers. Its four-cylinder engine was cast in pairs and had a 5-inch bore and a 5½-inch stroke. It delivered 40 hp from its 432 cubic inch displacement, with tremendous torque. Later it was bored out to 5.125 inches, which raised displacement to 454 cubic inches and the power output to 45 hp.

The sliding-gear transmission was mounted close behind the engine, but carried separately from it, and had three speeds with direct drive on top gear. A propeller shaft enclosed in a torque tube took the drive to the rear axle—an advanced type of construction that had been tried experimentally by Ford and was to be adopted by Buick in 1907.

Front and rear axles were attached to the pressed-steel frame by semi-elliptical leaf springs; the rear ones free to support the weight without having to carry any driving thrust, since the torque tube handled those duties.

The brake system was fairly typical for its day, with internal-expanding shoes in drums carried in the rear wheels, and an external-contracting band brake carried at the forward end of the propeller shaft. All wheels were shod with 36 × 4½ inch tires. Accurate performance figures are not available for the Royal Tourist, but it was known as a fast car, so the 4-40 must have been good for 55 mph to 60 mph. Generally a car of lighter construction than the high-powered Winton and Peerless models, its acceleration must have been quicker, especially from standstill to 30 mph.

So great was the soundness of the Royal Tourist that few chassis changes were undertaken in the next few years. The model range was expanded, and in 1908 included a G-3 limousine with a $5,000 price tag. By 1911 the same basic four-cylinder engine had been developed to deliver 48 hp, but by that time the Royal Tourist was beginning to fall behind. It was not keeping up with technical trends and in 1911 the Royal Tourist Motor Car Company (which had been so renamed in 1908) merged with the Croxton-Keeton Motor Company of Massillon, Ohio, to form a new organization, Consolidated Motor Car Company, which folded within a year. The Royal Tourist plant was taken over by F. B. Stearns and continued its existence as the home of great cars.

Robert Jardine signed up as chief engineer with Jeffery in 1911 and moved to Racine, Wisconsin. In 1913 he was working as a consulting engineer for Mitchell-Lewis Motor Company in the same town, but the following year went to Chicago with the Rich

Tool Company, becoming its chief engineer and director. He served as chief engineer of Wilcox-Rich in Detroit until his death in 1936.

9. NATIONAL MODEL L, 1907

Indianapolis still has its Speedway, but its great cars exist only in museums. The seat of Marion county gave birth to several great makes of car, the first of which was the National (Fig. 1-9.)

After only three years' experience in building gasoline driven cars, National produced a great one in the form of its 1906 Model L. Because of changes made for its second year of production, it is the 1907 model that is described in these pages.

It was created on the drawing board of W. Guy Wall, who had been responsible for the design of all previous Nationals. In 1900, he was one of the co-founders of the National Automobile and Electric Company, with Arthur C. Newby and William E. Metzger as partners.

A. C. Newby was a scion of a wealthy Hoosier family, and one of four men responsible for construction of the Indianapolis Motor Speedway in 1909. Metzger left National after a few years and made his name as sales manager of Cadillac. He was later involved with Studebaker and the IMF (Everitt-Metzger-Flanders) car.

W. Guy Wall was born in Baltimore, Maryland and graduated in civil engineering from the Virginia Military Institute at Lexington, Kentucky. He also held a degree in electrical engineering from the Massachusetts Institute of Technology. He was

Fig. 1-9. 1907 National Model L.

named chief engineer of the retitled National Vehicle Company in 1901, and the company produced electric cars for two years before his first model driven by an internal combustion engine was ready.

Wall had begun to experiment with gasoline engines in 1901, but apparently without success, for the Model A National of 1903 was powered by an engine bought from an outside supplier. This Rutenber engine had four separately cast cylinders. It carried a cone clutch and a three-speed transmission with a progressive shift. Wall kept up with the state of the art and used shaft drive to a bevel-gear rear axle. The engine sat vertically in the front of the pressed-steel frame. At the nose was a cellular radiator, with fan and water pump contained in the radiator assembly.

Model B was a direct successor to Model A, using the same engine, appearing as a 1904 model. National's first four-cylinder engine of its own manufacture went into the Model C of 1905, an elegant $2,500 prestige car visually distinctive by its shiny circular radiator shell.

With a 4.25-inch bore and a 5.00-inch stroke, the engine had a displacement of 283.7 cubic inches and delivered 24 to 30 hp at relatively low rpm. All valves were mechanically operated by a single camshaft, and arranged in L-head configuration. Cylinders were cast separately and mounted on a common crankcase.

Lubrication was by splash to pockets in the crankcase walls, from where the oil would run through drilled channels to the crankshaft and camshaft bearings. Sight-feed oilers were fitted on the dash, along with a compression release button for cranking, an oil supply relief rod, and ignition coil.

The cone clutch had cast aluminum pressure plate and cover, with leather faces. An interlocking device disengaged the clutch whenever either brake was applied, to avoid stalling the engine.

The engine was mounted in a sub-frame, with the transmission bolted on to form a unit. It had double ball-bearing countershaft transmission with three forward speeds and direct drive on top gear. The rear wheels were shaft-driven via a bevel-gear pinion and ring gear assembly.

Model C set the pattern for several generations of cars from Wall's office. It used the Apple system of an engine-driven generator to recharge the storage battery, an unusual refinement then found in only one or two other makes of car. The National also carried a dry-cell battery as a spare. Wall was very safety conscious, and to guard against breakage in the steering linkage causing the car to go out of control, he provided a second tie rod.

Model C was given a heavier companion in the shape of Model D, equipped with a 4-cylinder 35-40 hp engine that introduced the ball-bearing crankshaft in National's power units. Model D used a 3-speed and reverse gearbox and shaft drive. It followed the now established chassis layout with a pressed steel frame and engine sub-frame. Built on a 104-inch wheelbase, it had a cast aluminum body and a list price of $3,000.

During 1906 all National engines were given ball-bearing crankshafts and camshafts, dual ignition with two separate spark-generating and firing systems. That included not only the Model C, which continued in production, but also the new Model L, a 75-hp model in the $5,000 price class.

Model L was National's first six. Other sixes in production in 1906 were Ford, Franklin, and Stevens-Duryea. The National six had individually cast cylinders, just as the company's four-cylinder engines. It also was notable for its seven-bearing crankshaft with an aggregate bearing width of 14 inches.

For 1907 the National L received a new T-head engine, giving a crossflow head and better breathing. This unit was manufactured in a new engine plant, leased from the India Chain Company.

Earlier transmissions had been shifted in a quadrant type of gate, now an H-pattern shift was adopted for the Model L.

The engine had two separate ignition systems, one with coil and battery, the other with a high-tension magneto.

Model L brakes used dual concentric drums, one within the other, for each rear wheel, both with internal-expanding shoes. One set of drums were pedal-operated, the other worked by the hand brake lever.

The Model L remained in production until 1911 and was improved at frequent intervals. For 1908, the engine had cylinders cast in pairs instead of singly, and the rear suspension that year was changed from semi elliptical to platform springs

W. Guy Wall was to continue his superb work for National for many years, as will be seen from examples to be dealt with later.

10. STEVENS-DURYEA MODEL U, 1907

Another contender from New England, rivaling the Columbia and Locomobile for excellence, was the Stevens-Duryea, manufactured in Chicopee Falls, Massachusetts (Fig. 1-10).

It was designed by J. Franklin Duryea, brother of Charles E. Duryea, and partner in the design and construction of the Duryea single-cylinder automobile of 1893. He had no formal engineering training, but was an expert mechanic, and became a competent design engineer.

It was in 1901 that the J. Stevens Arms & Tools Company of Chicopee Falls, Massachusetts, decided to go into the automobile business, and invited Frank Duryea to be their engineer.

Frank Duryea began his career as a toolmaker for the Ames Manufacturing Company in Chicopee Falls in 1891, and joined his brother Charles in Springfield, Massachusetts, in 1892/93 to undertake construction of a motor vehicle Charles had designed. Tests revealed serious shortcomings in the design, and Charles took off for Peoria, Illinois, to sell bicycles, leaving Frank to develop the machine.

Frank entered an improved prototype in the 1895 Chicago Times Herald auto race, and won the event over five other cars with an average speed of 5.05 mph. This brought Charles back to Springfield, where they went into production with the Duryea car, building a total of 13 vehicles in 1896.

They sold their company in the fall of 1898 to a group of New York businessmen who called themselves the American Automobile Company, which was out of business before the turn of the century. Charles returned to the Midwest to make three-wheelers while Frank stayed in New England and linked up with the Stevens organization.

The first model he designed for Stevens was a Stanhope buggy powered by a horizontal two-cylinder engine placed in the rear. It had tiller steering, tubular frame, and belt drive. It was listed at $1,200 and had a top speed of 30 mph.

The firm changed its title to the Stevens-Duryea Company in 1904, and Frank Duryea prepared a new four-cylinder model for 1904, with a front-mounted engine and shaft drive to the rear axle. This design ripened into the Model R of 1905, the car that built Stevens-Duryea's reputation.

It was driven by a 20-hp L-head in-line four with nondetachable head and separately cast cylinders. Displacement was 212 cubic inches (3.875 × 4.50 inches bore and stroke).

Built on a 90-inch wheelbase it had a pressed steel frame, right hand drive, wheel steering, gearshift and handbrake outside the cockpit. Tires were 30 × 3½ inches.

Equipped with an aluminum side-entrance tonneau body, it had a curb weight of 1,650 pounds and a list price of $2,500. It was a quality car, known for its reliability rather than its performance.

Fig. 1-10. Stevens-Duryea Model U of 1907.

For customers demanding more power and speed, Frank Duryea prepared a six-cylinder design.

The first six was the Model S, introduced as a 1906 model, selling at $5,000. Its engine was an L-head design with individually cast cylinders and the flywheel in front, gear-driven water pump on the side of the crankcase, and progressive-shift transmission. With a bore and stroke of 4.75 × 5.25 inches, it had a displacement of 558 cubic inches and was rated at 50 hp.

Model S was built on a 122-inch wheelbase and shod with 36 × 4-inch tires on the front axle and 36 × 5-inch tires in the rear. Despite the massive 3,700-pound weight of this giant touring car, it had lively acceleration and a maximum speed of 60-65.

But the new 1907 Light Six, Model U, was the more intelligent, more efficient car. It listed for $3,500, compared with $6,000 for the Model S. As is so often the case, the less ambitious project led to the greatest car. After Model U was launched, Model S became known as the Big Six.

The Model U engine had 3.875-inch bore and 4.375-inch stroke, giving a displacement of 309.5 cubic inches. The cylinders were cast singly, and the crankshaft ran in four main bearings. It had jump-spark ignition and a modern cellular radiator, multiple disc clutch and a three-speed sliding gear transmission with progressive shift pattern.

The gearbox was bolted to the engine in the usual Stevens-Duryea manner, with the flywheel at the front, and the whole power unit assembly was carried in a three-point suspension system—two wings extending from the front of the crankcase to the frame side members, with a single central mounting around the transmission output shaft to a frame crossmember.

Model U had a lower-built chassis than the S, with a 114-inch wheelbase and 34 × 4-inch tires all around. Complete with canopy, the five-seater touring car weighed a mere 2,500 pounds. It got a top speed of 56 mph from its 35-hp engine, with a 3.00:1 final drive ratio using a straight bevel pinion and ring gear assembly.

For 1909 the U engine was enlarged to 336 cubic inch displacement by lengthening the stroke to 4.75 inches. Power output was unchanged, but low-range torque was substantially improved.

Model S was discontinued in 1908, its place being taken by an elegant Model Y with a 40-hp six derived from the Model U. It led in turn to a new generation of Stevens-Duryea sixes in 1911, beginning with the excellent Model AA. We will encounter further examples of the great cars from Chicopee Falls at a later point in history.

11. PIERCE GREAT ARROW 6-60, 1908

Not all cars that put the adjective "great" into their names were really great. The Great Smith and the Great Western missed by a wide margin. So did the Great Eagle and the Great Southern. But the Great Arrow truly deserved its name (Fig. 1-11).

The 1908 Six-60 was absolutely magnificent, and the maker's advertisements stressed smoothness and quietness more than power and speed. A point was made of the lack of vibration and ease of starting.

A product of Buffalo, New York, it had a pedigree that commanded respect: it was built by the George N. Pierce Company which had been in the automobile business for eight years.

George Norman Pierce was born in a village near Waverly, New York in 1846. He attended local schools and was graduated from a business college. His first job was as a clerk in a home-appliance firm in Buffalo, New York. By 1872 he had obtained majority control of the business and reorganized it as the George N. Pierce Company.

A businessman named Charles Clifton was named treasurer of the Pierce Company in 1897, after it had gone into bicycle manufacturing. It was Clifton who was mainly responsible for spreading the company's activities into automobile building. A steam car was built in 1900, but that project was soon given up. Later that year, Clifton went to Europe to look for new ideas for the kind of car Pierce should produce, and fastened on the de Dion-Bouton Motorette, a light quadricycle of primitive design and therefore easy to make.

The first Pierce Motorette was based on a Diamond three-wheeler powered by an imported de Dion-Bouton engine. The next Motorette was a four-wheeled carriage with a rear-mounted de Dion-Bouton engine, built on a 54-inch wheelbase.

Neither Clifton nor Pierce had any clear idea how to evolve the Motorette into a modern automobile. As fate would have it, their problems were over when a young Englishman came to see the Buffalo plant and irrevocably changed the company's fortunes. His name was David Fergusson, than 30 years of age. He hailed from Bradford in Yorkshire, and had an engineering degree from the Bradford Technical College.

He had years of experience in railroad locomotive, steam engine, and gas engine engineering. He had also worked briefly with Edward J. Pennington on car designs in London in 1896, and came to America with Pennington in 1899. He worked briefly with the E. C. Stearns Company in Syracuse on a steam car project, while privately starting to design a gasoline automobile. This was to be the design that he took to Pierce.

Imported de Dion-Bouton engines were used up to 1903, when Pierce began building its own single-cylinder engine, designed by Fergusson and being, by and large, a scaled-up de Dion-Bouton unit.

The car Fergusson had designed from scratch went into production as a 1903 model. It had a 15-hp two-cylinder engine mounted under a hood in front and chain drive to the rear axle, and it was called Arrow to distinguish it from the Motorette which was then phased out.

In 1904 Fergusson designed his first four-cylinder car, which was also the first to carry the name Great Arrow. It went into production in 1905 as a 24-28 hp touring car with a T-head engine of 269.5 cubic inch displacement (4.25 × 4.75 inches bore and stroke). It had shaft drive to the rear axle, with a three-speed transmission and column shift(!).

It had a cast aluminum body, with a copper hood and fenders fabricated from sheet aluminum. It weighed just under 2,000 pounds as an open touring car and was priced at $4,000. With a product like that, success could not elude the Great Arrow, and Pierce built a huge new factory at Buffalo in 1906. The two-cylinder models were discontinued, and two four-cylinder types adopted: the 28/32 and 40/45.

By 1907 their designations were simplified as "30" and "45". Wheelbases got longer and frames and bodies lower. The day of the six-cylinder Great Arrow was fast approaching.

Two six-cylinder models were added for 1908, a 40 hp and a 60 hp vehicle. Fergusson created the sixes by adding two cylinders to the "30" and "45" four-cylinder engines. This was relatively simple, for all Pierce engines were made with separately cast cylinders. Fergusson designed a seven-bearing crankshaft for the sixes, that was a chrome-nickel steel forging of extremely high tensile strength.

Jump-spark ignition was used, with storage battery and high-tension magneto. Radiators were of the cellular type. The cone clutch was leather-faced with cone inserts. The three-speed

Fig. 1-11. The 1908 Pierce Great Arrow 6-60 from Buffalo, N.Y.

column shift was carried over from the four-cylinder models, with shaft drive to the rear axle. The brakes had both external bands and expanding shoes working on drums in the rear wheels.

Both the 40 and the 60 were built on the same chassis, with its 130-inch wheelbase and 56-inch track front and rear. Front tires were 36 × 4-inch, the rear ones 36 × 5-inch. The 6-40 was listed at $5,500 and the 6-60 at $6,500. For 1909, Pierce built only six-cylinder cars, with a steady output of six cars a day, all with a quality and finish that impressed everyone who saw them.

11. MATHESON 6-48, 1908

Mathesons were great cars before the company produced its first six, but the 6-48 was a major step and the one that best represents the work of Matheson's brilliant chief engineer, Charles R. Greuter (Fig. 1-12).

The Matheson rivaled the Packard for precision engineering, the Pierce-Arrow for choice of high-grade materials, the Locomobile for ambition of concept and styling, and had a level of technical sophistication all its own.

The company was founded by two brothers, Frank F. and Charles W. Matheson, in Grand Rapids, Michigan, in 1903. They had made a fortune in the furniture business, and had bought cars in the early days of the century. Soon, they began entertaining notions of how cars could be improved, and set out to build cars that would satisfy their own stringent demands.

Since they were businessmen and industrialists, not engineers, they determined to get the best talent money could buy. Their choice fell on Greuter, who was then building a small car of exquisite design and construction in Holyoke, Massachusetts.

Charles R. Greuter was born in Philadelphia, Pennsylvania but educated in Switzerland, where his parents moved when he was two years old. In 1880 he graduated from Winterthur Technical College, and went back to America with his fresh engineering degree. He worked for various engine manufactuers in New England, and in 1888 began design work on a new type of stationary engine. He built his first complete engine in 1893, and shortly afterwards was able to attract enough capital to set up a factory for manufacturing small marine engines. His one-cylinder, two-cylinder, and three-cylinder engines soon became favorites of small boat builders in the Boston area.

About 1900 he began experiments with an overhead camshaft engine. This was something few others had attempted anywhere in the world, the first on record being John Wilkinson, the engineer who later went to Franklin and was responsible for the design of its cars for over 25 years. (Wilkinson had designed an overhead-camshaft engine in 1897, but it was never put into production.)

Greuter was certainly unaware of the existence of Wilkinson's solution, and set out to find his own. Moving the camshaft to the top of the cylinder head was simple, but driving it posed a problem. Greuter thought out a method that would assure close mechanical control of the valve timing, using a vertical shaft, driven by bevel gears from the crankshaft, and driving the camshaft via a similar bevel gear set.

The overhead camshaft became a feature of the one-cylinder and two-cylinder engines he made for installation in the Holyoke car, which he began producing in 1901. It was these vehicles that brought him to the attention of the Matheson brothers.

When they traveled to see him at Holyoke, he showed them the prototype four-cylinder engine, also with an overhead camshaft and the valves splayed above hemispherical combustion chambers. Greuter had created the first hemi-head engine, and the Matheson brothers recognized its merits. They offered to purchase his whole business, and put Greuter on the payroll as chief engineer of Matheson. He accepted.

Incidentally, the Matheson brothers were not alone in appreciating the value of Greuter's hemi-head design: A. R. Welch of Pontiac, Michigan, copied it for the Welch car in 1904—an ambitious design that failed due to insufficient testing and development.

Fig. 1-12. Matheson's 6-48 of 1910, designed by Charles R. Greuter.

Producing the cars was the next challenge for the Mathesons. They did not have plant capacity in their home town, and considered moving to Detroit. But they went to Wilkes-Barre, a mining and manufacturing town in Northeast Pennsylvania, which boasted of raw materials on the spot, availability of skilled workers, attractive real estate prices, and easy financing through enlightened bankers. While the plant was being set up, Matheson assembled six cars in leased premises in Grand Rapids, with all later ones to be built at Wilkes-Barre.

The first Matheson had a 24-hp four-cylinder overhead camshaft engine with individually cast cylinders, three-speed transmission, and chain drive to the rear wheels. It was a fine car, but not powerful enough to satisfy the Matheson brothers. Greuter then designed his Big Four, a 40-45 hp unit of similar layout. It was to be the mainstay of Matheson production for six years, upgraded to 50 hp. But Frank and Charles Matheson asked Greuter for still more power.

He responded by creating a 60-65 version, scaled up from the Big Four which then became the smallest. The 1906 Matheson cars were built on a pressed steel frame with a 125-inch wheelbase. The chassis had forged nickel-steel axles and nickel-steel transmission gears and casing. A four-speed gearbox became standard, but chain drive was retained.

Curb weights ranged from 2,890 to 3,160 pounds and prices from $6,000 to $7,000. Standard equipment included a compressed-air starter, steering gear of the irreversible type, rear wheels with internal-expanding brakes, and contracting-band brakes on the sprocket shafts. The Matheson was a luxury car, with body work that matched the Matheson brothers' taste in furniture. As for speed, they could top 60 mph with either engine and any body style.

The 60-65 hp model was discontinued when Greuter began preparing his overhead-camshaft six in 1907. For 1908, the model range included a Runabout, Touring Car, Landaulet and Limousine, all with the 50 hp Bit Four of 471 cubic inches displacement, all built on the same 128-inch wheelbase. The chassis layout remained basically unchanged, retaining the chain drive system and dual brake systems.

Late in 1908 the six-cylinder Matheson was unveiled, a magnificent vehicle, indeed, with its 125.5-inch wheelbase and shaft-driven rear axle.

While the fours continued with individually cast cylinders, the Matheson six had its cylinders cast in pairs. With 4½-inch bore and 5-inch stroke, it had a displacement of 477 cubic inches and a rating of 50 hp. The camshaft drive was refined to make the engine quieter rather than more powerful, the camshaft itself remaining firmly lodged overhead. A dual ignition system was fitted, with two plugs per cylinder, one fired by coil and battery, the other by Bosch magneto. Lubrication was by a splash system of the constant-level type.

A racing clientele sprang up around the Matheson, and it went on to a distinguished career in road races, hill climbs, and board-track events. Louis Chevrolet drove a Matheson in many races, and the demand for Matheson cars grew all around the country. But the Matheson brothers never expanded their factories to keep up with the order flow.

This sealed the Matheson's fate, and the marque disappeared in 1913, after a total of only about 1,800 cars had been produced since the start of production in 1904. Charles R. Greuter returned to the Boston area and set up an engineering shop in Brookline. We will meet him again in connection with other great cars.

Frank and Charles Matheson became Dodge dealers and Frank handled Dodge at the retail level until 1928, when he quit the car business to open a warehouse and operate in real eastate. He died at the age of 95 in 1967. Charles, four years his junior, went to New York as a Dodge factory representative in 1920, and the following year was named vice president of Dodge. In 1924 he went to Oakland as sales Manager, Four years later he moved to Chrysler as vice president in charge of sales, leaving in 1938 to become president of Reo in Lansing, Michigan, where car production had recently been phased out in favor of concentrating on the Reo Speed Wagon and other trucks. Two years later he was dead at the age of 64.

12. LOZIER MODEL H, 1909

A New Yorker, in the same upstate sense that the Pierce-Arrow was a New Yorker, the Lozier was built in the small town of Plattsburg on Lake Champlain. It may seem an unusual place to manufacture cars, but it was a perfectly logical site for a boat-building marine-engine plant, and it was with the purpose of making motor boats that Lozier had located there, long before its management had any idea of going into the automobile business. When it did, it was to produce a line of exquisitely engineered vehicles to designs by John George Perrin, using space available in the marine engine and motorboat works.

John G. Perrin was fresh out of Toledo High when George Burwell hired him for training as a future technical expert for Lozier's Cleveland Bicycle Co. Henry Abram Lozier had started the firm bearing his name in 1880 to manufacture bicycles with the Cleveland trademark in Toledo.

It was his son Harry who was responsible for the company's going into the automobile business, and who served as president of the Lozier Motor Car Company.

In 1903 he sent 28-year-old Perrin to Europe for a six-months' study of cars and how to make them. Perrin returned with his luggage packed with drawings, specifications, and notes on the leading French and German makes, including Mors, Darracq, Mercedes, CGV and Panhard-Levassor. By combining the best features of each, he designed the first Lozier car.

The engine was a T-head in-line four, with mechanical operation of all valves. The rear axle was chain-driven via a 3-speed gearbox. It was built during 1904 and first shown in January 1905 at Madison Square Garden in New York City.

Perrin was not satisfied with simply building the car to European-type specifications—he also specified the use of materials and components imported from Europe. The Lozier car was built with steels supplied by Krupp in Germany and Derihon in Belgium. Carburetors were purchased in France, and Bosch magnetos were imported from Germany.

The first Lozier engine had four cylinders cast in pairs, with a bore of 4.5 inches and a stroke of 5.5 inches, giving a displacement of 350 cubic inches. It delivered 37 hp at 1,250 rpm. It was installed in a car known as Type B or 30-35 hp, of which the company produced 25 examples in 1905. Notable features included nickel-steel axles, pressed-steel frame, and ball bearings in wheel hubs and gearbox. It was built on a 115.5-inch wheelbase, with 36 × 4-inch wheels, and carried all-aluminum bodywork.

Shortly afterwards, Perrin left Lozier to go to work for Pope-Waverly in Indianapolis, transferring in 1906 to Pope-Toledo in his native city. But by mid-year 1906 he was back at Lozier, holding the titles of chief engineer, factory superintendent, and manager, at the age of 31.

Model B became C in 1906, and Model D was a new design, a 40 hp 4-cylinder listed at $5,500 as a touring car and $6,500 as a limousine. It weighed 2,800 pounds and had a 60-mph maximum speed. Model F was a modernized D for 1907, but Model E was a new model, a 60-hp 4-cylinder model with a 120-inch wheelbase, priced at $7,000 and $8,000 according to body type.

Type F evolved into Type G, selling at $4,000 in 1908. Type H was launched in September, 1907, with Type I following in November. In its Briarcliff version, Model H was a car of extremely rakish appearance, anticipating a style that was to become fashionable for the next decade and beyond.

The H engine was a four-cylinder, T-head unit rated at 60 hp. Square cylinder dimensions of 5.25 × 5.25 inches gave a displacement of 455 cubic inches.

Type I was a six-cylinder version of the same engine, with the chassis on a 131-inch wheelbase. The engine had a ball-bearing crankshaft and splash lubrication with assistance from an automatic oiler. It was water-cooled, with a gear-driven centrifugal water-pump.

Dual ignition was used, one with a Bosch high-tension magneto; the other by coil and battery. The four-speed gearbox provided selective shifts in the H-pattern that was to become standard in the industry.

The car was built on a 124-inch wheelbase and the wheels were shod with 36 × 4½-inch tires. The base price for the Briarcliff was $5,000, with an additional $20 for the cape top. The Limousine sold for $6,000.

Lozier production figures remained very low, for the cars were built to the highest standards of workmanship, with careful inspection and testing. The term high-grade is hopelessly inadequate to describe the Lozier's quality.

13. THOMAS FLYER 6-70 MODEL K 1910

Without any evidence that Winton, Ford or Thomas reserved the letter K for their most prestigious models, It remains a fact that the first of the great cars from each of them carried the same designation: Model K.

The 1910 Thomas Flyer Model K 6-70 was a high-quality touring car of staid appearance but overwhelming power and performance (Fig. 1-13). A glance from a knowledgeable observer was enough to reveal a very clean engineering design, with a T-head six showing marvelous workmanship and artistic sensibility.

Orginally introduced in 1908 with a 136-inch wheelbase, The Model K had a wheelbase of a full 140 inches in 1910. It weighed about 3,500 pounds, had a maximum speed of 70 mph, and carried a price tag of $6,000.

It looked like the coherent product of a single mind, but its ancestry makes clear that its technical makeup was a combination of elements created by various progenitors.

To begin at the beginning, Edwin Ross Thomas was a great American entrepreneur who started two new businesses in 1900; first, the Buffalo Automobile and Auto-Bi Company to make steam-driven bicycles and tricycles, and second, the E. R. Thomas Motor Company, also in Buffalo, to manufacture gasoline-powered motor cars.

E. R. Thomas built his first car in 1901. Oddly, it was called Model 16. If there were 15 earlier ones, they probably existed only on paper. Model 16 was produced under the direction of George Salzman, who was probably its principal designer. It had a horizontal twin mounted under the seat with two-speed planetary transmission and chain drive to the rear wheels.

During 1904 Thomas went to an in-line three-cylinder engine, installed in front, under a hood. The first such model had a curb weight of 2,000 pounds, and a list price of $2,500. This was the first Thomas model graced with the Flyer name.

In November, 1904, the factory built its first four-cylinder model, a 40 hp car, Thomas Flyer Model 25, priced at $3,000. A 50 hp model followed in 1905. It was powered by a 4-cylinder, T-head engine, and had a chassis with a 118-inch wheelbase. List price was $3,500.

H. J. Hass was chief engineer of the company then, and it was he who was mainly responsible for turning the rough ideas and outlines of E. R. Thomas into engineering drawings and specifications . . . up to 1905.

For in 1905, E. R. Thomas hired Gustave Chedru to be chief of the car design staff. A Frenchman, Chedru had worked for de Dion-Bouton, Richard-Braiser, and Clement-Bayard on car designs and engineering in France, and had come to America with Edison after working for Edison in Europe. At first, Chedru did surprisingly little to change the Thomas product.

The Thomas 4-50 Victoria of 1907 was built on a 100-inch wheelbase. It had a pressed steel frame, with the engine mounted at the front end, a sliding gear transmission and chain drive to the rear axle. Tires were 34 × 4½-inch on all four wheels. That car had a list price of $3,500. In 1907 Thomas also built a Limousine with

Fig. 1-13. The Thomas Flyer 6-70 Model K of 1910.

the same engine and drive train on a longer frame with a 114-inch wheelbase.

Thomas's first six was introduced in 1907 as the Model 27 Touring Phaeton. The engine had its cylinders cast in pairs and was coupled to a sliding-gear transmission with chain drive to the rear axle. This car was built on a 124-inch wheelbase and had a curb weight of 2,600 pounds. Its list price was $6,000. The same chassis was also available as a Type 30 Limousine with a 2,800-pounds curb weight and a $7,000 price.

The Thomas Flyer became famous as the winner of the fabulous New York-to-Paris auto race in 1908, when George Schuster drove a four-cylinder Model 35 a distance of 13,342 miles in 112 days (not including shipping days).

By 1908 Chedru was gone, and Thomas's chief engineer in 1908 was Frederick P. Nehrbas, who is credited with the design of the New York-Paris car. Obviously, however, its engineering elements can be traced back to Chedru. (No doubt Chedru was also responsible for the six-cylinder model that went into production in 1908).

The engine of the Model K consisted of six separately cast cylinders on a common crankcase. It was actually the same engine that was used in the four-cylinder Model F (4-60) with two extra cylinders. It had the same T-head valve configuration and the same bore and stroke, 5½ × 5½ inches, giving the 6-70 a displacement of 784 cubic inches. Jump-spark ignition was used, with a high-tension magneto. A new four-speed sliding-gear selective-shift transmission was adopted, placed centrally in the chassis, with chain drive to the rear wheels.

The cooling system featured a cellular radiator with two fans. The brake system had internal-expanding drums in the rear wheels and an external-contracting bank brake on the transmission jackshaft. Long semi-elliptical leaf springs were used for both front and rear axles.

Its body design was by A. A. Woodruff, Thomas body engineer. An ash frame, reinforced with metal plates, carried an aluminum body made of 16-gauge panels. The car weighed 3,600 pounds and had a maximum speed of 70 mph. The 6-70 was tractable, smooth, relatively quiet, with above-average ride comfort and easy handling.

The Thomas line for 1908 also included two lower-priced models, the 4-20 Towncar and the 4-40 Detroit. These were shaft-driven cars of more modern concept, designed by a group of former Oldsmobile engineers working in Detroit, quite independently of the Thomas engineering staff in Buffalo. They were built in a separate plant in Detroit by a Thomas subsidiary that was a spin-off of the parent company in Buffalo. Organized in 1909, it cam under control of Hugh Chalmers, who reorganized it as the Chalmers-Detroit Company.

Thomas Flyer Model K remained in production throughout 1910. But the E. R. Thomas Company was losing money and headed for bankruptcy; E. R. Thomas himself resigned in 1911, and in 1912 the company was placed in receivership. The creditors finally ordered its affairs to be wound up, and in March 1913 the assets of the E. R. Thomas Motor Car Company were sold at an auction to the Empire Smelting Company of Depew, New York, for $51,000.

Edwin Ross Thomas remained active in many other enterprises but never again became associated with the auto industry. He lived until 1936, dying at the ripe old age of 86. As for Gustave Chedru, he returned to France to become chief engineer for Etablissements Andre Dubonnet at Neuilly and built many prototypes with novel suspension systems and chassis configurations up to 1939.

14. CHADWICK SIX 1910

One of the rarest of America's great cars, the Chadwick was produced in very small numbers to the most exacting standard of materials and workmanship. Less than 300 Chadwicks were built throughout its existence from 1904 to 1915 (Fig. 1-14).

Lee S. Chadwick blatantly advertised the Chadwick car as being "The most powerful, the fastest, the strongest, the safest, the simplest, the quietest, the most easily controlled, the most dependable, the most advanced, the most luxurious car . . . available to the buying public."

Lee Sherman Chadwick had studied engineering at Purdue University and served as chief engineer for the two-cylinder Searchmont car built in Trainer, Pennsylvania, in 1902-03.

When the Searchmont venture folded, Chadwick bought the parts that had been made for a new four-cylinder model he had designed, leased factory space in Chester, Pennsylvania and built what was to become the first Chadwick car. With a bore and stroke of 4.50 × 5.00 inches, it had 318 cubic inch displacement, and an output of 24 hp. Yet the car was good for 60 mph!

Chadwick patented the cooling system, with its huge spun-copper jackets containing four or five times greater capacity than the cylinder displacement. To demonstrate its cooling capacity, Chadwick once ran a car in a speed contest without a fan belt, and the Chadwick still won.

An elaborate lubrication system relied on a shaft-driven force-feed oiler with direct oil pipes to each cylinder and main bearing. Crankpins received splash lubrication. Chadwick built his own carburetor, which was provided with a patented lever-adjustment allowing the driver to adjust jet-nozzle opening from his seat.

After incorporating the Chadwick Engineering Works Chadwick built his first six in 1906. It was a T-head design with cylinders cast in pairs, also using the surrounding copper jackets. This engine, however, was very disappointing to Chadwick for it failed to drive the car any faster than the four-cylinder models.

In addition to increasing the cylinder displacement of his six, Chadwick began exploring other ways of raising power output, and did much pioneering work with super-charging. He settled on a belt-driven centrifugal blower, and racing-type Chadwick sixes so equipped were timed at over 100 mph in 1905-06.

The supercharger became optional for the 1907-model Chadwick Six. That year Chadwick moved into a new plant at Pottstown, Pennsylvania and engaged John Thomas "Ted" Nichols as chief engineer. Together, Chadwick and Nichols created the production model that was going to be built from 1908 through 1910.

The engine was a new T-head design with 5.00×6.00-inch bore and stroke, giving a displacement of no less than 706.9 cubic inches. Output was 70-75 hp at 1,100 rpm without the super-charger. It was fitted with a patented Chadwick carburetor and matched with a 4-speed transmission. A cone clutch was built into the flywheel. Frame, shafts, and gears were made of chrome-nickel steel.

But Chadwick was unwilling to stray from chain drive to the rear axle. This was the one area in which he hesitated. In all other respects he was in the vanguard of technical evolution, if not out on his own, scouting for new technology, always ready to put it to use.

Aluminum was used for the body, which was mounted on a reinforced wooden frame and fastened to the frame with rivets. Genuine leather seats were used, stuffed with curled hair.

Bodies were built by the Reading Metal Body Company to Chadwick design and specification, until Harry Roumig, a foreman with Reading Metal Body, left to start his own business in the nearby village of Fleetwood and secured the Chadwick contract.

Fig. 1-14. Chadwick Six, 1910, one of America's rarest great cars.

Thus was born the Fleetwood body that was later absorbed by the Fisher brothers. The 1908 Chadwick Fast Runabout was listed at $6,500 and the Type 16 Limousine for $8,000. They may have been worth it, for production costs must have been atrociously high. And the Chadwick, despite its bulk and weight, was a high-performance car. In August 1909, a Chadwick set a new 10-mile world record in 8 minutes 23.4 seconds (71.5 mph).

Lee Sherman Chadwick retired from the automobile industry in 1911, and the company carried on for four more years, but the Chadwick cars were no longer built to the same standards after his departure.

Chadwick made a new career as chief engineer of the Perfection Stove Company of Cleveland, and never lost interest in car design, though his days with the auto industry were forever ended. He died in 1958, in Burlington, Vermont, where he had retired.

15. OLDSMOBILE LIMITED 1910

According to the maker's catalog, the Oldsmobile Limited "has created a new standard of luxury in motoring. The combination of the smooth-running, six-cylinder Oldsmobile engine, improved spring suspension, and large 42-inch tires, produces the easiest-riding car ever built." The Olds Motor Works in Lansing, Michigan, built 310 of these glorious, great cars in 1910 (plus 1,525 four-cylinder models).

Its six-cylinder L-head engine was rated at 60 hp, and the car was said to be able to reach 75 mph. The wheelbase was 130 inches, which, taken together with the tallness of the body structure, made the 56-inch track look narrow (Fig. 1-15). The frame was so high up, the car had a two-step running board. As a seven-passenger touring car, the Limited carried a list price of $4,600; a far cry from the Curved Dash model with its single-cylinder engine and 700 pounds curb weight, which could be bought for $650 in 1901, and put the Olds Motor Works on the map.

Ransom E. Olds had built his first car in 1897. It was a tiller-steered machine with a 5-hp engine, giving the car a top speed of no more than 18 mph. A company formed to build and sell it failed. Olds did better with the Olds Motor Works, established in Detroit in 1899, but his first design, priced at $1,250, attracted so few orders that Olds Motor Works seemed headed for sure failure.

In 1901, the company added a low-priced car, of utter simplicity, built on a 66-inch wheelbase. It had been designed by a young engineer, Malcolm F. Loomis, who had joined Olds right after graduating from the engineering school of Michigan Agricultural College in 1896.

This car put the Olds business on the express track. A sudden stop occurred in 1901 when the factory was destroyed by fire. Olds moved back to Lansing, and concentrated production on that one model, forever known as the Curved Dash Oldsmobile. It was the basis of a successful one-model program that lasted through 1905.

Big changes in policy were made in 1904, when R. E. Olds resigned and started manufacturing the Reo. Malcolm F. Loomis left at the same time, but Oldsmobile had an engineering staff that bristled with talent, and the new management under F. L. Smith, set out to compete in the middle-class and luxury car markets. George Willis Dunham, with the assistance of Theron P. Chase, led the engineering department, where Howard E. Coffin held a prominent position up to 1907.

First came the Model F, a two-cylinder car priced at $1,250, which evolved into the Model L in 1906. That was the year of the Model S, Oldsmobile's first four-cylinder car, selling at $2,250. The following year, Olds concentrated its production on one model, the AH four-cylinder, with a list price of $2,750. It was renamed Model M for 1908, and was quite successful.

The first six cylinder Oldsmobile was the Model Z from 1908, priced at $4,200. With its 4.50 × 4.75 inches bore and stroke, the displacement was 453 cubic inches and its output 48 hp. Built on a 130-inch wheelbase, it had a 3-speed transmission and shaft drive to the rear axle. It was a direct forerunner of the Limited, its price rising to $4,500 before it was discontinued at the end of 1909.

The Oldsmobile Limited was designed by Carl C. Hinkley, who had joined Oldsmobile in 1906 as assistant chief engineer and was given the title of chief engineer in 1907. Hinkley came from Lima, Ohio, and had studied engineering at the Case School of Applied Science. He had worked for Peerless in 1903, and with the Frank B. Stearns Company in 1904-05.

The engine Hinkley created for the Limited was a giant of 707 cubic-inch displacement, with 4.75-inch bore and stroke, and cylinders cast in pairs with integral T-heads. It was equipped with a Rayfield updraft carburetor and had Bosch dual-system magneto ignition. A leather-faced cone clutch took the drive to the four-speed selective-shift transmission, where a propeller shaft carried the power to the rear axle. The rear axle was suspended in a platform-spring system, and the front axle was carried by normal semi-elliptical leaf springs.

The Olds Motor Works had been absorbed by General Motors in 1909, so the Limited was indeed a GM car, and by far outstripped anything that Buick, Oakland or even Cadillac could produce in the way of luxury cars in that day. But the Limited was phased out in 1912, after 1,850 of them had been produced, when Charles W. Nash became president of Oldsmobile, and redirected the entire product philosophy towards the less glamorous and more utilitarian.

C. C. Hinkley left Olds in 1912 to design a new car for the Owen Motor Car Company in Detroit, and later that year joined the Chalmers Motor Company as chief engineer. In 1917 he formed Titan Motors Corporation to build truck engines for the U.S. government, and this firm developed into Hinkley Motors, which he led till it went under in the growing competition from Continental, Lycoming, and others in 1926. Then he joined Buda as director of engineering, and led the development of the Buda range of diesel engines. Hinkley died in 1936.

16. SIMPLEX SERIES 50, 1910

Perhaps archaic in many ways, rather than progressive in its layout and specifications, the Simplex was nevertheless a great car. Certainly, its performance was such that it left no doubt of it being a case where the polished example of established practice surpasses the first applications of superior principles. The origins of the Series 50 can indeed be traced right back to the 1901 Mercedes, which so influenced the whole world of automaking (Fig. 1-16).

The 1910 Simplex was designed by G. Edward Franquist, whose history of automotive engineering goes back to the year 1900; and Traugott J. Gott, an engineer from Strelitz in Mecklenburg (now East Germany) who had emigrated to America, and joined Simplex as chief draftsman in 1908. Franquist joined Smith & Mabley in 1903 and designed a car that was a direct copy of the 18/22 Mercedes. The company had been formed by Carlton R. Mabley, and A. D. Proctor Smith in New York City to act as importers of Panhard-Levassor, Mercedes, Renault and Fiat automobiles. Before long, they decided to start production of an American car built to European standards.

The car was named S & M Simplex, to distinguish it from the American Simplex made in Mishawaka, Indiana, and later, just Simplex. The Simplex name was taken from the Mercedes Simplex which formed the basis for the first model. Franquist copied most

Fig. 1-15. Olds Limited, 1910, "a new Standard of luxury in motoring."

63

of his designs from Mercedes models imported by Smith & Mabley, deviating in 1905 to make a copy of the French CGV (Charron, Girardot & Voigt).

The Simplex cars of 1904-12 were constructed in a building on East 83rd Street in Manhattan, by a small group of expert mechanics and machinists. Cylinders, axles, gas tanks, and dashboards were cast, soldered, and machined in this little factory. Frame members were bought from outside and assembled here. Only wheels, tires, electrical parts, and sundry minor items were purchased from outside suppliers.

Gradually, Franquist's confidence in his own engineering talent got the upper hand, and the 1907 short-stroke 50-series was not only a largely independent creation, but also the car that was to make the Simplex name famous in America.

The 50 series Simplex was a T-head four-cylinder unit with both bore and stroke of 5.75 inches, giving a displacement of 597 cubic inches. It was claimed to deliver 50 hp but almost certainly delivered a sizeable bonus beyond that figure. The cylinders were cast in pairs, and the enormous pistons were "gun-iron" castings from exactly the same material. An aluminum crankcase was fitted, containing a camshaft on each side. The exhaust camshaft could be shifted axially to relieve compression when starting the engine.

On both camshafts, the cams bore against rollers carried at the bottom of the pushrods, reducing friction losses in the valve gear. Each cylinder had two spark plugs, fired by a Bosch dual-magneto system. The magneto was driven by a shaft from the right side of the engine, while a similar shaft on the left drove the water pump.

An external tank served as an oil reservoir, and contained a small pump that fed oil under pressure to the crankshaft and camshaft bearings. This pump was driven by a vertical shaft mounted on the rear end of the right-side camshaft.

The Juhasz carburetor received gasoline under gravity pressure from a feeder tank under the hood, which in turn was kept filled from the main tank by a pressurized system utilizing exhaust-gas pressure.

A four-speed sliding-gear transmission was combined with the differential in the center of the car, with a jackshaft and chain drive to the rear axle. The transmission casing was made of aluminum.

The rear wheels free-wheeled on the axle but the hub was fixed to the drive chain sprocket. Radius rods took up the driving thrust and transferred the thrust loads to the chassis frame. Brake

Fig. 1-16. The 1911 Simplex 50 Speed Car.

drums in the rear wheels had internal-expanding shoes, actuated by the handbrake lever, while the sprocket shafts carried external-contracting bands operated by a linkage from the brake pedal. The Simplex was built on a 128-inch wheelbase, with both axles carried on semi-elliptical leaf springs.

The firm of Smith & Mabley went under in the financial crisis of 1907, and was taken over by Herman Broesel, who reorganized it as the Simplex Automobile Company. Broesel was a wealthy textile trader, who left the running of the car business to his sons, Carl and Herman Junior. Production continued in Manhattan until 1912, when Simplex moved to new premises in New Brunswick, New Jersey.

Chapter 2
The Early Years: 1911 to 1913

There can be no doubt that racing improved the breed in the formative years of the auto industry. Many car companies entered factory teams in selected events, and benefited from the publicity (when winning or placing among the leaders) as well as from the technical lessons learned in failures or when trying out new things.

17. NATIONAL SERIES V, 1911

Based in Indianapolis, National used racing as a deliberate part of its product development effort. And its racing successes contributed much to the nationwide reputation of the make (Fig. 2-1).

In November, 1905, a National had set a new stock car world record, covering 1,094 miles in 24 hours, a record that was still undefeated in 1909. But National's bestknown achievements in racing came after the introduction of the Series V in 1911.

As National's chief engineor, W. Guy Wall also learned from successes and failures of the cars of his rivals in racing, and was quick to adopt new features that could improve the quality and performance of the National.

The last National examined in these pages is the Model L of 1907. Along with its four-cylinder stablemates, the D, F, and H, it had its cylinders cast individually. In 1908 Wall began to use cylinders cast in pairs resulting in considerable weight savings, and lower production costs. Wall also gave in to fashion, for that year he buried the radiator with the circular shell and adopted a new shield-shaped.

In his racing cars, Wall had made a point of assuring easy engine interchangeability, so that the same chassis could compete in different classes, or be quickly refitted with a higher-powered engine after coming face-to-face with a speedier rival. In 1911 he took the step of utilizing the same principle in the standard production car. It was first applied to the Series V.

The same basic vehicle was available with a choice of two engines, a 40 hp four-cylinder unit, or a 60-hp six-cylinder engine. Both were T-head units with non-detachable heads and dual ignition with two plugs per cylinder.

Cylinder dimensions were the same in both: 4.875-inch bore and 6-inch stroke, giving displacements of 448 and 672 cubic inches, respectively. With the 40 hp engine, the car had a top speed with a normal touring car body of 60 mph, and the six could reach 70-75 mph.

They held the road well, for they were built with an uncommonly low center of gravity. Wall designed a drop-center frame with kickups over the axles, which lowered the body without taking risks in the areas of ground clearance or ride comfort. Frames were given deeper-section side members for 1913 to prevent any sagging while carrying heavy loads.

In 1911 the Series V engine had part splash, part pressurized lubrication. Splash was eliminated for 1912, the engine then working with full pressure lubrication. During 1912, Wall directed a lot of new experiments to make the engine quieter, and ended up with special cast-iron pistons having skirts of a new design, and camshafts with revised cam profiles. All this was done without loss of power, in fact, the 1913 models showed a slight gain in horsepower.

National was among the first to adopt electric starting, having standardized a Gray & Davis starter for the 1912 models. The driver engaged the starter by pushing on a separate pedal positioned next to the accelerator. On the 1913 models, electric lighting was made standard, too, with a Gray & Davis generator to charge the storage battery. The generator was driven by a silent chain from a sprocket on one camshaft. A tire pump was a permanent fixture, built into the front of the crankcase, with a detachable air hose reaching to all tires.

While National's racing drivers, like those driving Simplex racing models, preferred the right-hand drive position with outrigger brake lever and gearshift, National's non-racing clients tended to prefer the left-hand seat for driving in the manner

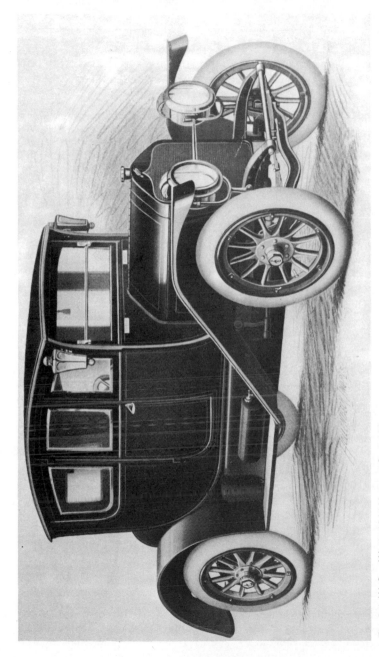

Fig. 2-1. W. Guy Wall's 1911 National Series V.

popularized by Ford's Model T. Consequently, Wall designed the Series V with the steering wheel on the left, and gearshift and hand-brake levers mounted centrally in the floor.

Chrome-nickel gears and shafts were used throughout the drive train, with a four-speed transmission and shaft drive to the rear axle. The concern that Wall always showed for quality also paid off in racing.

National was especially prominent in track racing, winning the Elgin National Trophy race in 1911, and the Illinois Trophy Race the same year. In 1911 a National also set a new stock-car record for the flying mile in 40.32 seconds (89.3 mph). In 1912 National won the Indianapolis 500 miles race, with Joe Dawson at the wheel, and an average speed of 78.7 mph, powered by a four-cylinder engine enlarged to 490 cubic inch displacement.

In the market place, National was up against a lot of hot, local competitors, such as Stutz, Marion, Premier, and Marmon. On the national level, National was competing in a flexible price class bordered on the lower side by the flagship models of Hudson, Cole, Buick, and Cadillac, while having a margin on the high side from the low-line models of Packard, Locomobile, Peerless and Pierce-Arrow.

18. PACKARD SIX-48, 1912

Ever since the Model L of 1904, Packard stayed in the forefront of the quality-car market. Because of the advanced design of the company's first four-cylinder model, subsequent evolution over the next half-decade seemed almost stagnant. Clearly, the emphasis at Packard was not on innovation, but on material strength and mechanical reliability. After the $3,000 Model L came the Model S with a $4,000 list price, basically an upgraded and enlarged version of the same design (Fig. 2-2).

The departure in 1905 of Charles Schmidt (who joined Peerless in Cleveland) no doubt had a great deal to do with the temporary freezing of Packard's car design. Never one for daring innovation, J. W. Packard recommended careful, step-by-step, extrapolation of the established models and Henry B. Joy went along with him. In fact, they hesitated so long in appointing a new chief engineer that it became unnecessary. One man grew into the function of leading the engineering staff so well that the naming of Russell Huff as chief engineer in 1907 merely put the official seal of approval on the existing state of affairs.

A native of Leesburg, Ohio, he had studied engineering at the Case School of Applied Science and joined Packard in Detroit in 1902 at the age of 25. Thus, he was one of few qualified engineers at Packard prior to Schmidt's arrival, albeit lacking in experience. He gained self-confidence by dint of on-the-job training, and carefully nurtured plans for greater Packards of the future.

The first results of his growing independence of engineering thought were combined in the Series 30 of 1907. It was known internally as the Model U, powered by a four-cylinder T-head engine, cast in pairs, with a bore and stroke of 5 × 5½ inches, giving a displacement of 432 cubic inches. Understressed for the ultimate in reliability and long life, it delivered 30 hp at 650 rpm.

Walter T. Fishleigh was executive engineer for the design team that was responsible for this project. Series 30 was built on a chassis with 123.5-inch wheelbase, and was available with closed bodywork in addition to the usual open tourer and cape top models, all with a basic price of $4,200.

Packard had produced only 700 cars in 1906, but Joy had started a major plant expansion that year, and in 1907 over 2,000 Packards were built.

Russell Huff and Henry B. Joy were convinced there was a market for a lightweight high-quality car, which led to the design of the Series 18 (Model N). It was a short-wheelbase car with a smaller edition of the Series 30 engine, introduced in 1909. It was a true Packard, but the traditional Packard clientele failed to realize it, and remained overwhelmingly faithful to the Series 30. Both were kept in production, however, through the 1911 model year.

These Packards still had the gearbox in unit with the rear axle casing, combining all gears inside one package, which added dramatically to the unsprung weight. Still, Packard tried to minimize the unsprung weight by making both the gearbox and final drive housings of aluminum.

Huff and his assistants were preparing revolutionary changes in the technical makeup of Packard cars, including the engines as well as the chassis. They were getting ready to produce six-cylinder engines and shaftdrive chassis carrying the transmission adjacent to the engine.

The first such Packard was the Six-48, making its debut in 1911 as a 1912 model. It was mainly Huff's work, and among those who share credit for its design are Owen R. Skelton, who had joined Packard in 1907 and worked on transmissions and axles; and Allen Loomis, an extremely inventive young man who had come to

Packard in 1906 as a research engineer. During his ten-year stay with Packard, Loomis took out 39 patents, most of which came to be used on Packard cars.

In its original version, the six-cylinder engine was a T-head design, bearing a direct relationship to the four-cylinder T-head engines. Its cylinders were cast in pairs and had a bore and stroke of 4½ × 5½ inches, giving 525 cubic-inch displacement. It ran much faster than the older T-head engines, delivering 75 hp at 1,720 rpm. (The number 48 refers to horsepower calculated under the ALAM formula.) The Packard Six actually delivered 48 hp at less than 1,000 rpm!

With this engine, Packard went to force-feed lubrication, with an oil pump driven by a worm gear on the camshaft delivering oil under pressure to all crankshaft bearings and the wrist (via holes drilled in the connecting rods). The camshaft bearings, however, still relied on getting a splash from the swinging cranks.

During August, 1912, Packard announced a stablemate for the Six-48 in the form of a Six-38—a design that had been started considerably later. With this model, Packard adopted the L-head engine, placing all valves on the same side, concealed by aluminum covers mounted on spring clamps. Cylinders were cast in pairs, with non-detachable heads, and while the Six-38 had the same stroke as the Six-48 and therefore could use the same crankshaft, it had a smaller bore of 4 inches, which reduced the displacement to 415 cubic inches and maximum output to 60 hp.

The Six-38 was equipped with an electric starter (combined with the generator) while the Six-48 relied on handcrank starting throughout the 1912 and 1913 model years. With the Six-38, Packard switched to left hand drive, and moved the gearshift and handbrake levers, not to the middle of the chassis, but next to the driver's door, for left-handed operation. This layout was adopted also for the Six-48 in 1914.

Under Skelton's influence, Packard began using helical-cut gears for the pinion and ring gear assembly as early as 1913. The gears were developed by a Swiss engineer, Ernst Widhaber, who had gone to work for the Gleason Works in Rochester, New York where the gears were manufactured.

For 1914, the engine program was revised, both sixes now being composed of two blocks of three cylinders. Simultaneously, L-heads replaced T-heads on the larger engine, reducing its production cost by utilizing greater sharing of components.

Fig. 2-2. Packard Six-48 of 1912.

Wheelbases ranged from 115.5 to 138 inches for the 1914-model Six-38, going up to 144 inches for the Six-48. Customers paid $4,150 for a Six-38 touring car and $5,200 for the Limousine in the same series. The Six-48 five-passenger phaeton was listed at $4,750, and the six-passenger Brougham at an even $6,000.

In 1912 Packard's manufacturing complex in Detroit included 30 separate buildings with a combined floor space of 38 acres. At full capacity, it gave work to 7,000 people, representing no less than 80 trades. At that time, there were more than 18,000 Packards running on American roads.

J. W. Packard had resigned from the presidency in 1909, and Henry B. Joy held that office until he was named chairman in 1916.

Russell Huff left Packard in 1914 and worked as a consulting engineer with Dodge from 1916 to 1925, but resigned due to ill health, and died in St. Petersburg, Florida in March, 1930.

19. ALCO 60 HP, 1912

Few Americans had heard of the Alco until it won the Vanderbilt Cup races in 1909 and 1910. In the latter event, it covered 278 miles at an average speed of 65.18 mph. Starting in the 1909 race as a complete outsider, a challenger of unknown potential, it had beaten an international field of reputable racing cars, and impressed all who saw it with its speed and stamina. It was built in Providence, Rhode Island, by a subsidiary of the American Locomotive Company, its trade mark being an acronym of the parent firm's title (Fig. 2-3).

The six-cylinder engine that powered the giant Alco touring car of 1912 was essentially the same as that which powered the 1909-10 racing car. It was a T-head design with cylinders cast in pairs, and non-detachable heads.

In production tune, it delivered 72 hp from its 578.5 cubic-inch displacement (4.72-inch bore and 5.51-inch stroke). One plug per cylinder was fitted with Bosch magneto ignition. Exhaust valves were the same size as the inlet valves (2.3125 inches across the head). A Newcomb carburetor prepared the mixture from fuel fed under pressure from the rear-mounted tank.

Lubrication was a combination of force-feed and splash, with an oil pump driven by a spiral bevel gear from the exhaust camshaft. Cylinders, pistons, and wrist pins had splash delivery only.

The centrifugal water pump was contained in a separate housing and driven via an Oldham coupling, and a six-blade fan, belt-driven from the crankshaft. The two-piece, horizontally split crankcase was made of cast aluminum. The cylinders were vanadium steel castings, and the crankshaft was machined from a solid billet of vanadium steel.

The Alco engine was a high-precision unit, built with a strong focus on quality and only a glance at the cost. The Alco was a high-priced car, advertised at $6,000 with a standard touring body in 1910, but that was certainly not enough to recoup the production costs for the small volume of cars turned out. The automobile department lost about $600,000 a year during its seven years' existence, and no more than 5,000 Alco cars were built in that time.

American Locomotive Company started the automobile department as a sideline in 1906, building French-designed Berliet cars under license. For couple of years, the cars were sold as Berliet or American Berliet, their production supervised by French engineers from the Lyon Factory. But in 1908 the general manager of the automobile department, Charles E. Davis, decided the business would be better off without the license, and set up a drawing office with B. D. Gray as chief engineer.

Davis had an engineering degree from Worcester Polytechnic Institute, and laid out the Alco Six in considerable detail, leaving the calculations, checking, material specifications, and other routine matters to Gray. Together they retooled the huge Providence plant, formerly used for building railroad locomotives, for car production.

The resulting 60 hp Alco was fabulous. Built on a 134-inch wheelbase, the touring model weighed 4,125 pounds and could

Fig. 2-3. The Alco 60 HP circa 1911. Body style remained the same through 1913.

reach 85 mph. Of course there was still a lot of Berliet influence in the design; the T-head engine configuration came from Berliet, and it is perhaps more than a coincidence that Berliet also brought out its first six-cylinder engine in 1909.

Berliet used chain drive on all its cars until the 14 CV model of 1907, and Alco used chain drive on the 1909-model 60 hp. The four-speed, all-ballbearing transmission, encased in aluminum, was mounted well back in the chassis, which placed the jackshaft and sprockets level with the forward spring eyes of the rear suspension, and gave conveniently short drive chains.

For 1910, Alco went to shaft drive. The gearbox was moved forward, shortening the drive shaft from the flywheel-mounted disc clutch. An open propeller shaft with universal joints at both ends took the drive to the all-steel rear axle. Because the jack shaft disappeared in this redesign, the contracting band brakes it carried on the chain-drive model were lost, and had to be combined with the internal-expanding rear-wheel drums.

The 1910 chassis was carried over to 1912 and 1913, but the 1913 model was given three-quarter-elliptical rear springs and Truffault-Hartford shock absorbers. At the same time, the brake system was refined, and the torque arm between the rear axle and the transmission casing was fitted with a universal joint at its rear end. Bigger tires were mounted on the rear wheels, measuring 37 × 5 inches, while the front tires remained at 36 × 4½ inches.

About mid-year in 1913, W. H. Marshall, president of American Locomotive Company, ordered the automobile department closed. A prototype called New Alco Light Six was shown in January, 1913, designed and built by the Crane Motor Company of Bayonne, New Jersey, but it was never produced for sale under that name. Instead, it became the Crane-Simplex.

B. D. Gray left the company and never worked in the automobile industry again, but Charles E. Davis went to Warner Gear Co. as general manager. The American Locomotive Co. stayed in the railroad prime-mover business as long as it was viable, and then began to diversify, reorganizing as Alco Products in 1955. Its operating assets were sold to a subsidiary of the Worthington Corporation and it became Citadel Industries in 1964.

20. MARMON "32", 1912

Long before there was a speedway there, Indianapolis was the home of several makes of interesting cars. There are similarities and parallels in their histories, with the cars emerging from obscurity to fame by virtue of their technical advances, lively performance, and indisputable quality. Although Marmon achieved popular acclaim much later than National, Marmon was to survive National by about a decade (Fig. 2-4).

The Marmon has a longer history, too, but its first great car was the Model "32" introduced in 1909. It was developed, year by year, so that by 1912, there was a high-grade, light car of modern construction, so well balanced in its concept and detail engineering that it could not be denied a place in the list of the 100 Greatest.

Powered by a four-cylinder T-head engine, it was to account for the bulk of Marmon's production for nine years.

The credit for the design of the car goes to Howard C. Marmon, son of company founder, Daniel W. Marmon, who had taken control of the E. & A.H. Nordyke Company of Richmond, Indiana, in 1866 and reorganized it as the Nordyke & Marmon Company. Its main business was making flour-milling machinery. Howard was born in Richmond in 1876, attended Earlham College there, and got his engineering degree from the University of California at Berkeley in 1898.

He began to design the car of his dreams in 1898 and talked his father into letting him build it in a corner of the engineering shop. The car he built in 1902 was a lightweight machine powered by an air-cooled overhead-valve V-twin engine which was most notable for featuring forced lubrication of the crankshaft bearings.

The engine was mounted in front, with a three-speed transmission and shaft drive to the rear axle. Engine, clutch and transmission were mounted in a subframe with some degrees of pitch freedom, so that the propeller shaft could work without universal joints.

Howard's car so impressed his elder brother Walter, who had inherited the business, that the family firm steered itself into automobile manufacturing. At the age of 23, Howard found himself chief engineer of a car factory. This called for a production prototype which Howard quickly designed and constructed.

It was called Model A and was a direct development of his first design, in terms of chassis layout and features. It had the same 84-inch wheelbase, but had more power, in the form of an air-cooled V-4. After a test period, Howard redesigned it as Model B, which went into production in 1904. It was priced at $2,500, an extremely stiff price or a 2,000-pound, four-seater tonneau built on a 90-inch wheelbase. Yet it was a realistic price in view of what went into the Marmon in the way of imagination, engineering skill, patient development work, good materials and skilled work.

The Marmon C-35 and D-36 followed in 1906, also powered by air-cooled V-4 engines. Bodies were made mostly of aluminum, and the cars made a good reputation for the name of Marmon in the market place.

No big changes were made throught 1907, though Howard designed and built several experimental cars with air-cooled V-8's in 1906. In 1908 Marmon was among the first to use drilled crankshafts with pressure lubrication to main and crankpin bearings. Even wrist pins were lubricated with oil supplied through tubes attached to the connecting rods. From 1905 onwards, he was refining his engineering philosophy and bringing it more into line with that of other leading makes, resulting in the 1908-model Marmon which broke completely with earlier principles. The sub-frame disappeared, V-4 engines were discontinued, and air cooling discarded in favor of water-cooling.

Marmon went to water-cooled in-line four-cylinder engines in 1909, with two series: the 40-50 hp Model H, and the smaller Model 32. Model H was discontinued in 1910, but the Model 32 lived on until 1918. It was a high-performance car due more to its lightweight construction, excellent balance and roadholding, than to brute power. The Model 32 engine was a 317 cubic-inch T-head four, almost typical of current Indianapolis fashion. The engine was built up around a tunnel-type crankcase with cylinders cast in pairs.

Both crankcase and sump were aluminum castings. The crankshaft ran in three main bearings, with force-feed lubrication. The drive train featued a disc-type clutch at the flywheel, with a long propeller shaft to a three-speed transmission built into an extension of the rear axle (compare with the Packard "30").

The frame had pressed steel side and cross members riveted together, with a basic body structure of cast and rolled aluminum.

After the "32" came the "34" which must be recognized as one of the 100 Greatest in its own right.

21. WINTON SIX MODEL 17, 1912

Like most other car makers, Winton found itself in a period of transition at this time, gradually working its way out of the archaic and into the progressive era. The automobile was beginning to shed the last vestiges of horse-drawn carriage engineering, and auto industry executives and engineers had begun to face the reality of the situation they had created, with its consequent need for a rational, industrialized approach to automaking (Fig. 2-5).

Fig. 2-4. The Marmon "32" of 1912, a high-grade, light car.

Fig. 2-5. Winton Six Model 17 of 1912.

Winton's ambitions never did go in the direction of mass production, but only to modernize its concept of the great car. Alexander Winton was a man of conservative tastes, and his business still had the title of Winton Motor Carriage Company as late as 1912. The Cleveland factory was up to date in machinery and equipment, and manned with highly skilled workers, most of them specialists in their own trades, from machinists and fitters to carpenters and electricians.

Winton and his collaborators had a strong determination to continue to make great cars, which naturally meant keeping up with the greatest. And for a long time, they succeeded.

Since 1907, Winton had been building six-cylinder cars exclusively. In the years that followed, the Winton underwent only minor changes that were either superficial or evolutionary. Wheelbases were lengthened, suspension systems revised with an eye on restful riding, and seat cushions and upholstery carefully worked in pursuit of improved comfort. Body design was modernized in keeping with current trends, which meant lower back seats, smoother lines where the hood meets the cowl, and more flowing fender lines, with bigger and heavier fenders. More closed model bodies became available in response to customer demand, but for Winton, the standard model remained the open tourer with canopy top.

Winton went into 1912 with one single chassis, Model 17, built on a 136-inch wheelbase and a track half-an-inch wider than the industry norm of 56 inches. With the standard touring car body it weighed about 3,900 pounds, and while it did not have startling power of acceleration, it had an impressive top speed of about 75 mph.

The engine was enormous and inevitably reminiscent of a giant marine engine rather than a high-performance automobile. The six cylinder were cast in pairs, with water jackets completely surrounding each cylinder, and wide open spaces between each pair, due to the need for extra space to accommodate extremely wide main bearings of the double-ball-race type. Single-race ball bearings were used on the crankpins.

The four-bearing crankshaft also had large-diameter main and crankpin journals, with generous overlap, but lacked counter-weighting. A huge flywheel was suggestive of a two-cylinder unit—not a smooth-running six.

The crankshaft was offset relative to the cylinder center line against the cylinder walls in one of the first examples of this method of reducing side thrust in the pistons. Winton also used an aluminum crankcase that was split vertically for easy access to crankshaft bearings, without disturbing any other mechanical parts. Thus, the Winton engine showed no lack of refinement or of imagination in the minds of its creators.

It was an L-head design, with a long camshaft driven by helical gears from the front of the crankshaft. The timing gear train was also intended to drive a centrifugal water pump, bolted to the front pair of cylinders, and even to the fan, through an adjustable spring-tension clutch. Force-feed lubrication was assured by an eccentrically driven pump located externally, at the rear end of the oil sump.

With its 4.5-inch bore and 5-inch stroke, the Winton Six had a displacement of 477 cubic inches. It was rated at 48.6 NACC hp, and actually delivered between 60 and 70 hp.

Winton used right-hand drive through 1911, with hand brake and gearshift inside the driver's door, but the following year the steering gear and column were relocated on the left side, and gearshift and hand brake levers moved to a central position.

The four-speed gearbox was a separate assembly, linked to the multi-plate clutch and flywheel via a short shaft, and driving the spiral bevel rear axle through an open double-jointed propeller shaft. Both front and rear axles were carried on semi-elliptical leaf springs in 1911-12. A new rear suspension was adopted for 1913, with three-quarter elliptical springs.

Brake drums in the rear wheels were equipped with both internal-expanding shoes and external-contracting bands. Tires were 37 × 4-inch in 1911, 37 × 4½ inches in 1913, and grew to 37 × 5 inches in 1915. It was in 1915 that Winton finally abandoned the compressed-air starter and went to electrical equipment for starting and lighting.

Prices for the Model 21 of 1915 started at $3,250 for the four-passenger touring car and two/three-passenger roadsters; the six-passenger touring car was listed at $3,500. Model 21 was also available with a range of closed bodies, including a sedan and a landaulet, both listed at $4,600, and a three-quarter limousine listed at $4,350.

Winton sought a niche below the Packard, Peerless and Pierce-Arrow market, but ran head-on into competition with White, Locomobile, and National whose products were in some ways ahead of Winton's. And lower-priced challengers such as Oldsmobile, Chandler, and Hudson threatened the Winton from below, luring away its customers with attractive products at reasonable prices. Soon Winton was forced to make an abrupt change in marketing policy, which led to new and lower-priced cars. A lighter car was added in 1916, the Six-33, with prices starting at $2,285.

It was powered by a scaled-down version of the big L-head six, with a bore and stroke of 3.75 × 5.25 inches, which gave a displacement of 348 cubic inches and a real output of 50 hp.

The Six-33 was built on a shorter wheelbase of 128 inches, and the touring car had a curb weight of 3,300 pounds. But it was competing in a market with which Winton was unfamiliar, and the hopes Winton had entertained for it were dashed.

Technically, Winton cars were beginning to fall behind. They were soon surpassed not only in style but also in quality and excellence. After World War I Winton's market dwindled to the danger point. A proposed merger with Haynes in 1923 was never implemented, and, left to its own devices, the Winton Company went under in 1925, with its Captain, Alexander Winton, then 65 years old, still at the helm.

He was able to reorganize his business as the Winton Engine Company, manufacturing power units rather than complete vehicles, and he directed this firm until his death in 1932. The Winton Engine Company was taken over by General Motors, and reorganized in 1937 as the Cleveland Diesel and Engine Division.

22. S.G.V. J-SERIES, 1913

The art of making motor cars lost some of its mystery for American engineers and entrepreneurs after the first decade of the twentieth century. A supplier industry had sprung up, so that would-be auto makers could order everything needed, as from a mail-order catalog, and simply arrange for the assembly of parts and distribution of product. Precision tools and machines were available, and the ranks of skilled men swelled at all levels, due to education and experience on one hand and immigration from Europe on the other. At the same time, financiers and investors had recognized the automobile industry as a major vehicle for fortune-building (Fig. 2-6).

Mass production was beginning to make its mark, with Ford, Willys, Buick and others fighting to outproduce each other. A U.S. court of appeals ruled in 1911 that Ford (and other non-licensed auto makers) had not infringed the Selden patent, which had been a deterrent to many wishing to go into the car business. Now the doors were wide open, and over 1,100 companies were registered in America for the express purpose of manufacturing automobiles. Some were stock promotions, and some were honest attempts to meet demands whose existence was well-proven.

Louis Chevrolet was in the hospital, recovering from a racing accident, and the Dodge brothers, tired of being subcontractors to Ford (no matter how profitable), were laying plans to build a complete car of their own.

Such was the scene upon which the S. G. V. car arrived in 1911. It was an expensive, high-grade car of excellent quality, with the most modern engineering then seen in the U.S., built by a small concern that had no illusions about mass production, but whose product was an undeniably great car.

Fig. 2-6. Sternberg, Graham and Van Tine's S.G.V. J-Series, 1912.

The initial S.G.V. stand for Sternberg, Graham and Van Tine. Herbert M. Sternberg was vice-president and Robert E. Graham (no relation to the Graham brothers who later produced the Graham-Paige) was secretary and treasurer.

Neither had any previous experience in the automobile business, and left production up to the partner behind the third initial, Harry Alfred (Fred) Van Tine, who had been associated with the auto industry in engineering and technical posts since 1902. He had previously worked in New York City, center of auto imports, and had used the opportunities which that location offered to become thoroughly familiar with European car design and engineering practice. His favorite was the Lancia, and he was probably quite deliberate in copying design features of the Lancia when drawing up the first S.G.V.

The S.G.V. Company was formed in Reading, Pennsylvania, taking over the plant and assets of the defunct Acme Motor Car Company, The Acme had come into being in 1903, and after several tentative starts with low-priced cars, the company tried the opposite end of the scale, and by 1910 was offering a six-cylinder touring car of intelligent design (by Oliver Bickel), listed at prices up to $5,000, with a no-mileage, no-time-limit warranty. Too few customers who had the money to buy an Acme ever learned of its existence, let alone its excellence, and the enterprise failed, probably from the combined lack of publicity and promotion.

Today there is no question about the high ideals behind the Acme, for it was built by a remarkably selfcontained outfit, which produced its own engine, transmission, steering gear, frame and bodies in its Reading plant. This plant became the home of the S.G.V. and Van Tine must have found the atmosphere and environment congenial, for he never strayed from the prestige-car concept.

He kept some of the Acme men of proven qualifications, and brought in C. Tufts, who had formerly worked for the Pullman Company in York, Pennsylvania, as chief draftsman. Van Tine was more concerned with quality than with appearance; above all, he had a strong sense of the practical, and did not build his cars on an elephantine scale. Instead, the S.G.V stood on a 118-inch wheelbase, with 34 × 4-inch tires all around.

The four-cylinder engine was mounted entirely inside the wheelbase and drove the rear axle via a multi-plate clutch, four-speed transmission, and propeller shaft. The engine was cast en bloc, with 3.875-inch bore and 4.375-inch stroke, which gives a displacement of only 206 cubic inches. It had an NACC rating of a mere 24 hp, but its real output was 35-40 hp, and its performance rather lively, thanks to lightweight construction.

The car had jump-spark ignition with a high-tension magneto, and a low-profile cellular radiator. The driver sat on the left, and had the gearshift lever and handbrake mounted centrally, for right-hand operation.

The shift was of the selective type, which was now becoming general, and the hand brake acted on contracting bands on a drum carried on the transmission, while the brake pedal worked expanding shoes in drums mounted in the rear wheels.

For 1914 a USL electric self starter was listed as a $100 option. The S.G.V. was also available with the Vulcan electric gearshift, which allowed the driver to change speeds by pushing selector buttons mounted on one of the steering wheel spokes. By 1915 closed-body models cost $4,000, with the roadster or touring car models listed at $3,200.

That was the last year of the S.G.V. car, for the company went under in 1915, and was purchased by John A. Bell, who moved it to Newark, New Jersey, but was unable to restart production.

C. Tufts stayed in Reading, and found work with the Daniels Motor Car Company. 'Fred' Van Tine went back to the retail end of the automotive business where he was active until his death in 1925.

23. LOCOMOBILE SIX-38, 1913

Throughout its existence as a make of car, Locomobile remained one of America's greatest. It was one of the first great cars made in this country, and under the technical leadership of A. L. Riker, the Locomobile advanced an envied position—on the race track, in the market place, and in the minds of men (Fig. 2-7).

How the Locomobile evolved since our examination of the 1904 model can be quickly related. The basic chassis formula Riker had found in 1904 was not changed for five years, Locomobile continuing with four-cylinder engines and chain drive through 1908. His engines evolved more quickly, the F-head with automatic inlet valves giving way to a modern T-head design in 1906.

The typical Locomobile engine was built in several sizes, all with cylinders cast in pairs and copper jackets. The biggest in 1906 had 1,032 cubic-inch displacement and enough power to propel a racing chassis at speeds up to 110 mph! This combination won the Vanderbilt Cup races in 1908.

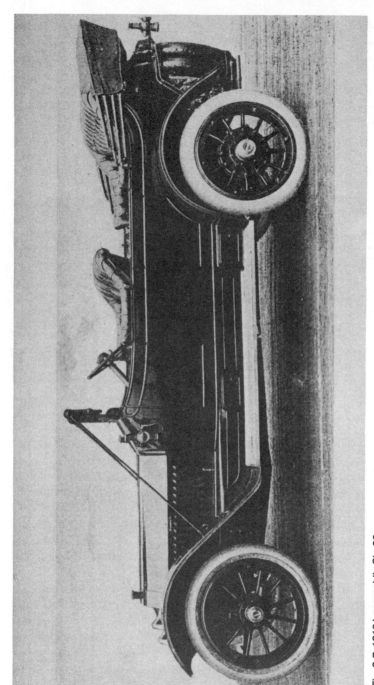

Fig. 2-7. 1913 Locomobile Six-38.

The 1907 production program crystallized into two series, Type E and Type H, rated at 20 hp and 35 hp respectively. Though the numbers sound low, they were spirited cars with real power outputs of about 35 and 45 hp.

Both had four-cylinder, T-head engines and chain drive. The driver sat on the right, with gearshift and brake levers outside the cockpit. The Model E touring car was built on a 96-inch wheelbase and had 32 × 4-inch tires on all wheels. The same 229-cubic-inch engine went into the Model E limousine, built on a 106-inch wheelbase, which had a list price of $3,800 ($1,000 more than the touring car).

Model H had a 251-cubic-inch displacement and both the touring car and limousine bodies were mounted on a chassis with a 120-inch wheelbase. The limousine had 34 × 5-inch tires on the rear wheels and 34 × 4-inch ones in front. The Model H five-passenger touring car cost $4,500 and the limousine $5,800.

The first modern Locomobile came in 1909, and was known as Model 30. With this design, Riker went to shaft drive, using a four-speed transmission mounted adjacent to the engine, and an open propeller shaft to a spiral bevel rear axle. The engine was rated at 38 hp but delivered about 50 hp from its 286 cubic inch displacement.

The Locomobile 30 was built on a 120-inch wheelbase and had a low frame, with semi-elliptical springs on both front and rear axles. Coachwork was elegant, because of classic proportions, even if the designs were fairly simple. List price for the touring car was $3,500.

Of course, Riker had assistants who steered the Locomobile's evolution more in the direction of the Pierce-Arrow rather than the Stutz or the Mercer of the time. Among them must be mentioned the head of the drawing office, a Swedish-born engineer named Frank G. Alborn, who joined Locomobile as a draftsman in 1900 and stayed with Locomobile until 1920. He later became chief engineer of White Motor Co. in Cleveland, where he created some notable new trucks.

Albert B Schulz had been working in association with A. L. Riker at Locomobile since 1902 and was named assistant chief engineer in 1905. Schulz stayed on as assistant chief engineer until 1916, when he went to Mercer in Trenton, New Jersey, as chief engineer.

Another influential man in product development at Locomobile in the early years was an English engineer, Alfred J.

Poole. He had come to the U. S. at the age of 23 with impeccable credentials from the works manager's office of Pennington in London; the experimental shop and drafting room of Humber in Coventry; and the Daimler test department, also in Coventry. He ran the test and assembly shop for Simplex for a couple of years, and then joined Locomobile as an experimental engineer about 1906. He left Locomobile in 1911 and went to Bosch Magneto (later United American Bosch) where he stayed until 1931.

The first Locomobile Six was basically a Riker creation, continuing the T-head design, with cylinders cast in pairs. The first one was an enormous 469 cubic-inch engine delivering about 80 hp (despite its official rating as a 48 hp engine). It was first installed in the 1911 Model Six-48, certainly a great car in every sense of the word. But the more modern Six-38 from 1913 is a more interesting and admirable car. The Six-48 was a brute; the Six-38 a refined performance car. Though the Six-38 was a very big and heavy car, it became known as the Little Six.

With bore and stroke of 4.25 × 5.00 inches, its displacement was 425.5 cubic inches and a real output of 60 hp. Like the Big Six, it had cylinders cast in pairs with non-detachable T-heads, and the crankshaft ran in seven main bearings. The crankcase was made of manganese-bronze alloy, and the oil sump of cast aluminum. The gearbox casing was also a manganese-bronze casting.

A Disco electric starter was fitted, and the wet-cell battery was automatically recharged by an Adlake generator. The transmission was a four-speed countershaft type with selective shift. The first models had right-hand drive, but Locomobile changed to left hand drive in 1914.

The 1913 Six-38 was built on a 128-inch wheelbase, which was stretched to 132 for 1915. Tire size was 4½ × 36 on all four wheels. The rear axle was a one-piece steel casting. Axle springs were semi-elliptical in front and three-quarter elliptical in the rear, manufactured from special spring steel.

List prices in 1915 were $4,400 for the four-passenger torpedo, $5,400 for the seven passenger limousine, $5,500 for the landaulet and $5,700 for the Berline.

A. L. Riker continued as technical director of Locomobile until 1921, when he settled in Bridgeport as a consulting engineer. Later he moved to Fairfield, Connecticut, where he died in 1930.

24. KISSEL KAR 60, 1913

During the teens of the century, there were many parallels between Oldsmobile in Lansing, Michigan, and the Kissel Motor

Car Company, located inland across Lake Michigan in Hartford, Wisconsin. Both had their base in the low-priced market, and yet both made brief, meritorious excursions into the luxury car market. Both produced a small number of expensive cars with surprising flair and then quietly reverted to their stock in trade (Fig. 2-8).

The run-of-the-mill Kissel Kar was a four-cylinder machine of modest power and mediocre performance, priced to compete with the Studebaker, Chalmers, Buick, Jackson, Velie, and Oakland. Suddenly, in 1913, Kissel came out with a six-cylinder machine with all the allure and performance of a Winton, Stearns, or Peerless (to mention only three great cars from Cleveland).

How could this happen? It's a short story, but the answers are not obvious. Kissel was not a pioneer automaker (having started production in 1906), but the company build practically every part of its vehicles in-house, relying on outside suppliers only for tires, electrical systems, and other special equipment. This gave Kissel Motor Company a dimension of freedom that most Detroit companies did not have at the time.

Louis Kissel was German, having been born there in 1838 and emigrated to Wisconsin at the age of 19. In 1869 he started the Hartford Plow Works with his sons, George, Otto and William. He later founded the Hartford Lumber Company, the First National Bank of Hartford, Hartford Electric Company, and the Northrup Tenteal Fur Company. It was in 1905 that he, with George, Otto and William, started the Kissel Motor Car Company.

The first models had four-cylinder engines, steel-frame chassis, and shaft-driven rear axles. The designs were apparently bought from independent consultants and Kissel's serious blacksmiths and machinists turned them into a workable car. Two years went by while Kissel produced cars without having its own product-engineering office. That was not created until 1908, when Louis Kissel hired Herman David Palmer and named him motor and chassis engineer shortly afterwards.

Palmer was also born in Germany and educated at the University of Cologne; while he was a sound mechanical engineer, he had no actual experience in car design and manufacturing when he joined Kissel. He developed the Kissel Kar four-cylinder models, and in 1909 designed a six-cylinder engine, a 505 cubic-inch unit with square cylinder dimensions (4.75-inch bore and stroke).

Very few of those were built, and the bulk of Kissel's production as late as 1913 was made up of four-cylinder cars of 30, 40 and 50 hp. But that year the mighty '60' appeared. It was an in-line six of the L-head type, with cylinders cast in pairs.

According to a report in *The Horseless Age;* "All parts are ground to size and lapped in with the part which it fits, the piston in the cylinder, piston rings into their grooves, etc. As the motor is assembled, each part is weighed and carefully balanced—first, the crankshaft by itself, then the flywheel and connecting rod. When the motor is finally assembled it is driven on block by a belt, and then under its own power until it is thoroughly limbered and ready to be mounted in the chassis."

The engine had splash lubrication, assisted by forced feed from a gear-driven oil pump via tubes to all accessible parts. A silent chain was used for the camshaft drive, in place of the gear train used on previous models. Electric starting was adopted, along with Ward-Leonard electric lighting. The 60 inherited a leather cone clutch from earlier models but had its own four-speed sliding gear transmission, with direct drive on third gear and overdrive top.

Kissel made its own transmissions, with gears cut from chrome-vanadium steel blanks, and ball-bearing mounted shafts. The transmission was mounted separately from the engine, further back in the middle of the chassis. The Kissel used shaft drive, having an open propeller shaft with universal joints at its front and rear ends.

The rear axle was of the full-floating type, with huge brake drums, 14 inches in diameter and 5 inches in width. The service brakes were of the external-expanding type, and the emergency brake system had external-contracting bands acting on the same drums.

Kissel Kar bodies were designed by another German-born technician, J. Fredrich Werner, who had acquired his engineering experience with Opel in Russelsheim. He came to America in 1905 for an assignment with Studebaker, and later joined Kissel.

Standard equipment for the 60 was only slightly more complete than for the lower-priced Kissel Kars and included a pantasote top and cover, glass front, electric lamps, shock absorbers, demountable rims, Stewart & Clark speedometer, double tire irons, Solar black-enameled and nickel-trimmed dash and tail lamps, robe rail, foot rail, horn, jack, tire pump, tire repair kit, and a set of hand tools.

Fig. 2-8. The 1913 Kissel Kar 60 of Hartford, Wisconsin.

Great as the Kissel Kar 60 was in the reality of its hardware, it was a failure in the marketplace, and the company phased it out in 1914, at a considerable loss.

Kissel's next six appeared in 1915 and was a small-block unit (with the cylinder block cast in one piece) of 341 cubic-inch displacement, rated at 42 hp, and matched with a three-speed transmission. Its price, body style for body style, was about $1,000 lower than for the previous year's 60 hp model, and it was well received.

But the 60 was not to be Kissel's last great car, and the next one to come along was another masterwork by the same Herman Palmer.

25. STUTZ SERIES B, 1913

Mention Stutz, and everybody thinks "Bearcat." The two names are forever associated. Stutz came into being as a make of car via the race track, and for years it seemed the factory existed only for racing's sake. Bearcats were great at winning races, and the design was stark, purposeful, and exciting. It was made in both four-and six-cylinder versions, selling at moderate prices of $2,000 and $2,125, respectively, in 1914 (Fig. 2-9).

Bearcats probably accounted for two-thirds of Stutz's production in the years 1912-18, and about three-quarters of the Bearcats were the lightest model with the four-cylinder engine.

While the Bearcat was rough and uncomfortable, as a short-wheelbase open roadster with bucket seats bolted to the frame, and fuel tank, toolbox, and spare wheel strapped on behind, Stutz also produced a number of touring cars with comfortable bodywork. Stutz used the Bulldog trade name in advertising a four-passenger touring car with minimal bodywork, and there was also a Roadster that was not a Bearcat, the difference being mainly in the fact that the Roadster had doors and the Bearcat did not.

These were race-bred, high-performance cars, engineered to make high-speed driving safe, and yet selling at very attractive prices. The 1913 Series B six-passenger six-cylinder touring car, complete with canopy top, was listed at $2,400. It was built on a 130-inch wheelbase (the four-passenger touring car had a 127-inch wheelbase, and the roadster's wheelbase was 124 inches). The price included Solar electric headlights, Esterline electric generator, and magneto ignition. Stutz's first closed-body model was a Series B sedan for 1914, with a list price of $3,800.

As a product of Indianapolis, the Stutz could not avoid direct comparison with the city's leading makes: National, Premier and

Pathfinder. The Stutz would soon surpass them, and eventually survive them.

The man behind the car, whose name it proudly bore, Harry Clayton Stutz, had no formal training as an engineer, but educated himself to be a superb mechanic with a superior understanding of technology. He was a farmboy from Ansonia, Ohio, who fled the farm to get a job with a sewing machine manufacturer. Later he went to work for the National Cash Register Co., and while there began to design and build his own car. It was a makeshift rig, built mainly from scrap parts, totally devoid of refinement, but said to have run reliably for several years.

From this experience, Stutz realized he had a lot to learn about cars and began a total-immersion course in on-the-job training, working for an axle company, a tire company, and a carburetor company, and then designed his dream car in 1904, the American Underslung, so called because the axles crossed the frame on the top side. He sold the design to the American Motor Car Co. of Indianapolis, who started production in 1905.

The following year, Harry C. Stutz was invited to become chief engineer and factory manager by Carl Graham Fisher, president of the Marion Motor Car Company (and one of the co-sponsors of the Indianapolis Speedway in 1909). Stutz accepted, and stayed with Fisher for almost five years.

By 1909 he was dreaming of new and different cars, however, and in his eagerness left the steady and secure life at Marion for the risks of the new and adventurous Stutz car. His prototype finished (eleventh) in the Indianapolis 500 miles race in 1911, and a batch of replicas was quickly built and sold to active race drivers.

He found backing to set up an organization known as the Ideal Motor Car Company of Indianapolis, which later developed into the Stutz Motor Car Company. Production of the Series A Stutz, a car that was notable for its four-cylinder T-head engine and the rear axle with its four-speed transmission built integrally with the final drive unit, began in 1912.

In the fall of 1912, Harry C. Stutz designed and built his first six-cylinder prototype, which went into production as part of the Series B for 1913. The six-cylinder Series B was a remarkably modern-looking car; in a quick examination today, it could easily be mistaken for a 1923 model.

It had a T-head engine with cylinders cast in pairs, like the four-cylinder units which made up the bulk of Stutz production.

With a 4.25-inch bore and a 5-inch stroke, its displacement was 425 cubic inches. It delivered about 50 hp, which was more than enough to give the car the kind of performance that would startle Stutz's rivals.

The engine was a remarkably clean design, with a water-jacketed intake manifold on the right and an exhaust manifold on the left, flanged to a large-diameter exhaust pipe. Below the exhaust manifold was mounted the centrifugal water pump, gear-driven from the camshaft. The water pump shaft extended both ways, driving the electric generator at the rear end and a pulley with belt drive to the fan in front. A new four-inch thick honeycomb radiator was mounted at the front cross member.

The chassis had right-hand steering, with a gearshift lever mounted inside the door, on the driver's side. Gemmer steering gear was used, with a Timken front axle. The drive line followed the pattern established with the four-cylinder models in 1912. Rear as well as front springs were semi-elliptical with Velvet auxiliary springs mounted at the rear end.

Few changes were made for 1914, but for the 1915 model year, the six-cylinder Series B evolved into the 6-F Series. The engine had its bore reduced to 4 inches, and though the displacement shrank to 377 cubic inches, power output was maintained at the 50 hp level. The new engine retained T-head construction, but was built up from two blocks of three cylinders; and a simplified three-speed transmission replaced the earlier four-speed design (though the gearbox location was not changed). During 1915, however, Stutz discontinued production of the six-cylinder engine in order to concentrate on the 390 cubic inch T-head fours.

Harry Stutz sold the Stutz Motor Car Company to a group of New York bankers in 1916, who poured new money into the enterprise, modernized and enlarged the plant, and then sat back to wait for the payoff.

As early as 1914, Harry Stutz had branched out into designing the H.C.S. car, whose trade mark was made up of his initials, yet he remained active in the Stutz Motor Car Company until 1919.

H.C.S. built a cut-price copy of the Bearcat, powered by Weidely or Continental engines, selling for only $1,475 in 1915. Later, taxicab and fleet models were built. But the H.C.S. enterprise went under in 1925.

In 1926 Harry Stutz retired to Orlando, Florida, and settled on an orange farm. Later he came back to business with some interesting aircraft designs, and was promoting them up to the time

Fig. 2-9. Stutz Series B, 1915.

of his death in 1930, after failing to recover from an appendicitis operation.

26. HUDSON MODEL 54, 1913

While Oldsmobile was making a tactical retreat from the luxury-and-prestige market after its experience with the Limited, Hudson was preparing to enter it. The comparison with Oldsmobile is both relevant and poignant, for the Hudson was designed by former Olds engineers, led by Howard E. Coffin, who had left Oldsmobile after the departure of R. E. Olds, in disagreement with S. L. Smith's management and policy (Fig. 2-10).

Olds had been successful in the rock-bottom price bracket, and Smith was steering the company towards big, high-powered, expensive cars. The Hudson Motor Car Company was formed to build low-priced cars, and met with success in its chosen market segment. And yet, within three years of its creation, its leaders were proposing to go the same route to which they had been opposed while working for the Olds Motor Works, and which Olds was —seven years later—ready to pull out of.

The Hudson Motor Car Company was organized in Detroit in 1908 as an offshoot of the Chalmers-Detroit Motor Company, financed mainly by J. L. Hudson, owner of a leading department store. Roy D. Chapin was elected president, and Howard Coffin vice president and chief engineer.

Chapin and Coffin had met at the Olds Motor Works in 1902 and became fast friends even though their respective backgrounds were strangely disparate. Coffin was seven years older than Chapin, who was only 22 when they met. Chapin came from a well-to-do Detroit family while Coffin was an Ohio farmboy. Both broke off their college studies, but for different reasons: Chapin because school bored him; Coffin because he had to go to work to make a living. When Coffin joined Olds, he had worked as a photographer for about a year, while Chapin had five years' experience with the postal service. He had also built a gasoline engine in 1897 and made his own steam car in 1899.

Coffin had gone far enough in the engineering school of the University of Michigan to feel confident of his ability to design a complete car. Chapin was ready to do anything as long as it was in a car factory. Coffin was given a drawing board, and Chapin's first job was to file transmission gears. In 1901 Chapin was chief test driver, and three years later, sales manager. Coffin was named director of the experimental department in 1903 and chief engineer of Olds in 1905.

Both left Olds in 1906. Coffin had designed a new light car that Olds did not want to produce, and Chapin sold it to E. R. Thomas. It became the Thomas-Detroit (later Chalmers-Detroit), and in 1908 Chapin and Coffin launched a new venture, destined to be the Hudson.

Hudson took over the factory of the defunct Northern Motor Car Company and began production in 1909, with Model 20, a four-cylinder roadster selling for $900. It was soundly engineered, built on a 100-inch wheelbase, with the drop-forged front axle carried on semi-elliptical leaf springs and the semi-floating, shaft-driven rear axle borne by three-quarter elliptics.

The 199 cubic-inch engine was of L-head design, cast in pairs, with splash lubrication and oil circulation to the mains by means of a plunger pump with sight-feel oilers on the dashboard. Connecting rods and crankshaft were steel forgings, and the three-speed transmission had an aluminum casing.

A touring car on a 108-inch wheelbase was added in 1910, and for 1911, Hudson introduced a new and more powerful car, Model 33, on a 114-inch wheelbase, with a 318 cubic inch engine, cast en bloc with its transmission bolted to the clutch bell-housing.

Model 33 evolved into Model 37 by mid-year 1912, with a new cast-en-bloc engine notable for its use of nickel-steel valves and bearing-cap bolts, aluminum crankcase, and helical-cut steel timing gears. The transmission was bolted to the engine, and the

Fig. 2-10. The Hudson Model 6-54 of 1913.

open propeller shaft was double-jointed. Model 37 was built on a 118-inch wheelbase, and was priced from $1,985 to $3,250 according to body style and equipment.

Concurrently with the preparation of Model 37, Coffin had designed a six-cylinder engine and developed a bigger chassis to carry it. That became Model 54, announced in August, 1912. The engine was conceived as two blocks from Model 37, each minus one cylinder, put end to end on a common crankcase, with a three-bearing crankshaft, carefully balanced but not counterweighted. With a bore of 4.125 inches and a stroke of 5.25 inches, the Model 54 engine had 421 cubic-inch displacement and delivered 55 hp at 1,500 rpm.

The engine was mounted well back in the channel-section, pressed steel frame, with a large-diameter flywheel and 11-inch oil-bath wet clutch with cork inserts. The all-roller-bearing three-speed transmission was bolted to the engine, and drove the full-floating pressed-steel rear axle via a double-jointed open propeller shaft. Delco electric starting was used, with Delco ignition and lighting also. A magneto provided sparks for ordinary running, with a dry-cell battery ready in reserve.

Suspension was by 37 inch long semi-elliptical springs in front and 50-inch long three-quarter elliptics at the rear all using phosphor-bronze bushings in the spring eyes. The front axle was a one-piece drop forging. Wheel spindles were heat-treated and carried roller-bearing hubs, and king-pins were made of nickel-steel. The rear wheel hubs also had roller bearings, driven by flanges on nickel-steel drive shafts. Artillery wheels, with 10 spokes for the front wheels and 12 spokes at the rear, carried 36 × 4½-inch demountable clincher tires.

The driver grasped an 18-inch-diameter steering wheel which worked a worm and wheel type of steering gear made of hardened steel. The rear wheels carried brake drums of 16 inches diameter, the brake pedal activating external bands and the hand brake lever working internal shoes.

Built on a 127-inch wheelbase, the Hudson 54 weighed about 3,750 pounds and had a maximum speed of 65 mph in full rig. The engine had tremendously strong torque, which enabled it to go from standstill to 50 mph in 21 seconds. Clearly, Coffin had engineered a car of very high performance, capable of outrunning many higher-powered and more expensive cars.

It was attractively priced, the five-passenger touring car being listed at $2,450 and the seven-passenger limousine at

$2,750. Hudson also offered Model 54 as a naked chassis, priced at $2,250. While the Hudson 54 did not have the same level of interior luxury and finish as the Pierce-Arrow, for instance, it definitely did have better performance.

For 1914 Model 54 received a four-speed transmission and the wheelbase was stretched to 135 inches. That year Hudson phased out its four-cylinder models and introduced Model 40 as a scaled-down version of the 54, on a 123-inch wheelbase.

Model 54 remained in production through 1915, the Phaeton then listed at $2,350 and the Limousine at $3,500. Howard Coffin experimented with V-8 and V-12 engines in 1915-16, but Chapin and other executives steered the model range back into the medium-priced field, with great financial gains for the company.

Model 40 became Model 42 and received a new engine, cast en bloc, with many improvements in 1915, and for 1916 the company went to a one-model policy with the introduction of the Super Six, an excellent car on a 125.5-inch wheelbase, with a base price of $1,375 (and $1,900 for the standard sedan).

The engine was a new design by a Hungarian-born engineer, Stephen I. Fekete, featuring a counterweighted crankshaft and high (5.0:1) compression.

Its 289 cubic inches were enough to deliver 76 hp at 2,450 rpm, which gave sparkling performance, and the Super Six went on to a very distinguished racing career. Private customers found its fuel economy excellent—up to 14 mpg, compared with the 9-10 mpg of the best of the Model 37's. This engine was kept in production until 1929, and the Super Six was the mainstay of Hudson production for a full dozen years.

27. KNOX "66", 1913

Most of us, even those who are familiar with the history of the Knox car, usually think of it as one-cylinder light utility vehicle rather than a splendid, high-powered luxury car. The fact is that Knox produced a surprising variety of motor vehicles, culminating with the "66." (Fig. 2-11).

The Knox, like its designer and builder, was a product of Massachusetts, but it is difficult to pinpoint regional characteristics in the car. Knox delivery vehicles were suitable for service in any metropolitan center, and Knox touring cars were capable of running on any American highway that existed at the time.

Harry Austin Knox was no graduate engineer, but a very skilled mechanic, and some have called him a mechanical genius.

Fig. 2-11. The 1913 Knox Model 66 "Torpedo."

He was a New Englander of Scottish extraction, born in 1875 in Westfield, Massachusetts. His formal education ended with graduation from Springfield Trade School at the age of 19.

He immediately began to experiment with automobile engines, and built a four-cylinder unit in 1895, which secured him a contract to design a car engine for the Overman Bicycle Company, then eager to get into the automobile business. He built three Overman cars in 1896 and 1897.

The following year he set up his own shop to manufacture cars bearing the Knox name. The Knox Automobile Company was organized in Springfield, Massachusetts in 1900, and its first product was a three-wheeler driven by a single-cylinder air-cooled engine. Knox made such a virtue of air-cooling that his vehicles were often advertised as the "Waterless Knox." Knox used spikes rather than fins, and his units were nicknamed "porcupine engine."

The first Knox four-wheeler dates from 1902, powered by a single-cylinder, air-cooled rear-mounted engine, which became the principal production model for 1903-04. For the 1905 model year, Knox added a model with four-cylinder, air-cooled engine.

Air cooling is usually considered primitive and has been unjustly given a label as "unrefined." But air cooling has the advantages of lower manufacturing cost and simplified maintenance for the owner, who has no water leaks or anti-freeze to worry about. The penalty is borne entirely by the owner, and comes in the form of noise. After some field experience with the four-cylinder Waterless Knox, the company decided to develop a water-cooled model.

Harry Knox apparently had no ambition to build great cars. He was utility-oriented, having added commerical vehicles to his product line as early as 1901, and the Martin tractor in 1910-12. He left the Knox Automobile Company in 1905.

It was Frank Trego who designed the water-cooled Knox engine and all Knox cars from 1908 on. He was an experienced automotive engineer when he came to Knox, having previously worked for Packard and Thomas Flyer.

The four-cylinder Model H was the first water-cooled Knox car, selling for $2,750 as a four-passenger touring car, complete with top, in 1908. Knox's sales literature claimed it scored "best on eight points." Apart from the prosaic best oiling system (forced feed, with internal leads), it was said to have the best clutch (cone-type, metal to metal). In what must be precocious use of a modern expression, Knox claimed its three-point engine suspension was the "Best Hang-up." Its sliding gear, selective type gearshift was described as the best transmission, while the shaft drive to the rear axle became the Best Drive. Knox claimed best cooling, since both water- and air-cooled models were available.

"Best capacity," Knox stated, without backing up the claim with anything further than the explanation "Always room to spare." The claim of best appearance invited the reader to look at the pictures, and the claim for best comfort led to the come-on: "Try and see."

Meanwhile, Trego was busy on the design of a six-cylinder Knox. It appeared as a 1910 model and was a real stunner . . . the Knox Six set a new stock-car world's record in Los Angeles in April 1910. Running on a one-mile board track, it covered ten miles in 7 minutes 22 seconds (81.45 mph). It was called Model 66 because of its horse-power rating.

The engine had a 5-inch bore and a 5.5-inch stroke, which gave a total displacement of 648 cubic inches. The cylinders were cast en bloc—one of the first ones to feature such construction, at a time when most fours were cast in pairs. It had overhead valves with pushrods and rocker arms, the rocker covers being tight-fitting aluminum castings intended to muffle the valve clatter. Cylinder heads were detachable—a feature Trego had introduced on the first Knox water-cooled fours.

A silent chain drove the magneto, with a separate chain drive to the camshaft from side-by-side sprockets on the nose of the crankshaft. The three-speed transmission was retained, but helical gears replaced the original spur gear type on the 1913 models. Buyers had a choice of where they wanted the gearshift lever, by the door for right-hand operation, or in the middle of the car. Ball bearings were used throughout the gearbox and final drive units.

Knox made its own front axles from steel forgings, but used Timken roller bearings for the wheel hubs and the upper steering knuckle pivot. Rear axles were full-floating type, with a pressed-steel differential housing anchored to the left and right axle tubes. A truss rod was added below the axle to assure stability. The 1913 Knox 66 loomed most businesslike, with its big wheels, long hood, and well-equipped body.

Knox also added a Little Six for 1913, the Model 46, which was a great car in its own right. But the Knox Automobile Company was losing money. The cars were selling well, but did not bring any profit to the manufacturer, who began borrowing heavily to secure working capital. Finally its financial obligations could no longer be met, and production ended in 1915.

Frank Trego had designed a V-12 aircraft engine, which he used to start a new venture, the Springfield Motor Company. He received important orders during World War I, and in 1919 set up Trego Motors in New Haven, Connecticut, which failed after a short period. As for Harry Knox, he lived on until June, 1957, when he died at the age of 82 in his home in Miami, Florida.

Chapter 3
The War Years: 1914 - 1917

After former general manager L. H. Kittridge became president of Peerless, he kept the business firmly anchored in the high-priced market. Prices for the 48-Six began at $5,000 (the same car was also known as Model 36 or Series K). It was a six cylinder model designed by Charles Schmidt, who had gone from Packard in Detroit to the Cleveland firm as early as 1905 and redirected its entire product-engineering course away from the Mooers tradition (Fig. 3-1).

28. PEERLESS 48-SIX, 1914

Peerless's first six had appeared in 1908, and was basically two extra cylinders added on to existing four-cylinder Model 18. The six-cylinder Model 20 shared the same cylinder dimensions: 4.875×5.50 inches, giving a displacement of 616 cubic inches (against 411 for the Model 18). These T-head engines were Schmidt designs, with few traces of Mooers engineering in their makeup.

Model 20 evolved into Model 25 in 1909, with an output of 50 hp, built on a 136-inch wheelbase. Carried over without change for 1910, it was simply renamed Model 28. The following year the engine was bored out to a full five inches, raising displacement to 648 cubic inches, but without increasing power output. The 1911 six-cylinder Peerless was known as Model 31. Model 30 was powered by a four-cylinder version of the same engine, built on a 123-inch wheelbase.

The Peerless range also included a smaller car built on a 113-inch wheelbase, powered by a 232 cubic-inch four-cylinder L-head engine, selling in the $4,000-$4,500 price bracket. The engines in Model 30 and 31 were, of course, T-head designs.

The 48-Six originated in 1912, along with a smaller companion model, the 38-Six (also identified variously as the Series-H or Model 35). Both were new T-head sixes with seven-bearing crankshafts and cylinders cast in pairs.

The 48-Six had 570 cubic-inch displacement, with 4.5-inch bore and 6-inch stroke. This was not Peerless's biggest engine, for Schmidt had also designed and put in production a 60 hp model, a giant 824 cubic-inch power unit with 5-inch bore and 7-inch stroke. But its weight was in the locomotive class, a massive 1,250 pounds or so, and that's difficult to rationalize for a passenger car. The 48-Six was no doubt the greater masterpiece (and the 38-Six a highly admirable creation, too, but overshadowed by the Series K).

Schmidt was a Frenchman, and he preferred to rely on French-made parts rather than trust American suppliers. The engine, transmission, and wheel bearings were imported. So was the ignition system, for a few years. For certain models, Peerless even imported axles and springs from France. He had full control, however, over the quality and precision of everything that was processed in the Peerless factory. Crankshafts were machined from solid billets of cast steel, and balanced together with the flywheel. Piston-and-connecting rod assemblies were classed by weight so that all were uniform inside each engine.

Schmidt had a team of first-class helpers, and at least one member deserves mention: G. W. Harper, the chief draftsman on the Peerless 48-Six. He was an old-fashioned engineer, educated at the Case School of Applied Science, widely known and respected for his thoroughness and accuracy.

For 1913, Bosch dual ignition with a single plug per cylinder replaced the former dual-plug arrangement. A new carburetor was adopted, with a butterfly throttle in place of the former piston-type air valve.

Peerless introduced an electric starter on its 1913 models. The starter motors came from Gray & Davis, and the system weighed about 175 pounds, including the battery. That year Peerless also went to electric lighting.

After more than a decade of using straight bevel final drive gears, spiral-bevel gears were adopted on the 48-Six for 1915,

Fig. 3-1. A 1915 Peerless 48-Six open touring car.

which was claimed to silence the rear axle. The transmission was a four-speed unit, with selective gearshift.

The 48-Six was built on a 137-inch wheelbase with 36 × 4½-inch front tires and 37 × 5-inch tires on the rear wheels. For comparison, the 38-Six had a 125-inch wheelbase, and the 60-Six had a 140-inch wheelbase.

Two four-cylinder models were built in 1912 but discontinued in 1913. One casualty was the 29 (Series D) with its L -head engine, and the other was the 33 (Series J), the successor to the 30.

Thus, for 1914 Peerless had sixes across the board. It looked as if Peerless had finally reached a rational production program, but when standardization came it was to be based on a V-8 engine, not a six. And before it happened, Peerless revived the four-cylinder car (Model 54) in 1915. Schmidt had been developing a V-8 since 1912, and it was put in production in 1916. At the same time, Peerless standardized one chassis with a 125-inch wheelbase and a choice of three body styles, with prices slashed to $1,890 for the touring car and $3,060 for the limousine.

The V-8 engine was a 322 cubic-inch T-head design that put out 80 hp at 2,700 rpm and remained in production as Peerless's only engine up to 1924.

29. LOZIER BIG SIX, 1914

When we last examined a Lozier, the factory was installed in a cozy and rustic environment on the west bank of Lake Champlain, as part of a motorboat works. In 1909, however, Harry A. Lozier moved the Lozier Motor Company to new premises on Mack Avenue in Detroit (Fig. 3-2).

His intention was not to turn the exquisite Lozier into a mass-produced car, but to benefit from relocating in what was fast becoming America's Motor City. These benefits extended from finding expert craftsmen to ready availability of special-purpose machine tools and materials, such as high-strength steel alloys, increasingly being specified by quality-oriented auto makers. Inevitably, Lozier learned much about the real cost of building cars by his boat-yard methods, and eagerly adopted an industrial approach to auto production. We see the first evidence of evolution in this direction in the new engines that Lozier made in Detroit.

The Lozier's reputation and performance rested on Perrin's basic engine concept, with a roller-bearing crankshaft, T-head valve gear layout with crossflow heads, and cylinders cast in pairs. Undeniably some of Lozier's individuality was lost in the process, as new engines were designed in growing conformity with the industry's norms. Detroit-built Loziers became increasingly equipped with cast-en-bloc L-head engines using plain crankshaft bearings.

Lozier's first six was Model I of 1908, which John G. Perrin created by adding an extra pair of cylinders to the Model H four. Bore and stroke were changed from 5.25 × 5.25 inches to a longer stroke of 5½ inches, while the bore was narrowed down to 4.625 inches. The Model I six was rated at 50 hp, but actually delivered 72 hp from its 554 cubic inch displacement. To accommodate this engine, the Model H chassis was lengthened from a 124-inch wheelbase to 131 inches.

Of course, this engine belongs in the Plattsburg generation, being a T-head, roller-bearing type. It was said to be quiet as well as tremendously powerful, easy and pleasant to drive, with the risk of mechanical failure so remote that a Lozier owner could regard a breakdown (other than tire trouble) as a virtual impossibility. As a result of Harry Lozier's experience in driving the Model I as his own personal car for a long period, he made a decision to go to an all-six-cylinder program, but the demand for Lozier's four-cylinder models was so strong that this idea was never implemented.

First of the new-generation sixes was Model J, announced in 1909, and discontinued at the end of 1910. The L-head engine was built up from two blocks of three cylinders, and had a plain-bearing

Fig. 3-2. Lozier's Big Six of 1914.

crankshaft. Built on a 116-inch wheelbase, it was a light car, obviously intended to replace the four-cylinder-models—but incapable of stirring up the same enthusiasm in the market place.

Perrin went to work on an upgraded successor to the J, which appeared at the end of 1912 as the Type 77 or Light Six. Powered by an L-head engine of 424.5 cubic inches (3.875-inch bore and 6-inch stroke) it was rated at 36 hp, though its actual output was about 50. Type 77 was built on a 127.5-inch wheelbase and carried a list price of $3,250.

As always, Detroit Lozier produced its own transmissions—a three-speed design with selective shift, and rear axles of the full-floating type with ball-bearing hubs.

The Light Six was well-received, and orders poured in during the winter and spring of 1913. But it was the Big Six that was universally recognized as the 'great' Lozier of its day. Model I had developed into Type 51 by 1911, with a 560 cubic-inch T-head engine. In April 1912 it was redesigned with left hand drive and central controls, and renamed the Type 72. The 131-inch wheelbase and $5,000 list price remained unchanged from Type 51 specifications. It weighed 4,950 pounds with a touring car body and had a maximum speed of 80 mph.

As a backup for the Light Six, Perrin redesigned the Model H, which had continued in production practically without change since 1909 and was offered at $4,000 in 1912. At the end of 1913 it was replaced by Type 84, the lowest-priced Lozier ever offered, listed at $2,100.

The engine for Type 84 was a new L-head design, with 4.25-inch bore and 6.5-inch stroke, giving no less than 369 cubic-inch displacement and a true power output of 56 hp. Unfortunately, not many were built, for in August 1914 Lozier was forced to suspend production. The company had fallen too deep into debt, and the creditors were unwilling to carry Lozier any longer.

The last of the Big Six Loziers, therefore, came to stand as a monument to the kind of automotive excellence Perrin's lofty ideals could produce, and at the same time served as a reminder of the fate that threatens car makers if realistic cost accounting is not exercised and heeded.

Harry A. Lozier remained in Detroit as long as there was any hope of getting the business on its feet again, running the Motor Patents Company as a sideline. In 1915 he went to Cleveland and formed the H. A. L. Company to produce a V-12-powered luxury car (with a Weidely engine). When this venture failed, he launched another project, the Lozier Brothers Company, this time in Philadelphia, in partnership with his elder brother Edward, to build a line of low-priced four- and six-cylinder cars. Production never got under way, and in 1917 he held a commission as a major in the motor engineering division of the U.S. Ordnance Department in Washington, D. C. He never produced another car, and in December, 1925 he died in Clearwater, Florida, from an attack of bronchial pneumonia.

As for John G. Perrin, his career as a car designer was far from over, and we shall meet him again in connection with further great cars of his creation.

30. McFARLAN SERIES T, 1914

Around 1910 many of America's wagon-builders and carriage makers had decided to become automobile manufacturers in the face of dwindling demand for horse-drawn vehicles. Studebaker did it, choosing to aim at the low-and medium-price market. Others aimed at the top: Brewster, Cunningham, and McFarlan, to name three of the most famous (Fig. 3-3).

The McFarlan Carriage Company had been formed in 1856 in Connersville, Indiana, by an English-born entrepreneur whose grandson was to take one of the family's subsidiaries into the car business.

His name was Alfred Harry McFarlan, who at the age of 28 began drawing up the layout and specifications of what he intended to be a "motor buggy" of reasonable price. By the time production started in 1910, the McFarlan was a high-grade six-cylinder automobile, fatefully launched on the path towards greatness.

The proximity of Connersville to Indianapolis must have influenced McFarlan in the direction of power and speed, which were touchstones for all local car makers. And in fact, we find that McFarlan cars were entered in local races in the first year of their existence. In 1911 McFarlan advertised its performance in the 200-mile race at the Indianapolis Speedway: an average speed of 65.49 mph with an average fuel consumption of 17 miles per gallon.

The first McFarlan cars were designed by Jesse Kepler, head of the Kepler Engineering Company of Dayton, Ohio, and were remarkably modern in concept, layout and execution. Despite the limited capacity of the factory, the 1910-model cars were priced no higher than $2,000 with touring car or tonneau bodies on a chassis with a wheelbase of 120 inches.

Fig. 3-3. The McFarlan Series T, 1914 from Connersville, Indiana.

Wisely, McFarlan decided to stay with manufacturing the chassis and bodywork its workers were most familiar with, and avoided going ahead with the idea of building its own engines.

A six-cylinder T-head engine of 248 cubic-inch displacement with its cylinder cast in pairs, produced by Brownell in Rochester, New York, was chosen. The transmission and rear axle, steering gear, brakes, and electrical equipment, were also purchased from outside suppliers. Frame, front axle, springs, and bodywork were made by McFarlan.

In 1911 the standard car from the previous year was renamed Little Six, and a new Big Six was added, powered by a 377 cubic-inch overhead-valve Brownell engine, which was bored out to 477 cubic-inch displacement in 1912. Built on a 128-inch wheelbase, it had a list price of $2,500.

For 1913 the Little Six was renamed Series S and the Bix Six became Series M. At the same time, the Series T was added. Series S was listed at $2,300 and Series M at $2,750, while the new Series T fitted in between, at $2,500.

The series T engine was not a Brownell but a Teetor, made by Light Inspection Car Company, Cleveland, Ohio. It was a T-head design with its six cylinders cast en bloc, of 452 cubic-inch displacement. It had a four-bearing crankshaft with plain bearings. The compressed air starter, which had been adopted for the Little Six in 1912, was also used on the Series T.

The three-speed transmission was combined with the rear axle, as on the Series S, whose chassis and 124-inch wheelbase it shared. The drive was taken up by a massive torque tube yoked to a cross member aft of the engine. The rear axle was of the full-floating type and carried on scroll springs of full-elliptical configuration, with swivel seats and spring eye bushings made of bronze. The front axle was carried on semi-elliptical leaf springs, and the steering linkage, which had been located ahead of the axle in 1912, was moved behind it.

No reliable performance figures exist for the car, but it probably reached 60 mph from standstill in less than 20 seconds, and top speed must have been a genuine 80 mph.

Coachwork being the traditional activity at the McFarlan plant, a variety of body styles proliferated, with nine different models offered for the Series T, including a number of closed bodies, such as the standard coupe, turtleback coupe, and limousine. The coupes were listed at $3,300 and the limousine at $3,700.

Series M and Series S were discontinued at the end of the 1913 model run, and a new Series X added. It was powered by a bored-out version of the same Teetor engine, 572.5 cubic inches in displacement. Both series had a new chassis built on a 128-inch wheelbase.

Gray pneumatic gearshift was offered as an option on both T and X cars. It was a preselective system, the driver setting the next gear to be engaged by moving a small lever mounted on the steering wheel (not on the column) whenever he wanted. The shift would occur when he pushed the clutch pedal to the floorboards.

In 1915 both Series T and X went to a 132-inch wheelbase, retaining the 56-inch track. Bodies were redesigned, with lower construction, and the model lineup considerably simplified. The four-passenger Series T touring car was listed at $2,590; the coupe remained at $3,300; and the limousine went to an even $4,000.

The Series T remained in production through the 1916 model year, with a production total of about 200 cars for its four years of existence.

31. PIERCE-ARROW "48", 1914

The Great Arrow disappeared in 1910 and the manufacturer formalized the trade make as Pierce-Arrow. Four cylinder models had been phased out in 1909, and three sizes of six-cylinder models were offered: 38 hp, 48 hp and 66 hp.

The latter was a huge machine with prices from $5,900 to $7,200, according to body style. The engine weighed about 1,450 pounds, had separately cast cylinders and was almost grotesque, with its 5-inch bore, 7-inch stroke, and 824.6 cubic inches. The touring car—on a 147.5-inch wheelbase—weighed over 5,000 pounds—limousines were even heavier. It was impressive rather than elegant, and too much of a truck to be called a masterpiece (Fig. 3-4).

Actually, it should not have come into being at all. Chief engineer David Fergusson wanted to build a V-8, but Charles Clifton overruled him and forced him to adhere to a six-cylinder policy. George N. Pierce died in 1910, and Clifton, now treasurer, sales director, and vice president, ran the company like a military outfit. The Buffalo plant had been expanded to a capacity of about 2,000 cars a year, and Clifton wanted to outdo each and every challenger in terms of luxury, opulence, size, comfort, power, strength, and quality.

The "48" was fully up to that task, and a magnificent motor car in every way, from its reinforced white ash frame and cast aluminum body to its superbly quiet yet immensely powerful 525 cubic-inch T-head six-cylinder engine.

The company's junior line, the "38," was competing at a level most car makers would consider top-of-the line, with its 134-inch wheelbase and 415 cubic-inch T-head six, listed at prices from $4,300 to $5,350.

Built on a 142-inch wheelbase, the "48" was majestic in its proportions as well as overall size, and equally suitable for city traffic as for the open road. In town, it was gentle and tractable, and on the highway, it ran with the steady beat of a steam locomotive rather than the fierce roar of a racing car. The engine was typical of Fergusson's rationale for making the best compromise between the technically ideal solution and what was possible with the existing tooling and machinery. Cylinders were cast in pairs, with 4½-inch bore and 5½-inch stroke.

Peak power was delivered at 1,750 rpm, but maximum torque was on tap from 750 rpm to about 1,000, and the engine would actually pull from 250 rpm and up. Actual power output was about 75 hp.

The crankshaft ran in seven main bearings, with an aluminum crankcase, which kept the complete engine weight to about 1,100 pounds. The flywheel was mated with a cone clutch, and the four-speed selective-shift transmission also had an aluminum casing.

In 1913, Charles Clifton laid down a new marketing policy. Up to that year, Pierce-Arrow, along with most of the industry, had introduced new models each year; suddenly Clifton decided to do away with the annual model change, and identify the cars by series instead.

The First Series was never given that label, but was understood to cover the 1913 models. For 1914, all cars were Second Series. (The "66" was identified as A-2, the "48" as B-2 and the "38" as C-2). The switch to the Third Series coincided with the start of the 1915 model year, and that put an effective end to Clifton's experiment.

A styling experiment from the same time turned out to be far more successful. The 1914 Pierce Arrow B-2 introduced headlamps mounted on the forward slope of the front fenders, a design feature patented by Herbert Dawley and assigned to Pierce Arrow, which became a hallmark for the great cars from Buffalo for as long as the firm existed. Separately mounted headlamps were listed as optional for many years, but most buyers preferred the fender-mounted design for its distinctiveness, and the option was eliminated in 1932.

The "48" engine was redesigned in 1918 with four valves per cylinder in T-head configuration. This enabled Fergusson to reduce valve gear inertia by going to smaller valves; and to improve engine efficiency by cutting back on valve overlap, no longer needed because of increased valve area. Better breathing gave improved low-range smoothness as well as an upward extension of the speed range: the "48" was still made from three sets of paired cylinders until 1920, when the company finally adopted one-piece engine blocks.

Charles Clifton became president of Pierce-Arrow in 1916 and chairman of the board in 1919. He was then 66 years old and acting as a brake on Fergusson's (and others) attempts to modernize the

Fig. 3-4. 1914 Pierce-Arrow "48" with 525 cu. in. T-head six.

product. During the period that followed, Pierce-Arrow fell from greatness, but fortunately not forever, as later chapters will show. And as for David Fergusson, we'll meet him again in connection with another make of car.

32. CRANE-SIMPLEX MODEL 5, 1915

By 1915, makers of great cars, such as Pierce-Arrow, Peerless, and Packard, had established certain images or identities, carefully built up over a decade or more. It was becoming increasingly difficult for outsiders, even companies that had been producing cars for just as long, to break into the exclusive upper-crust market, and it was practically unheard-of that a stark newcomer should claim its place in the elite and get away with it.

But that's what happened with the Crane-Simplex (Fig. 3-5). Perhaps it's not entirely fair to treat it as a total newcomer, since we have dealt with Simplex in an earlier chapter. On the other hand, the Crane-Simplex belongs to a totally different breed. Let me explain. As a corporate unit, Crane-Simplex came into being when the Simplex Automobile Company of New Brunswick, New Jersey took over the Crane Motor Car Co. of nearby Bayonne in July, 1915.

Henry Middlebrook Crane was a graduate of Massachusetts Institute of Technology, and at the age of 31 held the title of president of the Crane and Whitman Company, an engineering firm in Bayonne, New Jersey. Most of his earlier engineering work had been in the marine field, as designer and constructor of the Dixie speed boats (four wins in the Harmsworth Trophy contests).

Crane had started building Crane cars in Bayonne, New Jersey, in 1912, powered by large six-cylinder L-head engines. When this business was taken over, Simplex belonged to a group of New York investors, Goodrich, Lockhart & Smith, who had bought the assets from the Broesel family after the death of Herman Broesel, Sr. in 1912. The Simplex factory was moved from New York City to New Brunswick, where Broesel had a foundry. Crane's Bayonne plant was closed, and its equipment and personnel transferred to New Brunswick. The personnel included Henry M. Crane himself, who then set about creating the Crane-Simplex automobile.

No doubt it was going to be a great car; Henry M. Crane had never given a moments thought to any other type of car. It became a luxury car known for its high quality—the chassis alone selling for prices between $5,000 and $6,000.

Model 5 was built on a 143.5-inch wheelbase and had a curb weight of 5,400 pounds. The frame was made up of channel-section steel side members with a front sub-frame to carry the engine and transmission. Front and rear axles were carried on long semi-elliptical leaf springs.

The engine Crane designed was an in-line L-head six built up as two blocks of three cylinders on a common crankcase. So far in its structural makeup, it was not unlike the Rolls-Royce engine, created for the Silver Ghost in 1906.

But there were also important differences. Crane's was a long-stroke design, with 4.375-inch bore and 6.25-inch stroke, while Royce had square cylinder dimensions (4½-inch bore and stroke). More striking still, while Royce relied on a seven-bearing crankshaft, Crane ran his crankshaft in three main bearings only.

Crane's crankshaft was forged from electric-furnace alloy steel, surface-hardened by oil-quenching after machining. It had plain bearings, both mains and crankpin bearings having bronze shells lined with white metal. The crankcase was aluminum casting, with forged-steel main bearing caps.

From its 563.7 cubic-inch displacement the Crane engine delivered 110 hp at 1,800 to 2,000 rpm. Exhaust valves were made of tungsten alloy, and connecting rods were chrome-nickel steel

Fig. 3-5. The Crane-Simplex Model 5 of 1915.

drop forgings of H-section aspect. The carburetor was an updraft Newcomb-Simplex.

The engine had full-pressure lubrication, with an oil pump driven from the camshaft. The electric starter was a Bosch-Rushmore, geared directly to the flywheel, with its own clutch for disengagement. Each cylinder had two spark plugs, but both were fired from the same coil-and-battery ignition system. Rolls-Royce in contrast, used magneto ignition for one set of plugs, and coil-and-battery for the second set.

The Crane-Simplex had a four-speed unit with selective shift, bolted to the flywheel and clutch housing. It had shaft drive to a worm and bevel rear axle, with a torque tube to handle driving thrust.

Production of the Crane-Simplex ended in 1917, and the firm was absorbed into the Wright-Martin Aircraft Company, which had an important defense contract to produce Hispano-Suiza V-8 aircraft engines. For this, the New Brunswick plant was converted from cars to fighter-plane engines.

The Simplex car ended up in a strange post-war stew of companies formerly engaged in making fine cars, Hare's Motors, along with Mercer and Locomobile.

Henry M. Crane, in the meantime, had contacted his old M.I.T. classmate, Alfred P. Sloan, then president of General Motors, who hired Crane as his special assistant. Crane spent the rest of his career with General Motors, and was a special consultant to GM when he died at the age of 81 in January 1956.

33. STEARNS-KNIGHT, 1915

Among Cleveland's makers of great cars, one must definitely count the F. B. Stearns Company, and the 1915 models were not the first great cars produced by this fine firm (Fig. 3-6). The Stearns 30-60, for instance, from 1907, with its big 70-hp four-cylinder engine, certainly had greatness of a kind. Nor can one forget the enormous 45-90 of 1908, the company's first six, with an L-head engine of 800 cubic-inch displacement. How did the Stearns have its start?

Frank Ballou Stearns was a farmboy from Berea, Ohio who decided at the age of 14 that his life was going to be spent making cars, and in 1896, when he was 18, he put together a steam car in his father's barn.

Later he studied engineering at the Case School of Applied Science, and built about 50 cars between 1898 and 1900. Though

Fig. 3-6. Cleveland's 1915 Stearns-Knight.

Stearns began production with single-cylinder models, he had a four-cylinder prototype running in 1900. Realizing his basic need for expert, professional help in product engineering and manufacturing, he decided to hire a man to design new products and organize and run the expanded plant in Cleveland. And that man was destined to be James G. "Pete" Sterling, who went on to serve as chief engineer of the F. B. Stearns Company from 1901 to 1920. He had an engineering degree from Ohio State University, but no previous experience in designing cars.

After building a series of cars that can be characterized as tentative designs because thay were thoroughly engineered, yet explorative in their technical makeup, the company settled on a one-model policy.

In 1906 the F. B. Stearns Company made only one type of chassis, the 40-50 hp model in a 118-inch wheelbase. The 4-cylinder engine had a 4.875 inch bore and 5.875 inch stroke giving a displacement of 439 cubic inches. The firm claimed that a minimum of 2,100 work hours went into finishing each car, which gives a clear idea of Stearn's and Sterling's insistence on quality.

The 1906 Stearns weighed 3,000 pounds with a limousine body of cast aluminum. It had a pressed steel frame and semi-elliptical springs of 2½-inch width both front and rear. Tires were 36 × 4-inch in front and 36 × 4½-inch in the rear. Final drive was assured by double side chain to the rear wheels, and indisputably, the Stearns was in the great-car league from that time onwards.

In 1911 Stearns was first in America to adopt the Knight sleeve-valve engine. It was invented by an American, Charles Yale Knight, and consisted of an engine in which the normal poppet valves were replaced by double sleeves around each cylinder. A crank mechanism raised and lowered the sleeves to let their windows register with ports in the cylinder walls.

Knight patented his invention in 1905 but after failing to interest American car companies in it, he went to Europe where it was adopted by such famous makes as Daimler (of Coventry), Minerva (of Belgium), Panhard-Levassor (of Paris), and even Mercedes (in Stuttgart).

Despite such revolutionary changes, as a whole the Stearns product advanced in an evolutionary pattern, without sending shocks back into the factory or out to the clientele. Even more important changes were made with a minimum of fuss in production and without sending anything untested or unproven out into the market place.

In 1914, Stearns moved the gearbox from the rear axle to a central position. Six-cylinder cars had a four-speed unit, with selective shift. The gearbox was an all-ball-bearing design with shaft drive to a full-floating rear axle.

The 1915 Stearns-Knight six passenger touring car was listed at $5,000, and customers paid $4,850 for a three-seat roadster on the same chassis. The company also listed a Limousine at $6,100 and a Landaulet at $6,200. The cars were built on a 140-inch wheelbase, with weights of 3,300 to 4,500 pounds, according to body style.

The 489 cubic-inch engine had a bore and stroke of 4.25×5.75 inches, and was rated at 43.3 hp. Its actual output was about 65 hp, which gave road performance equal to most cars in its class, with a degree of silence that neither L-head nor T-head cars could come close to.

It was water-cooled, with a honeycomb radiator, and had jump-spark ignition with high-tension magneto. Starting was done by means of a Gray & Davis electric self starter.

The six disappeared at the end of the 1915 model run, and the company completely changed marketing tactics, with a speculative and dramatic dive into the low-priced field. The 1916 L-4 touring car sold for only $1,395, impressive value for a modern and economical four-cylinder model on a 119-inch wheelbase. A V-8 companion model (yes, the world's first V-8 Knight engine) was built on a 123-inch wheelbase and sold for $2,050.

But the days of Stearns-Knight's greatness were temporarily over. Frank B. Stearns sold his interests in the F. B. Stearns company in 1918, settled in Chesterland, Ohio, and devoted his technical talents to making improvements in the diesel engine and spent his spare time experimenting with organic farming. He died in 1955, at the age of 78.

J. B. Sterling left the company in 1920 to make his own car, the Sterling Knight, sponsored by a group of Cleveland businessmen headed by P. H. Withington. Sterling took over the plant of the former Stearns Aero-Parts Company and bought new land for an assembly plant. This venture lasted only a few years and in 1926 Sterling transformed his enterprise to making engines only, and was an important supplier to various truck builders up to about 1936.

34. PACKARD TWIN SIX, 1915

Smooth power was becoming a high-priority requirement for luxury cars by 1915, and the most obvious way to reduce noise and vibration was to add more cylinders. It has been seen how makers of fine cars made their transition from four to six cylinders. Some, like Pierce-Arrow, were unwilling to go further. But others, like Cadillac were first to develop a V-8, and several other manufacturers followed in short order (Fig. 3-7).

But the V-8 was no solution for Packard, who was justly proud of the smoothness of its sixes. In fact, the reasoning at Packard might have gone like this: "If the six is so smooth alone, two sixes must be twice as smooth." In any event, Packard simply chose to double the number of cylinders, going into production with a V-12 at a time when many auto makers had only recently graduated to the six. Not only that, but Packard discontinued its "38" and "48" sixes to produce V-12 cars exclusively!

The Packard Twin-Six engine was designed during 1913-14 by Jesse Gurney Vincent, who had joined Packard in 1912 as chief engineer and assistant to general manager, Alvan Macauley, who rose to a vice-presidency in 1913. Vincent was an engineer of vivid imagination, yet endowed with a great sense of the practical. A prolific inventor, he ended up holding more than 200 patents.

During his years at Packard, he raised the marque's reputation to new heights. Vincent was 32 years old when he came to Packard after a couple of years working on Hudson's engineering staff even though he had no formal training as an engineer. He was born in Charleston, Arkansas; grew up on a farm in Pana, Illinois; and quit school at the age of 17 to go to work as a machinist's helper in a steel works in East St. Louis.

He soon became an expert tool maker and machine setter, and put in five year's of correspondence-school studies in mechanical and electrical engineering. Most of the practical experience prior to joining Hudson was accrued from seven years with Burrough Adding Machine Company, where he rose from the rank of tool designer to superintendent of inventions.

Packard's V-12 was laid out with the banks disposed at a 60-degree angle, which gave evenly spaced firing impulses and an engine that had no equal in terms of balance. The three-plane, forged-steel crankshaft ran in four main bearings. It was an L-head design with detachable heads and all valves located inside the V. With its 3-inch bore and 5-inch stroke, it had a displacement of 424 cubic inches and was rated at 43.2 NACC hp. Real output was about 70 hp at 2,400 rpm.

The Twin Six had aluminum pistons and many other light alloy parts, including crankcase, flywheel housing, and transmission

Fig. 3-7. Packard Twin Six, 1915, an L-head V-12.

casing. It had full force lubrication throughout. The engine was set in motion by an electrical self starter, and used 6-volt coil and battery ignition. Both intake and exhaust manifolds were located between the cylinder banks, with pre-heating of the intake manifold accomplished by ducting the coolant through its base. The water pump was mounted externally on the right and driven by an extension of the generator shaft, which was driven by a V-belt from a pulley on the crankshaft.

The Twin Six was shorter than the L-head 404 cubic-inch six-cylinder engine it replaced, and remarkably similar in weight. Chassis engineering for the V-12 model was directed by Ormond E. Hunt, who had come to Packard in 1909 at the age of 25 and rose to become chief engineer of Packard by the time he was 35.

The transmission, which was bolted to the dry multiplate clutch and flywheel housing, was a three-speed design with selective shift. An open propeller shaft took the drive to the non-floating spiral bevel rear axle which was geared at 4.36:1. This ratio allowed the driver to run down to a walking pace in top gear and accelerate without snatch or stumbling, to a top speed of 72 mph (with touring car body). Both front and rear axles were suspended by semi-elliptical leaf springs, and the steering gear was of the worm and nut type—irreversible and demanding relatively light manual effort.

The Twin Six was introduced in May, 1915, and about 8,000 units were produced in the first model year.

The 1916 Twin-Six was listed at $2,600 as a 7-passenger touring car; $3,550 as a three-passenger coupe; $4,000 as a 6-passenger limousine; and $4,050 as a six-passenger landaulet or brougham, all built on a 126.5-inch wheelbase. Packard also offered the Twin-Six on a 135-inch wheelbase, with prices of $2,950 for the 7-passenger touring car at the low end and $4,600 for the Imperial limousine at the top end.

The closed-body models weighed well over 4,000 pounds, which naturally handicapped the car's accelerative capacity. But the engine was so silent, even on a wide-open-throttle, that the passenger got the impression there was something magic about the way the car gathered speed.

The Twin Six underwent few mechanical changes during its production life, which testifies to the essential soundness of its design. Body designs changed from year to year, and the Third Series, new for 1919, was a very modern-looking machine and well ahead of its time.

Henry B. Joy was elected chairman of Packard in 1916 (James W. Packard having resigned from the company in 1909), and Alvan Macauley then became president. J. G. Vincent was give the title of director of engineering, which he was to hold for the rest of his career.

The Twin Six remained Packard's only car line through 1919, and in 1920 a lower-priced six on a 116-inch wheelbase was added. Twin-Six production continued until the end of the 1922 model year when the V-12 was forced out to make way for Vincent's new straight-eight.

35. NATIONAL HIGHWAY TWELVE, 1916

Packard's Twin-Six had enormous impact on the market and the industry, and there was a rush to put competitive V-12 models into production. In a remarkably farsighted feat of concurrency, George Weidely had developed a V-12 which he produced for sale to auto makers. And W. Guy Wall at National, apparently without prior knowledge of Vincent's project at Packard, had gone ahead with a V-12 of his own.

The National Highway series was announced in the spring of 1915, with a choice of in-line six or V-12 engines. The six was purchased from Continental; the V-12 was a National product (Fig. 3-8).

While the Packard had been developed for maximum smoothness and tractability, the National V-12 was created for high performance. It has smaller displacement and higher specific output. Its Indianapolis heritage clearly shone through in its exhaust note as well as in its throttle response.

The National V-12 was built as two blocks of six cylinders, each inclined 30 degrees from vertical, with detachable L-heads. All valves were on the outside, just the opposite of Packard's layout. Wall's design necessitated the use of one camshaft for each bank, whereas all the valves on the Packard V-12 were operated by a single central camshaft.

The National Highway 12 engine had a bore and stroke of 2.75 × 4.75 inches, giving a displacement of only 339 cubic inches. The NACC rating was a conservative 36.3 hp, but the engine would spin fairly freely up to 3,000 rpm, and had a true output of at least 65 hp. It used a fork and blade type of connecting rod attachment to the crankpins, though by this time, most leading engineers had adopted the side-by-side configuration that Vincent chose for Packard's Twin-Six.

For 1917 the National V-12 engine was bored out to 2.875 inches, which raised the displacement to 370 cubic inches, and output to about 75 hp. It was difficult to find a production car of another make that could outrun the National Highway Twelve on the open road, for the National was also lighter in its construction than most other cars of its size and price.

The V-12 engine had full force-feed lubrication, high-tension magneto ignition, and electrical starting and lighting systems. Wall persisted in the use of a cone clutch rather than the more modern multi-disc clutch, but his three-speed, selective-shift transmission was up to date in every way. It was a compact design, robust, with high torque capacity, and bolted to the engine. An open propeller shaft took the drive to a full-floating rear axle with spiral bevel pinion and ring gear.

A. J. Paige, an engineer from Rose Polytechnic Institute, played a part in the soundness and quality of National cars. He held the title of assistant mechanical engineer in 1913 and worked mainly on chassis development.

Both sixes and V-12's alike were built on a 128-inch wheelbase. Both front and rear axles were carried by semi-elliptical leaf springs, and the wood-spoked wheels were shod with 36 × 4½-inch tires. All Nationals used a worm and gear steering system, giving very quick and accurate response. Brake drums were smaller than the car's performance levels would indicate as desirable, but the systems worked reliably, with internal-expanding shoes and external-contracting bands acting on the same drums in the rear wheels.

National's prices were surprisingly reasonable. The 1916-model Highway Twelve touring car could be purchased for as little as $1,990; the six-passenger touring car was listed at $2,020. Closed models were more expensive, and all came painted in National dark blue. The four-passenger coupe carried a price tag of $2,650 and the five-passenger sedan $3,200.

For 1917, National gave its customers a wide choice of colors, and the National stand at the New York automobile show included a four-passenger phaeton in yellow, a four-passenger roadster in white, and a seven-passenger touring car in gray, as well as the National blue coupe.

Despite the excellence of its products, the National Motor Vehicle Company ran into financial trouble. Management was blamed, and Arthur C. Newby resigned from the presidency in 1916, at the age of 51. He later started the Empire Automobile

Fig. 3-8. 1916 National Highway Twelve, another 12-cylinder.

Company, which also failed, and had no further connection with the auto industry. He died in 1933.

On Newby's departure, the National Motor Vehicle Company came under the control of a New York investment group and was renamed National Motor Car & Vehicle Corporation. W. Guy Wall stayed on, and production continued, with the V-12 in prominence through 1921. In May 1922, the National Motors Corporation was merged with the Kentucky Wagon Company (maker of the Dixie Flyer since 1915), Locomobile, Jackson, and Traffic Truck under the leadership of Emlen S. Hare.

Emlen S. Hare was a slick-super-salesman who had made his name and fortune in the Packard organization of New York and Philadelphia. He was named vice president of the parent company in 1918, but left Packard the following year to become president of Mercer. Next, he sought and won control of Simplex. Hare's Motors was no General Motors however. All his lofty plans collapsed, and the National went under in 1924.

W. Guy Wall opened an independent design consulting office in Indianapolis in 1925. He did some work for Stutz that year, and later helped various car makers and suppliers of parts to the auto industry in a multitude of engineering matters. He died in 1941.

36. CADILLAC MODEL 55, 1917

After a slow and steady climb towards the luxury-car market, Detroit's own Cadillac can be regarded as having achieved greatness with the introduction of its V-8 models in 1914 (Fig. 3-9).

The eight-cylinder Cadillac was an L-head design with a central camshaft and all valves located inside the V. With its 3.125-inch bore and 5.125-inch stroke it had a displacement of 314 cubic inches. Real output was 70 hp at 2,400 rpm on a compress ratio of 4.25:1, while the NACC rating was a mere 31.25 hp.

It was built up from two cast-iron blocks of four cylinders, each bolted on to the common crankcase at a 45-degree angle from vertical. The chrome-nickel forged steel crankshaft was a 'flat' or one-plane design running in three extraordinarily wide but small diameter main bearings. Main bearings were made of phosphor-bronze and lined with a special bearing metal developed by Cadillac. Connecting rods were mounted in a fork-and-blade arrangement, made with extreme precision. The machining and finishing of one pair of connecting rods (and pistons) was stated to involve 336 separate operations.

The camshaft was chain-driven and operated the valves via rollers and finger followers to relieve valve stems from bending loads. In the original version, cylinder heads were not detachable, but shared integral water jackets with the cylinder blocks. Each bank had its own shaft-driven water pump. The engine breathed through a one-barrel air-valve type carburetor mounted on a crossover manifold.

The Cadillac V-8 was not created in the Cadillac plant but designed and developed in a small shop in Mount Clemens, Michigan, masquerading as the Ideal Manufacturing Company where a team of engine experts could work in complete secrecy.

These experts were, of course, Cadillac engineers, and their leader was D. McCall White. McCall White was an English-born engineer who had experience from Arrol-Johnston, Daimler, Napier, and Crossley. He joined Cadillac in 1912 for the specific purpose of creating this new engine, under the supervision of Cadillac's engineering consultant, Ernest E. Sweet, who had designed Cadillac's first four-cylinder engine in 1905. Sweet was one of the original Cadillac stockholders and served as chief engineer for a number of years.

The first Cadillac of 1903 was a simple machine built on a 72-inch wheelbase powered by a single-cylinder 5 hp engine placed under the seat. It weighed 1,000 pounds and had a list price of $750.

The basic vehicle was a Henry Ford design. It became the Cadillac when Henry M. Leland took over the Detroit Automobile Co. and its plant, where Ford had been the chief engineer. Leland was the principal partner in a machine company that had contracted to build engines for Ford's venture.

Fig. 3-9. Cadillac Model 55 of 1917.

Rather than use the Ford-designed engine, Leland engaged A. P. Brush to design a new one, also to be produced by the Leland Faulconer Manufacturing Company. This firm was merged with Cadillac in 1905, and Leland was named general manager of the new Cadillac Automobile Company.

Cadillac added a two-cylinder, 9 hp Model E in 1905, and that same year also produced its first four-cylinder car, Model D, with a 30 hp engine, capable of 50 mph. Model D had a 100-inch wheelbase and a list price of $2,800.

All the while, production of the single-cylinder models B and F continued, with the E being replaced by the K and M twins in 1906. Then came the Model L, a 40-hp four-cylinder car priced at $3,750 in 1906.

Cadillac's Model G of 1907 was also a four-cylinder model, priced at $2,000 and equipped with a smaller engine of 20 hp, which was later increased to 25.

So strong was Cadillac's faith in the single-cylinder car, however, that a new one-lunger, Model T, selling at $1,350, was introduced in 1908 (when the lower-priced Model T Ford had a four-cylinder engine!)

Cadillac went to a one-model program in 1909, concentrating all its production on the 4-cylinder Series 30, offering three different bodies. All other models were dropped to let the factory build a great number of the Series 30. Output rose to 5,902 cars, or nearly three times more than the previous year.

Series 30 was to remain in production through the 1914 model year. It was the car that won the Dewar Trophy in England in 1909 for its use of precision-made interchangeable parts. It was also the car that introduced the Delco electric starter in 1912.

The engine for Series 30 was a 226-cubic inch T-head design with 4-inch bore and 4½-inch stroke. Cylinders were cast singly and the crankshaft ran in five main bearings. The three-speed transmission was of the sliding-shaft, selective-shift type, with shaft drive to the rear axle. The rear axle was carried by platform springs, combining one transverse leaf spring with the rear shackles of the usual longitudinal semi-ellipticals. The front axle had normal semi-elliptical springs. It had aluminum bodywork on a reinforced wood frame. This was the car that made Cadillac's success in the high-quality, medium-price market.

Cadillac made the complete car in its Detroit plant, including frame, axles, springs, and body. Its own facilities included a brass works and a sheet metal stamping unit.

The Cadillac V-8 was first used in Model 51 of 1914, a car priced at $1,975, and built on a 122-inch wheelbase. The chassis was directly derived from the former Series 30. It continued unchanged for 1915, and evolved into Model 53 for 1916. Aided by a new carburetor, its power output climbed to 76.5 hp. Greater variety in body styles led to a general rise in price. The roadster was listed at $2,000 and the Victoria coupe at $2,800; the brougham at $2,950 and the limousine at $3,450.

By 1917, Cadillac's Model 55 was one of the greatest cars produced in America. Wheelbase had grown to 125 inches and the landaulet's curb weight to 4,035 pounds. A longer chassis with a 132-inch wheelbase was in preparation.

Engine revisions included a change to detachable cylinder heads and the adoption of new, lighter pistons with an hourglass profile. Model 55 had a multi-plate clutch, three-speed transmission, shaft drive and a bevel-gear rear axle with a 4.43:1 final drive ratio. Standard tire size was 36 × 4½ inches.

The Lelands, (Henry M. Leland, the founder; and his son, Wilfred C. Leland, the president) left Cadillac in 1917. A go-getting GM executive who had come up through Buick's sales department, Richard H. Collins, took over the presidency. McCall White was named vice president and Sidney D. Waldon, formerly of Packard, was appointed chief engineer.

On the product front, Model 57 followed in 1918, available on either 125-or 132-inch wheelbase, with smaller and fatter 35 × 5-inch tires. No change was made in Model 57 for 1919, and it was renamed Model 59 for 1920. Power went to 79 hp and the prices ran higher, ranging from $3,590 to $5,190.

Cadillac had cast its anchor in the upper crust of the market, with a determination to conquer all opposition.

37. AUSTIN HIGHWAY KING, 1917

Cars from Michigan are usually associated, at least in thought, with Detroit and the notion of mass production. But the Austin from Grand Rapids in Western Michigan was the very antithesis of the stereotype, being produced in a quantity of little more than 1,000 units during its 16-year production life

The Austin was also a very great car, built with extreme care and attention by a small number of highly skilled and trusted men (Fig. 3-10). The Austin Automobile Company did not have the facilities to manufacture the major mechanical units on its own premises, but all components were selected only after great scrutiny and purchased from the most reputable suppliers.

The head of the firm, Walter S. Austin, had no thought of marketing in his head. His product was as far removed from market research as anything can be. Most probably he just wanted his car to be the kind of car that his friends and family would approve of, and in which he would be proud to travel.

The Austin family came to Grand Rapids from New York, and James E. Austin made his fortune in the lumber trade. His son, Walter Scott Austin grew up surrounded by carpenters, cabinet makers, and dealers in fine furniture. Doubtlessly influenced by the arrival of numbers of horseless carriages imported from Europe to Chicago in 1895-96, his mind turned to building motor vehicles on an American scale.

Walter Scott Austin began designing his first car in 1901. He was 45 years old when he first drove a car of his own construction in 1902. Walter and his father, James, found it satisfactory, and set up a factory at 86-92 Division Street in Grand Rapids, with machine shops, assembly, stockrooms, administration and drafting offices, all under one roof.

The first Austin car produced for sale dates from 1903. The paternal advisor and main backer, James Austin was to play a vital role in the production of the Austin cars, especially in the earliest period.

The product was a two-cylinder machine of general dimensions that were far larger than auto makers in those days were ready for. But Austin knew the value of space, comfort, and carrying capacity, and set about to develop the kind of power units that would be equal to the task.

By 1907 Austin was building a high-grade four-cylinder car of great allure, Model 35, with large-size wheels, a high frame, and side-entrance tonneau-type touring body. It had a list price of $3,000.

Built on a 108-inch wheelbase, the chassis had a straight angle-steel frame and a shaft-driven rear axle. A four-speed sliding gear transmission was used. The engine was an in-line four of 373 cubic-inch displacement, with 4.875-inch bore and a 5-inch stroke.

It was during 1907 that Austin introduced his Model L powered by an oversquare (5.5-inch bore and 5-inch stroke) engine 516.5 cubic inch displacement. This voluminous power plant delivered 50 hp at about 1,100 rpm and would run to 1,500 or 1,600 rpm, giving the car a top speed of more than 60 mph.

Model L was also built on a 108-inch wheelbase with a 56-inch track, and its wood-spoked wheels carried 36 × 4½-inch tires. The

Seven Passenger Limousine $5250

Fig. 3-10. The Austin Highway King of 1917 from Grand Rapids, Michigan.

complete touring car weighed no more than 2,500 pounds, not due to the use of exotic metallurgy, but to the simplicity and straightforwardness of Austin's construction. The price for the first Model L touring car was $3,500.

Austin's catalog for 1908 shows three different bodies being offered on the Model L chassis with the 60 hp four-cylinder engine (touring car, combination roadster, and detachable-top limousine).

Model X had a longer chassis to carry Austin's first six-cylinder engine, a 90-hp unit that was essentially the Model L four with an extra pair of cylinders.

Walter Scott Austin was interested in travel, and built his cars mainly for long-distance transportation. He was a charter member of the American Automobile Association, and a skilled driver himself. Austin was an early advocate of left hand drive, with central controls. He chose a four-speed transmission with selective shift for his first designs. Later, Austin designed a four-speed planetary transmission with a column shift.

A two-speed axle was made standard on the Austin as early as 1913. The reasoning behind it was to provide a highway range for high speed travel, and a low or normal range for city and suburban driving. The highway range was intended to bring smoothness, quietness, durability, and economy, all of which it accomplished). In 1918 Austin instigated a lawsuit against Cadillac for patent infringement of the two-speed axle, which was settled in Austin's favor about seven years later.)

Austin offered three series in 1913, the "55" with a list price of $4,000; the "66" which was priced $1,000 higher; and at the top of the line, the "77", for which Austin asked customers to pay an even $6,000.

The power unit was basically the same engine for all three, an in-line six of conventional design and construction. For the "55" it came with 4-inch bore and 5-inch stroke, giving 377 cubic-inch displacement.

The "66" had 4½-inch bore and 5½-inch stroke, with a displacement of 525 cubic inches, and the "77" had a displacement of no less than 668 cubic inches, with its 7-inch stroke and 4½-inch bore.

Twelve spark plugs were used in each engine, fired by separate high-tension magnetos. A compressed-air starter system was used, in combination with a tire-inflating reservoir, fed by the same pump.

Most other cars of this period had two separate brake systems, one worked by a lever and the other by a pedal. Austin did not like hand-operated brakes, and linked one system to the clutch pedal. The linkage was arranged so that continued depression of the clutch pedal after disengagement had occurred would apply the brakes. The driver could thus steer with both hands, while applying one set of brakes with the right foot and a second brake system with the left foot. The fact that both brake systems acted on the same two rear wheels was not in any way viewed as an anomaly, for front wheel brakes were widely believed to be unsafe.

On the 1913 models, three-quarter-elliptical springs were used for the rear axle suspension. Two years later, the rear axle was supported by two cantilever leaf springs on each side, claimed to give a softer and easier-riding car. The springs were not exposed to the same risk of breakage that a set of single semi-ellipticals would have been. And, though Austin was probably only vaguely aware of it at the time, or thought his customers would be, the dual-cantilever setup substantially reduced the unsprung weight and improved rear wheel traction and adhesion.

The 1915 six cylinder Austin engine was a long-stroke design with 4½-inch bore and a 6-inch stroke, giving 572.5 cubic-inch displacement. The 1915 Austin "66" was built on a 141-inch wheelbase and the manufacturer offered a choice of seven different body styles: A runabout at $3,600, and a close-coupled open car at the same price; five- and six-passenger models with four-door touring car bodies also selling at $3,600; four- and five-passenger limousines at $4,200; and a seven-passenger limousine at $4,700.

By 1916 Austin had reduced his range to three models: a dickey-seat roadster listed at $2,800; a sedan listed at $3,800; and a vestibule-brougham at $4,000. The 1916 models were built on a 142-inch wheelbase, and customers had a choice of wood or wire wheels. The two-speed rear axle was continued, with a three-speed selective-shift gearbox. The 1916 engine was smaller and lighter, of 371 cubic-inch displacement (3.875 × 5.25-inch bore and stroke), of cast-en-bloc construction.

A second model was offered in 1917, powered by a Weidely V-12 engine. This became Austin's main vehicle for the rest of the company's existence. Production ceased in 1918.

The Weidely engine had 389.5 cubic-inch displacement and weighed 750 pounds—no more than some sixes of similar displacement. With its 3.6:1 compression ratio, it delivered 75 hp at 2,000 rpm.

Walter Scott Austin withdrew from the auto industry and had a good income from interests in real estate and other fields. But his mind could never let go of auto engineering, and as late as 1950 he took out a patent for a hydraulic transmission system.

He was beginning to age, however, and in 1960 he had a stroke from which he never really recovered. He died at the age of 99 in his home town of Grand Rapids in 1965.

38. MARMON 34, 1917

Marmon presents an almost unique case for greatness, having achieved such recognition in 1912 for a four-cylinder car with a list price of $2,400—far below the typical "great" car of the era (Fig. 3-11).

Shortly after launching the successful 32-series, the Nordyke & Marmon Company in Indianapolis also entered the high-priced luxury car market with a couple of six-cylinder models. The "41" and "48" went into production in 1914, with wheelbases of 132 and 145 inches, respectively. Prices for the "41" started at $3,250 for the four-passenger touring car, while the "48" seven-passenger touring car was listed at $5,000.

Chassis design was essentially the same for both, with a channel-section pressed steel frame, semi-elliptical leaf springs on both front and rear axles, three-speed transmission and shaft drive. Tires were 36 × 4½-inch on all four wheels for the "41" and the "48" carried the same size on its front wheels, but bigger 37 × 5-inch ones on the rear wheels.

The "48" engine was a development of the T-head four used in Series 32, with its six cylinders cast in pairs. A 4½-inch bore and 6-inch stroke gave the engine a displacement of 572.5 cubic inches. It had low-range torque worthy of a Mack truck and delivered about 90 hp at the top end of its 2,400-rpm speed range. This engine was used in a number of special racing chassis based on the 32-series, and these Marmons were entered in 103 races over a three-year period, winning in 54 of them.

A very different engine was installed in the "41," with its cylinders made up in two blocks of three. Bore was reduced to 4.25 inches and the stroke shortened to 5.5 inches, giving a displacement of 468 cubic inches and delivering about 75 hp.

These models could not become popular, for they were too high-priced for that. Nor did they contribute much to uphold the reputation of the Marmon make, for they were somewhat lacking in distinction from rivals with a stronger background in that market, such as Locomobile, Peerless, and White.

Howard Marmon, meanwhile, was making plans for a one-model policy, whereby the four-cylinder 32-series and the "41" and "48" sixes would be replaced by one and the same car.

The designer of the original Cadillac engine, Alanson P. Brush, joined Marmon's engineering staff in 1913. Another engineer named Fred Moscovics also joined Marmon that year. They worked with Howard Marmon on the project that became the "34."

A. P. Brush was then 35 years old, and had just sold his Brush Runabout Company to the builders of the Car-Nation. Fred Moscovics was two years younger and had formerly worked for Continental Tire Company, designed the Allen-Kingston car, and served as vice president of the Bristol Engineering Company in Bristol, Connecticut, where he created a prototype motor taxicab, perhaps America's first.

The Marmon "34" became a showcase for advanced technology and daring metallurgy. The engine was an in-line six with pushrod-operated overhead valves, made almost entirely of aluminum. It had a one-piece cast aluminum block with cast iron liners, and an aluminum crankcase. The cylinder head was cast iron, and the crankshaft a steel forging. Aluminum parts included the pistons, oil pan, valve cover, water pump body, engine mounting brackets, fan pulley, and intake manifold. Aluminum was also used for the clutch housing, gearbox casing, and differential housing.

The body was made of aluminum, too (including the radiator shell), and mounted on an unusual frame of thin-gauge steel with side members up to 10 inches deep at the center and incorporating the running boards as part of the framework.

Marmon's extensive use of light alloys is estimated to have saved about 25 percent of the weight the car would have had if made from conventional materials. The "34" stood on a 136-inch wheelbase and with standard touring car body weighed only 3,295 pounds.

The 340 cubic inch engine had a 3.75-inch bore and 5.125-inch stroke, and the chrome-nickel steel crankshaft ran in four main bearings. It weighed 110 pounds and the complete engine about 550 pounds. Maximum output was 74 hp at 2,450 rpm (the NACC rating was 33.75 hp).

The drive train was as modern as anything on the market, except for use of an old type cone clutch. The three-speed gearbox had a selective shift gate, the propeller shaft was double-jointed, and final drive was of the spiral bevel type. The rear axle was equipped with three-quarter-floating hubs. Rear leaf springs were made to work with a progressive rate, and the car had first-class

Fig. 3-11. The low-priced Marmon 34 of 1917.

ride and handling. The driver sat, of course, on the left, and steered via a worm and wheel mechanism.

The Marmon 34 had a top speed of 65 mph with the 4.00:1 final drive and could reach 70 mph with the optional 3.75:1 axle. The former was naturally quicker from standstill to 50 mph, taking 19 seconds to do that, compared with 22 seconds for the higher-speed model.

Marmon's advances in the "34" included a 12-volt electrical system and wire wheels mounted with 34 × 4½-inch tires. And this fantastic package of a car was available at only $2,750 in touring car form.

Sensational as Marmon's use of aluminum was, it's senseless to pretend that it did not give trouble. Howard Marmon redesigned the engine for 1920, adopting a cast iron block, cast in two units of three cylinders each. A new three-bearing crankshaft was adopted for this engine, which weighed about 675 pounds.

It continued in production through 1929 without further structural changes, and steady development work raised its output to 84 hp at 2,700 rpm in the final version. Marmon produced over 11,000 cars of the "34" model, which was succeeded in 1924 by the "74"—a car with a new and more conventional chassis powered by the same engine.

Chapter 4

A New Decade Begins: 1920-1925

By the time of America's entry in World War I, Detroit was the nation's center of mass-production. It was to the manufacturers of Detroit that the Federal government turned for motive power for its ships, road transports, and airplanes. Out of these circumstances was to come one of America's greatest cars—the Lincoln. Specifically, it started with the Liberty aircraft engine, which was produced to government-approved specifications by several companies (Fig. 4-1).

39. LINCOLN MODEL A, 1920

When tenders were being offered, it was recognized as a tremendous opportunity by Henry M. Leland, president of Cadillac, to regain independence for himself from General Motors, where he was unhappy about having to carry out William C. Durant's orders, whose aim and portent was usually at variance with his own ideas and principles

With the assurance of a Liberty contract, Leland and his son Wilfred handed in their resignations at Cadillac, formed the Lincoln Motor Company, and took over the Detroit plant of the defunct Lozier Company.

The name Lincoln was Leland's own idea. He wanted a name to rival Cadillac's. Seeking a personage of equal or greater stature in the minds of Americans, his choice fell on Abraham Lincoln, the U.S. president for whom Leland had once voted as a young man.

Leland was awarded a contract for 6,000 Liberty engines in World War I, and by January 1919, Lincoln had produced 6,500.

Fig. 4-1. The 1919 Lincoln Model A.

But, in taking stock of his situation at that moment Leland realized that he had a work force of 6,000 men, a big factory with no marketable product, and a lot of creditors waiting for settlement. Going back into the automobile business seemed the answer to all his problems, and out of that came the Lincoln car.

Leland had such a great reputation, not only within the industry but among the public, that Lincoln's sales organization was able to take orders for 1,000 cars before the Lincoln automobile had even been unveiled, on the strength of his name alone.

A car designed by an old man of 77—how could that possibly be a great one? Leland was no ordinary old man, for his mental powers were as formidable as ever, and his concern with quality and precision undiminished. His assistant, however, was then a mature 45: Ernest E. Sweet had left Cadillac along with the Lelands in 1917. He had joined the machine business of Leland & Faulconer & Norton in 1893, fresh from a common school education in his home town of Wayne, Michigan, and had been active in the Cadillac organization since its foundation in 1902. It has been suggested that Sweet's share of credit for the design of the first Lincoln car is no less than Leland's and that seems a fair assessment.

Wilfred C. Leland had nothing to do with the technical side of the business. He was the administrator, secretary and treasurer all rolled into one. But he was no car man. He had "no gasoline in his blood," as a Ford executive said of him. Actually, Wilfred had wanted to be a physician and actually spent a year and a half taking a pre-med course at Brown University. In 1890, when Wilfred was 21, father Leland talked him into moving to Detroit and offered him a job with the tool company. Their later paths were inseparable.

Lincoln Motor Company went into production with its Model A in the summer of 1920. It was a big car, with wheelbases of 130 or 136 inches, a pressed-steel frame, and semi-elliptical leaf springs on both front and rear axles. Notable advancements were the use of shock absorbers as standard equipment, Alemite chassis lubrication, and thermostatically controlled radiator shutters.

The full-floating rear axle was driven via a torque tube and straight bevel gears. The transmission was a three-speed design, rugged and heavy, coupled with a multi-plate clutch.

The engine was a V-8, with surprising differences from Cadillac's. The Lincoln V-8 was laid out with the banks disposed at an included angle of 60 degrees (compared with the Cadillac's 90-degrees layout). This gave uneven spacing of the firing impulses, but in such a pattern as to counteract primary and secondary unbalanced forces rather than amplify them.

The Lincoln did inherit the fork-and-blade connecting rod arrangement which was also used by Cadillac, but the Lincoln crankshaft ran in five bearings. Thus, it certainly had higher internal friction losses and greater bearing loads, but crankshaft balance was probably better, despite the absence of counter-weighting of any kind and the engine ran quieter, with less vibration.

With its 3.375-inch bore and 5.00-inch stroke, the Lincoln V-8 had 357.8 cubic-inch displacement and a maximum output of 81 hp. It had two cast-iron blocks of four cylinders, mounted on a common aluminum crankcase. It was an L-head design with a single central camshaft and all valves located inside the V. The camshaft was driven by chain from the front of the crankshaft. To aid cold starting, the head carried a primer cup for each cylinder, into which the driver poured gasoline (this was common practice until choke mechanisms were perfected).

Lincoln's standard bodies were not pretty. Designed by Angus Woodbridge, whose major qualification for the task was being married to Henry M. Leland's daughter Martha, they had little in their appearance other than size to lure buyers.

Lack of styling probably affected the Lincoln's downfall, for sales began to dry up in 1921. Profit margins which had been narrow went into the negative, and Henry M. Leland's ability to borrow fresh funds from the banks was frustrated by an erroneous tax claim of $4 million against Lincoln. When the error was achnowledged, it was too late to save the company.

The Lincoln Motor Company fell into receivership in November, 1921, and was put up for sale on February 22, 1922. On that date it became the property of Henry Ford who paid $8 million for it. Total output prior to Ford's takeover was 3,407 cars. Still in stock at the time were 241 unsold cars.

Ford kept the father-and-son team of Lelands in charge of Lincoln, but that led to a situation that could only end in conflict, just as conflict had arisen between the Lelands and Durant at GM. The outcome will be narrated in connection with another great Lincoln of some years hence.

40. PORTER MODEL 45, 1920

America's most expensive car in 1920 was the Porter, a truly magnificent machine featuring sophisticated engineering as well as tasteful and speed-oriented design. The chassis alone cost $6,750, and the Porter touring car, lowest-priced of the six body styles in the catalog, was offered at $9,200.

It was in a class of its own among domestically produced automobiles. Only imports came with comparable prices. Of course, it was not the price that made the Porter so great . . . its greatness is solidly based on hardware (Fig. 4-2).

The Porter was a big car, with wheelbases up to 132 inches, but its bodies were as low as the frame (and practical considerations) would allow. The frame was made of pressed steel with straight side members, and both front and rear axles were mounted on semi-elliptical leaf springs. Strangely, the chassis was made only with right hand drive. Bodies bore a certain likeness to the Rolls-Royce, not only in radiator and hood design, but in overall proportions. The likeness was particularly striking in the case of wire-wheeled Porters (others had artillery wheels).

The Porter was built by an obscure firm with the title American & British Manufacturing Company, which operated out of a spacious factory in Bridgeport, Connecticut, where it had produced naval artillery during World War I. It had a decent machine shop and skilled workers.

140

Fig. 4-2. America's most expensive car of 1920, the Porter Model 45.

Making cars was perhaps a logical peacetime activity for this organization, but it had no prior experience with such products, and wisely decided to hire expert help. American & British signed up an engineer of a caliber that weighed far more than the company's six-inch guns, a man named Finley Robertson Porter.

F. R. Porter was famous as the designer of the T-head Mercer Speedster and Raceabout, and as chief engineer of Mercer from 1910 to 1915. The Mercer business was an offshoot of the John A. Roebling Sons Company, with a plant in Trenton, New Jersey. There, under Porter's direction, Mercer produced high-performance sports cars to rival anything the men of Indianapolis could build.

By birth, Porter was an Ohioan, born in Lowell, in 1872. His education can only be described as spotty; he left school at the age of 11, and as an adult took correspondence courses in mechanical engineering.

He broadened his knowledge by working in a number of different industries, and got involved with automotive engineering by being engaged by Charles C. Worthington, a well-known pump manufacturer, to design a steam car. The prototype was unsuccessful, and the last job Porter held before joining Mercer was managing a brass works in Pennsylvania.

The end of Porter's days with Mercer came after a disagreement with Charles G. Roebling. Porter wanted to stay with the T-head engine, while Roebling wanted to use a lower-cost L-head unit designed by Erik H. Delling. After Porter quit, Delling was named chief engineer of Mercer.

Porter moved to Long Island and took over the plant of the defunct Metropol Motor Company in Port Jefferson. He found wealthy backers and started to build the FRP car, a high-performance racer, also available with sports or touring car bodies. The most notable element in its engineering was the engine.

Porter went to an overhead camshaft, driven by a vertical shaft and worm gears, with a crossflow head. The four-cylinder FRP engine was cast en bloc, with 4.60-inch bore and 6.75-inch stroke, giving a displacement of 448.7 cubic inches. An output of 170 hp at 2,500 rpm was claimed for this engine.

FRP production ended after about 10 cars had been built, and Porter went on the government's payroll as head of the aircraft engine test establishment at Wright Field near Dayton, Ohio. His efforts to revive the FRP after the armistice led him into contact with American & British. He was engaged as a consultant, and his son, Robert Brewster Porter, was named chief engineer.

The engine for the Porter car was a detuned version of the FRP unit, with identical dimensions, but lower output, variously quoted as 120 hp and 140 hp at 2,500-2,600 rpm. The Porter was still one of the most powerful cars in production in 1920. While the FRP had been conceived for racing, the Porter was intended as a civilized family car. It is easy to see where the horsepower disappeared as mufflers went on and valve timing was altered to reduce clatter and roughness.

American & British had no facilities for making coachwork, and concentrated on chassis production. An agreement was made with Blue Ribbon, a Bridgeport carriage maker, to build Porter bodies. Some chassis also went to Brewster, Demarest, and Fleetwood.

Owners of Porter cars recall their great speed. A car that would top 80 mph in those days must have impressed anyone who could muster up the courage to keep his foot on the accelerator long enough to actually *cruise* at that speed. However, their recollections also include memories of high fuel consumption and frequent breakdowns.

In 1921 the Porter seven-passenger touring car was listed at $10,500 and the limousine at $12,500. Shortly afterwards Rolls-Royce opened a branch factory at Springfield, Massachusetts, and Americans could buy the American Rolls-Royce for less than the price of a Porter. By 1922, American & British discontinued car production, after having turned out no more than 36 complete units.

Porter then joined Glenn L. Curtiss to work on aircraft engine design and stayed there for a number of years. At an age when other men think of retirement, he set himself up as a consulting engineer, and during World War II he worked with both Bendix and Curtiss-Wright. He died at the age of 93 in his home in Southhampton, Long Island, in 1964.

41. DUESENBERG MODEL A, 1920

Duesenberg is primarily remembered not for the first car which bore that proud name, but rather the last ones to be built before the marque disappeared. Yet the very first Duesenberg was, in the context of its time and in comparison with its competitors, not only a great car but an advanced engineering achievement.

DUESENBERG "STRAIGHT-EIGHT" TOURING CAR

Fig. 4-3. Duesenberg's very first, the 1920 Model A.

It was called Model A and made its debut at the New York automobile show in November, 1920 (Fig. 4-3). Everything in its makeup and material specification spelled excellence. It was built on a 134-inch wheelbase with a frame having chrome-nickel steel side members, tempered-steel semi-elliptical leaf springs on both axles, and torque tube drive. Molybdenum steel was used for the rear axle, with a forged-steel differential carrier.

At a time when most auto makers were still resisting the use of front wheel brakes, and few had tried hydraulic brake operation, Duesenberg came out with a system of four-wheel hydraulic brakes (under Lockheed patents). A 16-inch drum with peripheral cooling fins was mounted on each wheel, all operated from a single pedal (as Duesenberg literature pointed out). The handbrake was connected to a contracting-band brake mounted at the front end of the propeller shaft.

And then there was the straight-eight engine, a masterpiece of design and craftsmanship. It had only 260 cubic-inch displacement, with its 2.785 inch bore and 5.00-inch stroke, but had a compression ratio of 5.0:1 and delivered 90 hp at 3,600 rpm—a rotational rate that had until then been associated strictly with racing and aircraft engines. True, those were the fields where the Duesenberg name had won its first triumphs.

The cylinder block was a single casting, with a detachable crossflow head also cast as one piece. Both were cast iron, while the crankcase and cam cover were made of aluminum. A single overhead camshaft was driven by vertical shaft and bevel gears at the front of the engine, operating splayed valves via neatly

144

sculptured rocker arms. The forged steel crankshaft ran in three main bearings and carried two integral counterweights. Aluminum pistons were used, and one spark plug per cylinder was fired by Delco coil and battery ignition.

An updraft Stromberg carburetor was carried on the intake manifold on the right-hand side of the block, while the exhaust ports discharged into a manifold on the left side. Force-feed lubrication was used throughout, with a gear-type oil pump. The engine was carried by a three-point suspension system, and the clutch bell-housing and three-speed transmission were bolted to the rear face of the engine block. Wire wheels were standard, carrying 33 × 5.00-inch tires. Duesenberg sold 92 cars in 1922 and 140 in 1923.

The Model A Duesenberg could reach 90 mph in stock trim with full bodywork, and in 1923 a standard five-passenger sedan ran for over 50 hours at Indianapolis Speedway with an average speed of 62.6 mph including stops for refuelling, tire changes, etc. Special racing Duesenbergs, powered by similar straight-eight engines, upheld the make's fame by racking up victory after victory in the most hotly contested events.

All these cars were designed by Fred S. Duesenberg, aided by his younger brother August. The family came from Lippe, Germany, where Fred was born in 1876. They emigrated to Iowa when Fred was eight years old. He grew up on a farm, and by the time he was seventeen he was making a living as a mechanic on windmills and farm equipment.

At the age of 21 he was making bicycles and racing them. His first step into the realm of automobiles came in 1902, when he joined Rambler as a test driver.

With Augie's help he opened a garage in Des Moines, Iowa, in 1903, and the following year they built their first car. Backed by a lawyer named Edward R. Mason, they started production of the lightweight two-cylinder model, called Mason, not Duesenberg. Appliance maker F. L. Maytag bought Mason in 1910, and renamed the car Maytag-Mason. The Duesenberg brothers were not part of the deal, however, and continued to build Mason cars in their own shop.

The first true Duesenberg racing cars, built in 1912, still carried the Mason label. They had a 230 cubic-inch four-cylinder engine, notable for its horizontal valves operated by long walking beams from camshafts on either side of the block.

In 1913 they moved to St. Paul, Minnesota, and formed the Duesenberg Motor Company. They became engine suppliers to other car makers on the strength of their racing reputation, and also built a line of powerful, high-speed marine engines.

During World War I the Duesenberg Motor Co. was enlisted in aircraft and marine engine production. They produced a 500 hp 16-cylinder Bugatti engine in a new plant at Edgewater, New Jersey, and also built a small number of 900 hp Duesenberg Model H V-16's. After the war, they decided to build complete touring cars as well as continue racing as a matter of company policy.

They sold the Edgewater plant to Willys-Overland, and sold the design for the four-cylinder walking beam engine to the Rochester Motor Co. They moved to Indianapolis, where the Model A was made.

42. PREMIER MODEL 6-D, 1920

"The aluminum Six with the electric gearshift," was Premier's slogan in 1920. This product of Indianapolis had long been renowned for technical innovation, but it did not acquire the image of a great car until its swan song in the early Twenties (Fig. 4-4).

The Indianapolis-based Premier company had been producing interesting cars since the turn of the century, and it was in 1916 that the aluminum engine and electric gearshift were adopted. The engine was a remarkably modern design with pushrod-operated overhead valves standing vertically along the cylinder axis. The camshaft was placed rather low in the side of the block, featuring a roller-cam and long, delicate pushrods to rocker arms above the head.

The six-cylinder engine was cast as a one-piece aluminum block with wet cast iron liners which gave a highly compatible rubbing surface for the light alloy pistons. The cylinder head was detachable; it was also a one-piece aluminum casting. The rocker cover was a simple pressed steel lid, bolted down to the rocker assembly.

The gearshift was a product of Cutler-Hammer in Milwaukee, designed to change gears in an ordinary sliding-shaft transmission by means of electromagnetic solenoids controlled by a quadrant mounted on the steering wheel. A normal clutch was retained, so there was really nothing automatic about it.

Premier ads made the point, however, that it enabled women drivers to shift gears without effort, and all drivers would be able to make quicker shifts, in traffic or when climbing hills. For some years Premier had exclusive use of this Cutler-Hammer device, but later, when the makers were given freedom to supply it to other car companies as well, it found few takers.

Both the engine design and the adoption of the electric gearshift are credited to A. L. Nelson, who was Premier's chief experimental engineer from about 1911 to 1919, when he was appointed chief engineer. Earl Gunn was chief engineer in 1916, succeeded a year later by Charles Crawford, who got the title of engineering director in 1919.

Premier had placed its first six-cylinder engine in production in 1907, and in 1913 settled on an all-six program. The early sixes were L-head designs with cast iron cylinders and heads. George A. Weidely was Premier's chief engineer in the early period, and created the first Premier with a four-cylinder air-cooled engine and shaft drive in 1905. As a runabout, it sold for $1,250, and as a side-entrance tonneau, for $1,500.

In 1906 Premier copied neighboring National's roundfaced radiator, and began setting speed records. In one test, the four-cylinder Premier 24-28 hp model covered 100 miles in 2 hours and 15 minutes (an average speed of 44.4 mph) while showing a spartan appetite, for it used up less than four gallons of gasoline (i.e. better than 25 miles to the gallon). In 1907, the Premier air-cooled four sold for $2,250, and a water-cooled six was added at $3,250. The engine was a T-head design with the cylinders cast in pairs, and the chassis was new, adopting semi-elliptical leaf springs all around instead of the full-elliptics used on the air-cooled models.

The first of the "modern" Premiers came in 1912, with the launching of the M-6. It had a new T-head six with two blocks of three cylinders, left hand drive and central controls. A compressed-air starter was used. Premier made its own transmissions and rear axles, using gears machined from nickel-steel drop forgings. Aluminum was used only for covering water jackets, and even pistons were made of gray iron.

Connecting rods were I-beam drop forgings, and the crankshaft was machined from a one-piece drop forging. With the M-6 Premier staked its first claim on a "great car" label. The Big Six, as it was known, delivered 60 hp from its 525 cubic-inch displacement.

The following year the Premier Little Six was added having virtually the same engine design but with reduced bore and stroke, giving 377 cubic-inch displacement. The two were consolidated into one new model, the 6-56, in 1916, with 415 cubic-inch displacement. This was a very big car, on a 134-inch wheelbase, with 34 × 4½-inch tires on wire wheels, full-floating rear axle, and worm-and-wheel steering. It was phased out after the overhead-valve aluminum-block engine went into production.

The aluminum six had the same 5.5-inch stroke as the 6-56 engine, but a smaller bore of 3.375-inches (instead of 4.00 inches), giving only 295 cubic inch displacement. Despite the 125.5-inch wheelbase of the 6-D in 1920, it was a relatively light car, with lively performance.

The standard touring car was listed at $3,525, and the seven-passenger Limousine at $5,800. Premier was noteworthy for its exceptionally roomy bodies, well laid-out and comfortable interiors, lavish equipment, trim and finish, and sleek styling. The V-front radiator led into a hood whose creased edge ran around the entire belt line. This 'Grecian' body edge was a patented design feature. Artillery wheels were standard now, with tire sizes to 32 × 4½ inches.

Crawford left in 1921, so A. L. Nelson was on his own—but had no budget for doing anything significant to move the product ahead. For 1921, the wheelbase was stretched to 126.75 inches, but few other changes were made. Despite successive price cuts, a drop in sales could not be arrested. The 1924 models had the same engine, and wheelbase was now 126.25 inches. Premier's prices had been slashed down to $2,535, with the top-of-the line closed model at $3,585 . . . to no avail.

By 1925 Premier was surviving only by building a line of taxicabs. Premier finally closed its doors in 1926.

43. WILLS SAINTE CLAIRE A-68, 1921

The dream of the perfect car never left the mind of C. Harold Wills, the man responsible for the Ford Model K in 1906 and the principal engineer on the Model T for 1908. That was the end of an era for him. It meant an end to all plans for new models, and Wills concentrated instead on developing new materials, especially better and more specialized metals. Ford paid him well, and in addition, he was an important Ford stockholder. But on his 40th birthday, he decided to spend his life differently.

He was an idealist in his view of the automobile, and he felt a personal need to indulge in more creative work than Ford was letting him do. In March of 1919 he resigned from Ford and made preparations to build his own car. He found a ready plant site in Marysville, on the shores of Lake St. Clair about 50 miles north east of Detroit, and that gave the car its name: Wills Sainte Claire (he changed the lake's name into feminine form for the car, as he would have done for a boat).

Fig. 4-4. Premier Model 6-D, 1920 featuring an aluminum six cylinder.

It was going to be his dream car. Not a giant road locomotive, but an exquisite gem, reeking of quality and the scientific use of the fine metals. It was powered by a 265 cubic-inch V-8 engine delivered 67 hp at 2,700 on a 4.1:1 compression ratio. From the three-speed transmission, there was torque tube drive to the spiral bevel rear axle. The standard touring car was built on a 122-inch wheelbase and weighed just 3,115 pounds, due to Wills's extensive use of aluminum and molybdenum throughout the chassis and drive train (Fig. 4-5).

Wills personally laid out the complete car and its engine, but hired well-known engineers to handle the detail design. Fred I. Tone was named chief engineer of Wills Sainte Claire. He had formerly designed the first Marion and the last American Underslung in Indianapolis, and spent years with Willys-Overland in Toledo. He and Wills met in 1917, when Tone was head of an inspection group for the Liberty aircraft engine which Ford had been awarded a contract to produce.

Another was Charles Morgana, who had come to Ford in 1916 as a buyer of machinery. He was formerly production manager of Maxwell-Chalmers, had worked with Briggs Manufacturing Company, and at the start of his career, had worked at the John R. Keim Mills (where William S. Knudsen had joined Ford). Morgana became a vice president of Wills Sainte Claire and handled all production matters.

Wills spared nothing in equipping his plant with the very best in precision tools and machinery, always with the accent on quality rather than quantity. They were setting up a plant with a very modern layout, but had no eye on productivity. That would be their downfall.

The product itself never let Wills and his men down. It was as close to perfection as anyone could have made it. Of course, thorough testing took its time, and the first cars were not completed till March, 1921. The price rose from the projected $2,000 to a full $3,000—due to higher manufacturing costs.

Much of the development effort was spent on the engine. It was no ordinary V-8, in the Cadillac/Lincoln mold. This was an overhead-camshaft V-8, more closely akin to the Hispano-Suiza W4R aircraft engine than to anything seen in a car before. Wills had no doubt been inspired by the Hispano-Suiza V-8 but in no way did he copy it. Wills used a 60-degree, not the 90-degree layout of the French motor. They shared the use of a single overhead camshaft per bank, with shaft drive, and integral construction (nondetachable heads).

But Wills used spiral bevel gears in the camshaft drive, instead of the straight-cut bevels of the Hispano-Suiza. Wills also added finger followers, interposed between the cam and valve stem, to avoid side thrust on the valves.

Light alloy enthusiast as he was, from his vanadium discoveries while at Ford to his extensive use of molybdenum in the Wills Sainte Claire, he shrank from going to aluminum for the engine block (which Hispano-Suiza had). The Wills Sainte Claire V-8 was made up of two cast iron blocks on a common crankcase.

Connecting rods were mounted in a fork and blade arrangement, while they ran side-by-side in the aircraft engine. Wills's crankshaft ran in only three main bearings, but Hispano-Suiza had used a five-bearing crankshaft. The latter also used tubular steel connecting rods but Wills chose H-section forged-steel rods.

Due to the use of eight cylinders, Wills was able to use a short stroke and a small bore (3.25-inch bore and 4.00-inch stroke). He also introduced a new refinement in the form of an automatic fan clutch with a centrifugal governor, so as to disengage the fan when its action was not needed. The Wills Sainte Claire was also the first car to use a backup light, automatically turned on when the car was put in reverse.

The car rode on semi-elliptical leaf springs, front and rear, and was steered by worm-and-gear. Wills himself designed the plain disc wheels, concave towards the hub, which mounted 32 ×

Fig. 4-5. Wills Sainte Claire A-68 of 1921.

6. 20-inch tires. The balloon-tire era was beginning, and Marysville was part of it from the start.

The A-68 was capable of cruising at 70 mph with the 4.45:1 final drive ratio, and gave an overall gasoline mileage of about 14-15 miles per gallon.

It had no particular reliability problems, but once something went wrong, repairs were invariably so complicated that they proved too baffling for service personnel in general.

Sales were slow, and production had to be cut back periodically. By 1923 the firm's capital was spent, and in a refinancing scheme, Wills lost the personal control he had enjoyed at the outset. The main thing was the survival of the car—and this time it stayed afloat.

44. CUNNINGHAM, 1922

Car styling did not start, of course, with the creation of the Art & Color Section at General Motors, but had existed as a notional part of car designing ever since the makers of automobiles devoted some attention to the appearance of their products. And that, counting bits and pieces, inside and outside, front, rear and sides, began when the American car emerged from its backyard builder-owner stage and a industry building transportation for the masses was formed.

We have seen how Packard made the fluted hood, National the round radiator, Pierce-Arrow the fender-mounted headlamps, and Premier the 'Grecian' belt line. One of the first to design the complete car with one overall styling theme was Cunningham, whose cars were remarkably handsome as well as being constructed in the best coachbuilding traditions. And to top it all, the Cunningham's engineering was also at a high level and not without originality (Fig. 4-6).

The Cunningham was built in a spacious plant on Canal Street in Rochester, New York, by a company that had several generations of experience in the manufactuer of fine carriages. James Cunningham, Son & Co. was formed in 1882 to carry on the carriage-making business started in 1838 when James Cunningham, an Irish immigrant from County Down and a partner named Kerr took over the Hanford & Whitbeck firm of coachbuilders.

The Cunningham heirs became interested in automobiles when models with closed bodies began to appear and the demand for horse-drawn carriages started its long decline. The

Cunninghams, like the Studebakers, were complete wagon builders, producing the frame, springs and axles as well as the body, and this naturally led their product philosophy towards the complete car instead of just the body.

Experimental Cunningham cars were running as early as 1907, apparently designed by the same engineering staff that was responsible for the carriages. They were powered by four- and six-cylinder Buffalo engines, but by 1910 Cunningham had prepared designs for its own power units, which were subcontracted to a reputable manufacturer. Transmissions, axles, radiators, and other components were purchased from leading suppliers.

The Cunningham Model H was built from 1910 through 1913, and was powered by an overhead-valve four-cylinder engine. With 4.75-inch bore and 5.75-inch stroke, it had 407.6 cubic-inch displacement and delivered about 40 hp.

Model H had a 124-inch wheelbase and 36-inch wheels. It had a chassis with semi-elliptical front springs and three-quarter-elliptical springs for the rear axle. This formula never changed throughout the life of the Cunningham car. A number of body styles were offered, and the 1911 touring car had a list price of $3,500. That year a Cunningham won the Standard Oil Trophy and the Chicago Motor Club 1,000-Miles Reliability Contest, showing speed as well as dependability.

Model S replaced the H in 1914—a bigger car with a 129-inch wheelbase and 37 × 5-inch tires. It inherited the same engine, now fitted with an electric starter. As a touring car, it was priced at $3,750. The closed models, Limousine and Landaulet, were listed at $5,000.

Shortly after car production got under way, back in 1910, Cunningham hired a chief engineer for the car branch. His name was Volney Lacy, and he was given responsibility for the development of the entire car. He also personally carried out the special assignment of creating a V-8 engine. The V-8 went into production in 1916, and Lacy began design work in 1912—well before he could have known about the preparations for a V-8 at Cadillac.

The Cunningham V-8, produced without major change through 1924, was laid out with the banks at 90 degrees and the crankshaft ran in three main bearings. An L-head design with a single central camshaft, it featured full forcefeed lubrication and magneto ignition with one spark plug per cylinder. Heads were detachable.

With a 3.75-inch bore and 5.00-inch stroke, it had a displacement of 442 cubic inches. Originally it delivered only 45 hp, but by 1922 output had doubled. Much of the credit for successful development work must go to C. Edward Franquist (of Simplex fame) who replaced Volney Lacy as chief engineer in 1918.

He raised the compression ratio, switched to coil and battery ignition, added counterweights to the crankshaft, and went from metallic to fibrous timing gears. He redesigned the induction and exhaust systems with a water-jacketed intake manifold, and raised oil pressure to 20 psi. Two wheelbases were available in 1922, 132 inches and 142. Customers had a choice of wire, wood, or disc wheels, carrying 33 × 5-inch tires. A tire pump was standard, and Cunningham even had an automatic windshield cleaning device.

The selective-shift transmission was a four-speed design, with direct drive on third and an overdrive top. The splined propeller shaft was open and double-jointed, to work freely in a Hotchkiss-drive system. The full-floating rear axle had spiral bevel final drive with 4.23:1 ratio, which gave the car a top speed in excess of 70 mph.

Frames were made of pressed steel, with all members heat-treated and hot-riveted. Mechanical brakes acted on the rear wheels only, via contracting bands for the service brakes, and internal-expanding drums for emergency and parking. The steering gear was of the worm and sector type, and the front axle had a reverse-Elliott I-beam profile.

Cunningham introduced four wheel brakes in 1925. At the same time, the company changed from a four-speed to a three-speed transmission.

About 1927 the V-8 engine displacement went to 471 cubic inches (bored out by 0.125 inch), and output climbed to 100 hp at 2,400 rpm. Prices were then given only on application, and usually resulted in quotes of about $6,000.

Cunningham had hoped the car business would be able to replace the sales volume that was lost when the carriage department closed down, but that never came to be. The Cunningham car was too exclusive in its character and price to have broad appeal. To keep its factories busy, and avoid laying off workers, the company began production of Cunningham-Hall airplanes in 1928.

The Cunningham V-8 car was produced in shrinking numbers up to 1933, and for the next three years, the factory concentrated on making bodies for other chassis, notably Ford V-8's. In 1936 the company went under and its affairs were wound up.

Fig. 4-6. The 90 HP 1922, Cunningham V-8.

45. HAYNES 75, 1922

The name of Haynes rivals those of Lambert and Duryea in seniority, since all three were building horseless carriages from 1892/93. Haynes was also the pioneer of auto-making in the Indianapolis area. However, it was not until the early Twenties that the Haynes made its place in the realm of great cars (Fig. 4-7).

Its creator was Elwood G. Haynes, whose basic expertise lay in chemistry and biology. He had studied at Worcester Polytechnic Institute and Johns Hopkins University, and it was during his years as a school teacher and superintendent for a natural gas company that he turned to metallurgical science.

His first car was built by two local mechanics, Elmer and Edgar Apperson (who later produced the Apperson car in Kokomo, Indiana), to Haynes's designs. It had a single-cylinder, two-stroke 1-hp air-cooled engine and chain drive.

The Haynes-Apperson partnership broke up in 1902, and the Haynes car evolved along fairly average lines. The first twin had been introduced in 1900, and the first four-cylinder models were added in 1904. Twins were dropped the following year, and Haynes concentrated on medium-priced models with four-cylinder engines for a number of years.

The first six was added in 1914, Model 26. It was designed by Frank N. Nutt, who had been named chief engineer of Haynes in 1909, when the founder wanted to devote more time to metallurgical studies than to cars. Nutt had joined Haynes in 1899 as a mechanic, fresh out of his high school in Los Angeles, and worked his way up, serving in succession as experimental engineer, project engineer, service engineer, draftsman, and design engineer. He was also an expert driver, and had driven in the Vanderbilt Cup Races on Long Island in 1904 and 1905 when he was stationed with the Haynes branch in New York City.

Haynes Automobile Company grew quickly in the years that followed. From an output of 1,400 cars in 1913, production soared to a record 7,000 cars in 1916. As for product evolution, Nutt was one of the first to develop a multi-cylinder concept, and Haynes brought out a V-12 in 1916. The engine was a lovely design, with pushrod-operated overhead valves, chain-driven camshaft carried centrally, cast iron blocks, and an aluminum crankcase. Bore was only 2.75 inches, but the stroke was fairly long at 5.00 inches, giving a displacement of 356 cubic inches, for an output of 55 hp.

It was first used in Model 40 of 1916, then continued in Model 46 of 1919, and Model 48 of 1920. During these years, power output rose to 70 hp. But it was a very expensive engine to manufacture, and it was phased out during 1921.

All along, Haynes had offered a companion model powered by a 50-hp 289 cubic-inch Continental L-head six, selling in the $2,500 price bracket, in contrast with the $4,000 selling price for the V-12. Elwood Haynes instructed Frank Nutt to design a better (and bigger)six, which went into production for 1922 in the car that became famous as Model 75.

The engine was just as powerful as the former twelve-cylinder unit, and much quieter, due to its L-head design and silent valve operation. It was also as smooth despite having only half the number of cylinders, which was mainly due to careful counter-weighting of the crankshaft. With its 3.50-inch bore and 5.185-inch stroke, displacement was 299.3 cubic inches. It was cast en bloc, with a detachable cylinder head. Despite its all-iron construction, and greater displacement, it was about 30 pounds lighter than the V-12.

Ignition was by coil and battery, and the engine was started by a push-button on the instrument panel. Exhaust heat was used to create a hot-spot in the intake manifold. A gear-type oil pump fed pressurized oil to all bearings. A dry-plate clutch faced the flywheel, with a three-speed transmission to complete the assembly. Final drive ratio was 4.60:1, which gave the car a top speed in excess of 75 mph.

Built on a 132-inch wheelbase, the Haynes Model 75 was not as heavy as that figure would indicate. As a touring car, its curb weight was 3,300 pounds, and the Limousine weighed about 4,100 pounds. Relative lightness helped assure its lively performance.

Fig. 4-7. The Haynes "75" of 1922.

Howard Wilcox drove a strictly stock 75 Speedster on the Indianapolis Speedway in March, 1922, with average lap speeds of 74 to 80 mph.

Six body styles were offered in the 75 series, including five- and seven-passenger touring cars, two-seater convertible (Speedster), coupe, sedan, and limousine.

Prices ranged from $2,395 to $3,395, which in all respects must stand as tremendous value. Haynes advertisements claimed that 95 percent of the car was made in its own plant. It had well-equipped machine shops, but did not have a modern assembly line. The body department occupied a huge floor space, and bodies were built up from a framework of wood, carefully fitted by skilled cabinet makers. Body panels were hand-shaped sheet aluminum. Painting was very thorough, with large areas reserved for slow room-temperature drying between coats of paint.

Model 75 was renamed Model 77 for 1923, but the car was essentially the same. Tire size came down from 34 × 4½-inch to 33 × 5-inch, which changed the gearing in favor of improved top-gear flexibility and acceleration, since the 4.60:1 final drive ratio was retained. Instead of fixed-hub wood wheels, Model 77 was available with detachable wood or wire wheels.

Financial troubles grew increasingly serious as competition in the price class Haynes had chosen sharpened in the face of reduced demand. A proposal to merge with Winton in Cleveland and Dorris in St. Louis won stockholder approval in 1922, but the plan fell through when Winton backed out.

Only the Continental-powered Model 60 was produced in 1924 and 1925, but despite prices as low as $1,295 for the touring car and $1,895 for the sedan, it failed to do well in the market place. Production of Haynes cars fell from 5,600 in 1922 to a mere 1,500 in 1925.

Elwood Haynes had retired in 1921, appointing A. G. Seiberling (a former Goodyear Executive) to take over the presidency of Haynes Automobile Company. Its bankruptcy in 1924 was a great shock to him, nevertheless, and he died in his home in Kokomo in 1925 at the age of 67. Frank N. Nutt joined AC Spark Plug as an experimental and research engineer starting what could have been a whole new career, but he fell ill in 1930 and died the following year, only 51 years old.

46. LA FAYETTE, 1923

One of the last great cars in the highway-locomotive tradition of the Oldsmobile Limited, which was giving way during the

Twenties to more intelligent solutions for carrying a normal complement of passengers and their luggage, was the La Fayette. The La Fayette was elephantine in its scale, pachydermic in its proportions, and prodigious in its performance (Fig. 4-8).

Built on a 132-inch wheelbase, and running on 36-inch wheels, the La Fayette had both stature and poise. It was tall and rode high off the ground, but its length gave it a well-balanced look. In 1921, the chassis alone sold for $4,750. Clients could get the Torpedo or the Touring models for $5,625; the Sedan was listed at $7,400; and the Limousine at $7,500.

Just as the Lincoln was created by one group of ex-Cadillac men to outdo the Cadillac, the La Fayette was the result of the efforts of another group of ex-Cadillac individuals to do better than the original.

La Fayette Motors Company was orgainzed in 1919 with a new plant at Mars Hill in Indianapolis by a group headed by Charles W. Nash, still fresh from his recent takeover of Jeffery in Kenosha, Wisconsin. Nash was a former General Motors president who set out on his own after W. C. Durant regained control of GM in 1916. His idea with the La Fayette venture was to provide a prestige car in support of the Nash, which was competing in the Buick/Oldsmobile market.

His engineering staff at La Fayette was headed by D. McCall White and E. C. Howard, with J. W. Applin as chief engineer. All three were former Cadillac engineers, leaving that company in 1919 at Nash's invitation. L. A. Menges was named chief draftsman, and J. P. Robertson held the title of works engineer.

Fig. 4-8. The distinctive 1923 La Fayette.

McCall White personally directed engine design. He laid down a V-8 with an angle of 108 degrees between the banks, with a bore of 3.25 inches and a stroke of 5.25 inches. That produced a displacement of 348.4 cubic inches and a maximum output of 100 hp—perhaps the first production car to reach that magic figure. The crankshaft was a high-strength steel forging and ran in five main bearings. It was successfully tested at over 4,000 rpm, though the engine was not capable of exceeding 3,000 rpm when installed.

It was an L-head design, innovative in that the valves were not in line with the cylinder axes, but inclined at 9 degrees. The ports, therefore, were aimed slightly towards the combustion space above the piston, rather than straight into the side chamber above the valve heads.

The engine was constructed with all major castings in aluminum, and mounted in the frame with a four-point suspension system, as this was thought to minimize rocking and vibration problems. The pressure-lubrication system was particularly comprehensive, with large capacity and an internal pump. The radiator had shutters with thermostatic control.

Clutch and gearbox were rugged units, not unlike Cadillac's, with a three-speed selective shift. Torque tube drive to the rear axle was used, putting driving thrust into a wide-splayed yoke on a chassis cross-member about halfway between the axles. Both front and rear axles were mounted on semi-elliptical leaf springs, notable for great length and very slight curvature.

Body engineering was very thorough, for both closed and open models, with an extra margin of quality put into all wear points, such as door hinges and locks, top mechanisms, spare wheel carriers, seat mountings, and window crank mechanisms.

But styling was not extraordinary. If the car had been built on a smaller scale, it would have looked plain. Not much imagination went into planning the impression one would get at first glance. No features made it stand out, no part of it was uniquely La Fayette. That was its greatest drawback in the price class in which it was competing, and may have played a part in its lack of success in the market place. By this time, cars like Packard and Pierce-Arrow had their own distinctive look, and many low-priced car makers were eagerly seeking visual identification at a glance—but usually without straying far from the stereotype elements that marked the era.

The La Fayette needed a seller's market to succeed; instead the luxury car market was entering a crisis when the car was launched. The organization was top-heavy, and overhead costs were excessive for its small production volume.

In 1924 Nash ordered the Indianapolis plant closed, and tried to bring La Fayette to Milwaukee. But whether his attempt was only half-hearted or whether he miscalculated, the end had come for the La Fayette.

Chief engineer J. W. Applin left to become a Durant and Star dealer in Franklin, Indiana. When D. McCall White was last heard of, in 1930, he was acting as assistant to the president of the Landis Engineering & Manufacturing Company in Waynesboro, Pennsylvania.

47. PACKARD EIGHT, 1923

No maker of high-priced cars made it painlessly through the slump of 1919-21, and that included Packard. Even Packard, which normally seemed secure as master of its own fate, was feeling the pinch. The Twin Six had successfully carried Alvan Macauley's one-model policy for close to five years when changing market conditions forced Packard to introduce a line of lower-priced models. Sales of the Twin-Six fell to 6,040 cars in 1920 (Fig. 4-9).

As a stopgap measure, Packard rushed a Single Six into production for 1922. It was an L-head engine with bigger bore and shorter stroke than the Twin-Six. Rated at 27.5 hp, it had 243 cubic-inch displacement.

That year the Twin Six was built on a 140-inch wheelbase, and the Single Six stood on a definitely compact 112-inch wheelbase. Since it was so much lighter, it still had acceptable performance. And it was a true Packard in terms of quality, appearance, and road manners. The Single Six was soon outselling the Twin Six by a ratio of seven to one, and no less than 13,433 of them were built during its first year.

In 1922, the Twin-Six wheelbase was shortened to 136 inches, and the price was slashed to a low $3,850. It was in the process of being phased out while J. G. Vincent was working since 1919 on its replacement: a straight eight.

In 1919 Vincent was given higher rank and a new title: Director of Engineering. He then placed Alfred Moorhouse in his old spot as chief engineer. They directed the design and development of the new car, which was announced as a 1923 model, priced from $3,650 to $4,950.

Fig. 4-9. 1924 Packard Eight.

Within weeks of its introduction, the new Packard Eight was known to be the smoothest engine in the industry. It was the industry's first straight-eight produced on an industrial scale, and it started a whole new trend. Straight-eights became a fashion that was to last 21 years. The Packard Eight had a production run through 1926 with no changes of any kind.

Packard did not build engines for all-out speed or acceleration, but for quiet operation, outstanding reliability, simple maintenance, and long life. The Eight had undersized valves and very mild cam profiles, and the compression ratio was only 4.5:1. With its bore and strokes of 3.375 × 5.00 inches, it had 358 cubic-inch displacement and in its initial form delivered 85 hp at 3,000 rpm.

The new eight was not just a single six with two more cylinders. It was a completely new engine, though bore and stoke happened to coincide with those of the six (after its stroke was stretched from 4½ to a full 5 inches).

In true Vincent style, it was an L-head engine with a detachable cylinder head. The cast iron, one-piece block was mounted on an aluminum crankcase. The crankshaft ran in nine main bearings and was drilled for pressure lubrication to mains, crankpin journals, and wrist pins. The oil pump was gear-driven from the distributor shaft. A single camshaft, located in the side of the block, was driven by chain from the front of the crankshaft. The cams bore against finger-type followers, which opened valves via cylindrical lifters.

One of its unique features was a gasoline-fired oven built into the carburetor body, from which hot gases circulated around the carburetor throat at the base to pre-heat the mixture. The exhaust

162

gas from this oven was drawn into the intake manifold further downstream.

The Eight was available in two chassis lengths, one with a 136-inch wheelbase, and the other with a 143-inch wheelbase.

Earl Gunn became chassis engineer for Packard in 1919, and was in turn succeeded by R. A Weinhardt in 1924. Therefore, the original Packard Eight is largely due to Gunn, while credit for its subsequent development must be handed to Weinhardt. The body engineer was A. L. Knapp, and E. F. Roberts was vice-president of manufacturing, having joined Packard as a toolmaker in 1903.

As one of the first in the industry, Packard introduced four-wheel brakes—a mechanical system—on the Eight in 1923. Bijur chassis lubrication was standard. This was a clever invention consisting of a central reservoir with its outlet controlled from a handle on the dashboard, connected via concealed passages to all grease points in the chassis.

Ride and handling were strong points in the Packard Eight. It was well balanced, with a pleasant, flat ride, and the worm and sector steering responded with great accuracy, as well as being free of kick and vibrations.

Both axles were attached to pairs of semi-elliptical leaf springs. After many years of torque tube drive, Hotchkiss drive was adopted for the Eight. At the same time, four-speed transmissions were brought back, after having been absent from Packard's production since 1915.

In 1927 Packard adopted the hypoid rear axle, the invention of a Swiss-born engineer, Ernst Wildhaber, and a development by the Gleason Works of Rochester, New York.

The Packard Eight had a top speed of 65-70 mph and would reach 50 mph in 22 seconds from standstill. It did it silently and with ease, and that's what counted for the Packard clientele.

48. STEVENS DURYEA, SERIES G, 1924

New England was still an auto manufacturing region of note as late as the mid-Twenties, with such firms as Locomobile and Stevens-Duryea producing fine cars in small series.

Stevens-Duryea was known for conservative management and conservative products. The company catered only to the prestige market, and though it took no shortcuts in quality, it seemed to resist advances in both design and production techniques.

Six-cylinder cars had been built in the Chicopee Falls plant exclusively since 1907, and since 1915 one engine had been standardized for all models. It was known as Model D and had a

4.44-inch bore and a 5.50-inch stroke, giving 472 cubic-inch displacement. A slow-running unit of tremendous torque, it delivered 80 hp at 1,800 rpm.

No important changes were made until 1920, when smaller wheels were fitted and the body was lowered, a rejuvenation process which caused a jump in alphabetic designation, the car being renamed Model E. Prices were now in the $7,000 to $9,500 bracket, and showroom traffic was as slow as a schoolyard on the first day of summer vacation (Fig. 4-10).

Thomas L. Cowles had served as the company's chief engineer up to 1921, and what happened to product development during this time can only be described as stagnation. When leaving Massachusetts, Cowles went to Studebaker as a truck engineer. His place was taken by a man of no lesser talent and stature than John G. Perrin, whose illustrious career had begun at Lozier.

After leaving Lozier in 1914, he worked for half a year on the engineering staff of Continental Motors in Detroit, and then served as chief engineer of Timken-Detroit Axle Company for nearly two years. He worked for the Canadian branch of Willys-Overland as manager of the plant in Toronto, 1917-18, where he directed the manufacture of the Sunbeam V-8 aircraft engine.

After the war, he was in charge of developing new types of Knight sleeve-valve engines for Willys, and in 1921 was approached by the Stevens-Duryea Company to come in as vice president and director of engineering. His immediate responsibility was to create an entirely new line of cars.

However, he was not given any real budget with which to work. A new engine was out of the question, for instance, so even his 1924 model had the same old six, with its cylinders cast in pairs and non-detachable heads, instead of a new, lightweight, cast-en-bloc unit. Everywhere he had to make-do with existing components if they were in any way good enough. Despite all this improvisation, he was able to create a truly great car.

Series G was built on a 138-inch wheelbase. The touring car weighed nearly 5,000 pounds, the sedan about 5,500. Three-quarter-elliptical springs were used to hold the rear axle, which was of the full-floating type, with spiral bevel final drive. The front axle was attached by means of semi-ellipticals in the normal way, and the front wheels were steered by worm and sector. Tire sizes varied, for the catalog shows that both 33 × 5-inch and 35 × 5-inch tires were available. Shock absorbers were fitted as standard for all four wheels.

The three-speed transmission was bolted to the clutch housing, and a long, double-jointed propeller shaft took the drive to the rear axle. Brakes were mounted on the rear wheels only, in the old-fashioned combination of external bands and internal shoes acting on the same drums.

The bodywork was the responsibility of Ernest T. Pearsons, who had come to Stevens-Duryea as body engineer in 1920 with a rich background in similar posts with Winton, Packard and Locomobile.

He patterned the radiator after the Mercedes and generally lowered the body sides down over the frame members, to give an appearance of greater modernity. The floor, of course, remained just as high, and the doorsills could not be lowered. Theft locks and automatic windshield cleaners were standard on all models, and a heater was fitted in all cars with closed bodywork. Bumpers, on the other hand, were not included.

The lowest-priced model was a seven-passenger touring car, listed at $7,500 in 1924. The two-seater roadster was priced at $8,150 and the four-passenger coupe at $9,000. For closed models, the company asked $10,175. About 100 cars in all were sold that year, and production came to an end in 1925. A number of unsold cars remained in stock, and one could buy a brand-new Stevens-Duryea until 1927.

John G. Perrin went to aircraft engine manufacturers Pratt & Whitney in Hartford, Conneticut where he remained until 1947. In

Fig. 4-10. Stevens-Duryea Series G of 1924, priced at $7500.

his later years, taught engineering at Trinity College in Hartford. He lived to the age of 88, dying in 1966.

49. CADILLAC V-63, 1924

In its continuing rivalry with Packard and under the pressure of competition from Lincoln, Cadillac was forced into an accelerated pace in product development. Its engineering staff found itself propelled by the obligation to raise its own sights about the Cadillac's future as well as to increase its efforts to uphold the make's self-proclaimed leadership (Fig. 4-11).

The year 1921 was one of momentous importance for Cadillac, for a new chief engineer was appointed almost simultaneously with the installation of a new president. Former treasurer of Cadillac since 1916, Herbert H. Rice, had early been given vice-presidential rank and was the obvious candidate to replace R. H. Collins when the latter resigned to take control of Peerless in Cleveland, taking his chief engineer, Anibal, with him.

Rice had joined the Pope Manufacturing Company back in 1893 and headed Pope-Waverly for many years. When the Pope empire collapsed, Rice organized the Waverly Automobile Company which he led until he linked up with Cadillac.

The man who assumed the functions of chief engineer to replace Anibal had been an assistant chief engineer for several years. Ernest W. Seaholm joined Cadillac in 1913 as a transmission engineer and had risen through the ranks.

Seaholm was born in Sweden, but came to the United States as an infant when his parents emigrated to New York in 1889. He grew up in Connecticut, and graduated from the Mechanics Arts High School in Springfield, Massachusetts, in 1905. That ended his formal schooling, as he went to work as a draftsman working for various clients, until he was hired by Clark W. Parker, an inventor who was working on a new drive system for cars and had contact with Henry M. Leland. Through Parker's work for Cadillac, Seaholm soon found himself a Cadillac employee.

To get back to 1921, the year was also notable for completion of a new Cadillac plant in Detroit, and the growth of the work force to 6,000 men. Two years later, Cadillac produced its 150,000th V-8 engine, and studies for an improved power unit were well along. The first-generation V-8 engine, and studies for an improved power unit were well along. The first-generation V-8 had some vibration problems that were viewed as more and more intolerable as the Cadillac car became more and more refined.

The second-generation Cadillac V-8 went into production in September 1923, unchanged in bore and stroke from the first one. The main area of modification was the crankshaft, which was redesigned as a two-plane rather than a single-plane type, and necessitated a revised firing order. Valve timing was also revised, with different lift and duration between inlet and exhaust valves, which meant adopting a new camshaft with 16 cams instead of only 8.

These developments were due to William R. Strickland, former chief engineer of Peerless and creator of the Peerless V-8 in 1916, who had joined Cadillac in 1922, counterbalancing Anibal's move.

Power output went up from 60 hp at 2,700 rpm in 1923 to 72 hp at 3,000 rpm for 1924. This was further increased to 80 hp in 1925.

With certain notable exceptions, the chassis was carried over from 1923, retaining the same 132-inch wheelbase and Kelsey artillery wheels carrying 33 × 5-inch tires. The big news was the adoption of Bendix-Perrot four-wheel brakes, in combination with a new reverse-Elliott front axle.

Rear suspension was unchanged from 1923 specification, with platform springs. Cadillac continued its use of a Timken axle with an open propeller shaft having a Spicer univeral joint at each end. The driving thrust was taken up by a single radius arm anchored to the differential housing and leading to a frame cross member about halfway inside the wheelbase.

Fig. 4-11. Cadillac's V-63, 1924.

A multi-disc clutch and three-speed transmission completed the drive train, and steering was by worm and sector. The V-63 was available in eleven body styles, standard bodies being built by Fisher for the first time. Standard Cadillac bodies from 1921-23 were designed by William N. Davis, who had joined the company as assistant body engineer in 1911. Standard equipment in 1924 included anti-theft ignition lock, electric horn, and automatic windshield cleaner. A Kellogg air pump for inflating the tires was mounted on the gearbox.

In 1925 Lawrence P. Fisher became president of Cadillac and the quest for greatness was intensified. A long-wheelbase chassis (138 inches) was added, and was in fact used for most of the Cadillacs that were built that year. The four-passenger phaeton was listed at $3,185 and the five-passenger sedan at $4,550.

Big changes were made for 1926, and about 250 pounds were sliced from the chassis, while maintaining the same wheelbase of 132 and 138 inches. Semi-elliptical leaf springs replaced the platform springs in the rear suspension and the frame was made of thinner-gauge channel-section steel members. The engine underwent a considerable redesign. Though bore and stroke went unchanged, connecting rods were shortened and all major castings lightened. About 130 pounds were stripped from the engine its accessories and mountings. Power output increased to 87 hp, mainly by raising the compression ratio to 4.7:1.

Performance was significantly improved, perhaps more by weight-saving than by the addition of more power. Still, Cadillac was a fast luxury car rather than a high-performance car with a deluxe body. The sedan could reach 70 mph and the open touring car perhaps 75 mph. Over-the-road fuel consumption averaged about 12 mpg.

At this time, Lawrence Fisher chose to cut prices, and the lowest-priced Cadillac in 1926 was a five-passenger brougham listed at $2,995. Cadillac gained new commercial strength and by the end of 1927 a quarter of a million V-8's were on the road.

For 1928 the wheelbase was pulled back to 130 inches and the chassis was lowered by the adoption of 32 × 6.75-inch balloon tires. The engine was bored out to 341 cubic-inch displacement, and power output climbed to 90 hp. A new counterweighted three-bearing crankshaft had been developed, and the new engine was even smoother-running than in the V-63. At the same time, a new twin-plate clutch and higher-capacity rear axle were adopted, and the following year Cadillac introduced the first in the world three-speed gearbox with synchromesh on second and top gears, based on the patents of Earl A. Thompson, an independent inventor who was speedily added to the Cadillac engineering staff. New projects then in the works would totally eclipse the V-8 with their grandeur a few years hence.

50. CHRYSLER, 1925

It was advertised as "A Thrilling Car That Drives With a Heretofore Unknown Ease," and fortunately the engineers responsible for making it had a lot better command of technical know-how than the advertising agency's copywriters had of the colloquial American language (Fig. 4-12).

Chrysler was the first medium-priced American car with a high-compression engine and advanced chassis specifications (four wheel hydraulic brakes, for instance). Its chassis was designed for a low center of gravity. Built on a 112.75-inch wheelbase, it was a relatively light machine—not in the Cadillac class. The Chrysler touring car had a curb weight of 2,705 pounds. It was powerful, fast and gave a fuel economy of 20 miles to the gallon. The company—which was formed on the ruins of the Maxwell Motor Corporation—sold 32,000 Chryslers in the first year. It was a more intelligent answer to the question of efficient personal mobility than was offered by any other car maker with similar ideas of status, image, and prestige.

Foremost among its wonders was the engine. It was a cast-en-bloc six with 3.00-inch bore and 4.75-inch stroke, giving a displacement of 201 cubic inches. An L-head design with a chain-driven camshaft, it also had a counterweighted crankshaft which ran in seven main bearings and a fully pressurized lubrication system.

Air cleaner and oil filter were standard, at a time when those items were not even found on some high-priced cars. Ignition was by coil and battery, and the pistons were of aluminum. With a compression ratio of 4.7:1, the Chrysler engine delivered 68 hp at 3,200 rpm. That is equivalent to 0.338 hp per cubic inch, a higher specific output than in any other American production car of its era.

The car had a vacuum-tank fuel system and a Stromberg updraft carburetor. The drive train included a dry multi-plate clutch three-speed transmission, and spiral bevel final drive in a semi-floating rear axle. The suspension system used semi-elliptical leaf springs all around, and the steering gear was of the worm and sector type. Wood-spoked wheels carried 30 × 5.77-inch tires.

The most extraordinary item, however, was the brake system. The car had Lockheed hydraulic brakes, with drums carrying external-contracting bands on all four wheels. An emergency brake mounted on the propeller shaft also consisted of a drum with an external-contracting band.

The 1925 Chrysler was available as a four-door touring car at $1,495, and as a phaeton at the same price. The range included a $1,625 roadster and a $1,895 Royal Coupe. The sedan was priced at $1,825 and the Brougham at $1,965. The Imperial had a price of $2,065 and the Crown Imperial $2,195. Chrysler even offered the naked chassis at $1,245.

The Chrysler car was the third attempt by a leading engineering group to satisfy the ideals of Walter P. Chrysler. Chrysler was a former railroad superintendent and locomotive production engineer who had made it to the executive level in the American Locomotive Company, but whose love for cars made him quit the rails and join Buick at half his former salary. That was in 1910, when Charles W. Nash was running Buick. Two years later, Nash was president of General Motors, and Chrysler was president of Buick. Like Nash, Leland, and many others, Chrysler did not thrive under Durant's rule at GM, and he quit in 1919. In 1920 a group of bankers hired him to head the reorganization of Willys-Overland, which was about to go under.

Part of his revitalization scheme was a new product, and to create it he hired the Zeder-Skelton-Breer Engineering Company in Newark, New Jersey. The three men behind that title were then the foremost brains available as consulting engineers to car makers anywhere.

Fred M. Zeder shared a railroad-mechanic's background with Chrysler, and also had graduated from the engineering school of the University of Michigan. He worked for Allis-Chalmers for a year, ran the EMF Laboratories for two years, and then served as chief engineer of Studebaker from 1914 to 1920.

Owen R. Skelton had met Zeder at Studebaker, where he went to work after seven or eight years with Packard. He had studied at Ohio State University and his first job in the auto industry was on the engineering staff of Pope-Toledo.

The third man, Carl Breer, was a Californian with an engineering degree from the Leland Stanford University. He met Zeder at Allis-Chalmers, but went his own way, through the Moreland Truck Co. and the Acme Electrical Auto Works, until the three united in 1920.

Fig. 4-12. 1925 Chrysler, featuring Lockheed hydraulic brakes on all four wheels.

Their first job for Chrysler—thought of as a "baby Lincoln"—was lost to Willys-Overland when Walter Chrysler took on the ailing Maxwell-Chalmers. The project ended up in W. C. Durant's hands after Durant had been forced out of GM. This car went into production as the Flint in 1921. Their second try was even more ambitious, and was planned as the "new Maxwell." It became the Chrysler car, and the Maxwell name was discontinued.

Oliver Clark did the styling for the first Chrysler. He was the body engineer, and the car's appearance just naturally became his responsibility. He captured the spirit of the advanced engineering that went into the mechanical parts, and gave it the modern look that contributed in no small measure to Chrysler's success.

51. PACKARD SIX, 1925

As the national economy progressed and the market for high-priced cars expanded, Packard found itself in an unusual situation. Despite the excellence of its modern-styled eight-cylinder models, it was the older six that the public wanted. The six outsold the eight at a ratio of better than four to one, which meant that without the six, Packard's production—and income— would have shrunk to a disastrous level.

President Alvan Macauley analyzed the situation correctly early enough to give wise and far-sighted instructions to the engineering and design staff. As the slump of 1921 was wearing off, Macauley confidently predicted a period of economic boom. His conclusion was that with increased purchasing power, the customers would not only want, but also be able to afford, more expensive Packards. Higher-priced products selling in larger numbers would boost Packard's profits. A fresh influx of cash was sorely needed after a string of lean years.

Together with J. G. Vincent and his assistants, Macauley formulated the recipe for a new Packard Six: A car with more power but smaller dimensions and lighter construction, that would put Packard up to par for performance without giving up any of its fabled smoothness, quietness, and tractability.

Greater emphasis was to be placed on styling—the Six had to look speedier and sportier, while the Eight was to remain classical and dignified (Fig. 4-13). Engineering refinement in both was to be brought to still higher levels, while interior design and equipment were improved in terms of functionality simultaneous with the substantial upgrading of comfort and appearance. All these changes, Macauley had reasoned, would amply justify the planned price increases, and he was again proved correct.

Fig. 4-13. Packard's 1925 Packard Six.

A new crankshaft had seven main bearings as before, but bearing diameters were increased to match those of the Eight, and a new balancing system with counterweights positioned next to center and end bearings was evolved by extended mathematical analysis. The new crankshaft was much heavier, and its oil passages were drilled in a different pattern.

The camshaft, driven by chain from the front of the crankshaft, was also beefed up and ran in seven bearings. It was rifle-drilled and its bearings received continuous lubrication. New roller followers replaced the former shoe-type follower, reducing both noise and friction in the valve gear. Valve spring anchors were changed from the C-profile to the slot-and-crosspin type.

Pistons were redesigned with a vertical drainage channel to duct surplus oil from the cylinder walls straight to lines leading to the Skinner oil rectifier (a combined oil cooler and filter) mounted on the exhaust manifold. Wrist pins received lube oil from a rifle-drilled passage through the rod web, instead of by the previous method of an external copper tube. Helical oilpump gears were adopted, and in the fan drive, a one-piece rubber V-belt replaced the former flat belt assembled from strips of leather.

Concurrent with the bore increase from 3.375 to 3.5 inches, raising displacement from 268 to 289 cubic inches, the flywheel received a fatter, heavier rim. The use of a dry multi-plate clutch continued with no change, but the three-speed transmission was redesigned. Holes were drilled in the gear webs to reduce their weight (and make shifting easier), spinning effect, and resonance.

Chief engineer Alfred Moorhouse personally supervised the engine and drive train development, while the new chassis was mainly due to James R. Ferguson, and the body design to Werner Gubitz.

One of the three main chassis design changes was the use of semi-elliptical leaf springs, shackled at the front end and anchored at the rear, for both axles. Packard did not use Hotchkiss drive (as Chrysler did) but provided a long torque arm to take up the driving thrust, relieving the springs of that duty. With the aim of reducing noise, the front end ot the torque arm was anchored in a new clamp with rubberized-fabric inserts.

The former drop-center front axle was replaced by one having straight beams pointing downwards from each wheel hub and meeting at a low point in the center. A new one-piece drag link was arranged to follow the suspension geometry and prevent shimmy. Steering gear was a worm-and-sector design.

The second change was the adoption of a mechanical four-wheel brake system, with internal-expanding drums on the front wheels. The rear drums had both inner shoes and outer bands, activated by hand brake lever and pedal, respectively.

The third change was the adoption of Bijur chassis lubrication, feeding oil to 45 points by merely pulling a hand-pump plunger. On the Packard, it was an integral part of the chassis design, with bosses and oil channels assuring correct metering, sealing, and simplicity.

The open propeller shaft was double-jointed, and the semi-floating rear axle was driven by spiral bevel (hypoid drive was still two years away). With 33 × 4½-inch tires, the final drive ration was 4.30:1, giving the car a top speed of 72 mph. When 33 × 5.77-inch tires were adopted in 1926, the axle ratio was adjusted to 4.66:1.

The six had a 126-inch wheelbase as standard, and a long chassis with 133-inch wheelbase was available. The pressed-steel frame had side members of 8 inches depth and 0.156-inch thickness. Special reinforcements were added in support of the front spring horns, inside the channels, and in the form of a tubular steel cross-member riveted in place.

Prices ranged from $2,585 for the five-passenger runabout to $3,675 for the seven-passenger sedan limousine. A five-passenger sedan was listed at $3,375 and a four-passenger sport model at $2,750. Ten body styles were offered in 1925, and the following year the five-passenger sedan and five passenger coupe were merged into a single model, the Club sedan, listed at $2,725.

The Six did exactly the job Macauley had intended, and Packard prospered. The market, in fact, was so buoyant that at the end of 1928 model year, the Six was discontinued in favor of producing two sizes of eight-cylinder engine. And J. G. Vincent had even more ambitious projects under way, as later chapters will relate.

Chapter 5
The "Roaring
Twenties" 1926-1929

While Locomobile had its financial ups and downs, the product never lost one whit of its quality, splendor, or greatness (Fig. 5-1). It remained one of America's finest cars to the very end. In 1912 Samuel T. Davis was named president of Locomobile. He was a graduate of the Rensselaer Polytechnic Institute, son-in-law of the founder, and had been with the firm since 1899. The technical side was directed by the versatile Andrew L. Riker, who had joined Locomobile in 1902.

52. LOCOMOBILE 90, 1926

Davis was a competent businessman and a car enthusiast, and the company prospered under his leadership. Unfortunately he died in 1915, at the young age of 42 and the company began to flounder. In 1919 it came under control of Hare's Motors, along with Simplex and Mercer.

Riker remained engineering director of Locomobile, and acted as design consultant to Hare's Motors, whose staff included several high-ranking ex-Packard officials such as H. D. Church, vice president in charge of product development; and Ormond E. Hunt as vice president in charge of production. Emlen S. Hare himself was a super salesman, foreshadowing such merchandising stars as E. L. Cord and Paul G. Hoffman, both of whom were to leave deep tracks in the record of America's auto industry.

But despite all the talent grouped at the top of Hare's Motors, the firm collapsed in 1921 and was dissolved the following year. A. L. Riker then went to work with an investment company in

Fig. 5-1. Barney Roos' masterpiece, the 1925 Locomobile 90.

Bridgeport. He was an independent consulting engineer from 1924 to 1928 and served briefly as vice president of the Ventilouvre Company in Bridgeport before a heart attack felled him at his home in Fairfield, Connecticut, in June, 1930.

The Locomobile Company fell into the hands of W. C. Durant, maker of the Flint, Star and Durant cars. Durant installed a trusted lieutenant, George E. Daniels, as president of Locomobile, and Daniels managed to recruit a brilliant former Locomobile engineer to return and take charge of the technical side. This man was Delmar G. Roos, usually called "Barney" by his friends and colleagues. His mind was occupied with radios and turbines when he left Cornell University with a degree in mechanical engineering in 1911, and he started his career with General Electric. After a year he went to Locomobile as an assistant experimental engineer.

Working under Riker was wonderful training, and Barney was promoted from engineer to electrical engineer to chief of research and experiments, in quick succession. In 1919 he accepted an offer from Timken Axle to take charge of engineering for its passenger car department.

Designing axles was too narrow a field for Barney and he jumped at the chance to become chief engineer of passenger car design for Pierce-Arrow in 1920. From this post in Buffalo, he returned to Bridgeport two year later. By 1924 he was vice president in charge of engineering and production at Locomobile.

His first-priority task was to modernize and develop the existing car in an attempt to bring it up to date, for it had hardly changed during the years he had been away. By 1925 he had developed a four-wheel mechanical brake system, which was unusual in that it had cooling fins on the front drums, and double drums with contracting bands in the rear wheels.

Second priority was to get a smaller, lower-priced car into production. That project led to the Locomobile Junior Eight, built in 1925 and 1926, and aimed at the market segment that was represented by Chandler, Auburn, Case, Rickenbacker and F. B. Stearns. The lowest-priced model was a touring car at $1,785, and the highest were a sedan and a brougham, both listed at $2,285. Of the 3,000 Locomobiles built in 1925, nearly 2,700 were Junior Eights. Modernization of the senior-series was suffering from the "to-little, too-late" syndrome.

The old 525 cubic-inch six with cylinders cast in pairs and integral T-heads was used through the 1925 model year. The cars were built on a 142-inch wheelbase and weighed from 5,000 to

5,750 pounds, according to body style. The chassis cost only $6,600 and the Victoria sedan was listed at $9,990. A Cabriolet was offered at $10,250.

Both chassis and body were built to the most exacting standards, but the designs dated from a time when stress calculations had been less accurate and engineers tended to include a portion of extra metal as a safety margin. The mechanical elements of the Locomobile had strength to spare, and as a result the car became disproportionately heavy, even for its size. Its four-speed transmission and spiral-bevel full-floating rear axle had capacity to handle the torque of an engine of twice its power.

For 1926 it was replaced by Barney Roos' masterpiece, the Locomobile 90, a prestige-type car conceived and developed with limited resources and not regardless of cost. Wheelbase was brought back to 138 inches, and curb weight ranged from 4,400 to 4,900 pounds. Its 371.5 cubic inch engine was an L-head design with 3.875-inch bore and 5.25-inch stroke, and a detachable head. It was cast en bloc, which in combination with the lower displacement saved about 300 pounds from the engine alone. The crankshaft was made of forged steel and ran in seven main bearings.

Chassis and drive train evolution also show the benefit of Roos' hand. A single dry-plate clutch replaced the former multi-speed unit, and a new lighter-weight, three-speed transmission was adopted. The new semi-floating, spiral-bevel rear axle was lighter, with lower excess torque and load capacity.

Semi-elliptical springs were used on both front and rear axles, and 33 × 6.75-inch balloon tires on woodspoked wheels replaced the earlier 35 × 6.75-inch ones. Cam and lever steering took the place of the old worm and gear system, and the brake system was entirely new, simple and modern, with internal-expanding drums on all four wheels.

Prices were cut dramatically, though the naked chassis still cost $5,000. The four-passenger 90 Sportif was listed at $5,500 and the 90 Roadster at $5,900. For $7,500 a client could become the owner of a seven-passenger Suburban Limousine, Town Car Brougham, or Cabriolet. In between were the 90 Victoria sedan at $7,300 and 90 Coupe at $6,950.

The number 90 reflected the engine's horsepower, which was among the highest in the industry, and enough to keep the Locomobile firmly in the ranks of high-performance cars.

Barney Roos, however, was not happy with his working conditions at Locomobile, and in 1925 he left, moving to Indianapolis as chief engineer of Marmon, only to relocate again the following year, this time moving just a few hundred miles north to South Bend, with the title of assistant chief engineer of Studebaker, where he was to create that company's greatest cars.

As for Locomobile, business went downhill well before the stock market crashed, and production ended in 1929. The following year Durant Motors declared bankruptcy, and no hope of survival could be entertained.

53. STUTZ AA, 1926

Harry Stutz left the company bearing his name in 1919, selling his shares to former vice president, Allan A. Ryan, the son of the largest shareholder in New York's Guaranty Trust Company. Ryan installed W. H. Thompson as president and general manager, but the company had no chief engineer and development slowed to a standstill.

The 1921 Stutz still had right hand drive, a holdover from the racing heyday, even after Pierce-Arrow had moved the controls to the left. The engine was a big T-head four delivering 90 hp, a derivative of the power plants that had made Stutz's reputation on the race track.

By the time the 1921 models went into production, ownership of the Stutz Motor Car Company had passed to Charles M. Schwab, president of Bethlehem Steel (and formerly the first president of U.S. Steel). Still it was not until May, 1922, that Stutz had a chief engineer.

His name was Charles S. Crawford, and he came from Premier. Actually, he had started his career with Lozier, joined Cole in 1910, been a purchasing agent for Empire, and factory manager for Westcott. He came to Premier in 1916 as assistant general manager and was a vice president at the time he left.

Crawford created a six-cylinder car for Stutz; with a 268 cubic-inch engine having pushrod-operated overhead valves and delivering 75 hp at 3,200 rpm. The 1923-model Six was built on a 120-inch wheelbase and retained the typical Stutz transaxle. Three body styles were available, priced from $1,995 for the touring car to $2,500 for the sedan.

Four-cylinder models, including the Bearcat, continued in production, with prices up to $3,115. The T-head four disappeared in 1924 when the Speedway Six appeared. It was a Crawford design with a new chassis having the gearbox attached to the engine instead of the rear axle, and 130-inch wheelbase. The engine was the same six as in 1923, with its output increased to 80 hp. This turned out to be inadequate and for 1925 it was given a new crankshaft with longer stroke, raising displacement to 289 cubic inches.

Schwab was not greatly satisfied with either the Stutz product nor the way the company was being run, and in 1925 he ended Thompson's presidency, replacing him with the dynamic Frederick E. Moscovics. He was both an engineer and a salesman, having spent ten years with Marmon, leaving a vice-presidency in 1923. He spent six months as vice president of Franklin in 1924, and quit in protest over not being given full executive powers.

Moscovics had firm ideas about what the new Stutz should be. It should be low and fast, safe and elegant. He had been making sketches and drawings for such a car for years, and now he was going to get it built.

He engaged Paul Bastien, who had formerly worked for Excelsior in Belgium, to do the chassis engineering; and brought in Charles R. Greuter to design the engine. W. Guy Wall, formerly of National, served briefly as a consulting engineer.

The Stutz with the low center of gravity stemmed from Moscovics's principles of a low frame with high horns over the axles, and the use of worm drive to lower the propeller shaft. Herbert Alden at Timken Axle Co. had developed a worm drive that was silent and reliable, and worked with relatively low friction, which Moscovics eagerly accepted.

Greuter was now of an age where other engineers called him "Pops" and deferred to his experience when it came to engines. Throughout the creation of the new Stutz, Crawford seems to have worked quietly as an administrative engineer, carefully avoiding interference with Moscovics, Greuter and Bastien. After the Matheson era, Greuter had operated his own experimental shop, worked for a carburetor company in Detroit, and designed motorcycle engines for Henderson. Since 1920 he had been developing an overhead-camshaft design, which was the basis for the Stutz Vertical-Eight, as it was called in the advertisements.

There was probably little discussion about the number of cylinders, since straight-eight Duesenbergs and Millers were forever setting new records at the Indianapolis Speedway. The Stutz had a bore and stroke of 3.1875×4.50 inches, and a displacement of 287 cubic inches. It had dual ignition with two plugs per cylinder, and ran with a 4.8:1 compression ratio. Output was 92 hp at 3,200 rpm.

The single overhead camshaft was chain-driven, though Greuter's plan had at first been to use a vertical shaft and bevel gears. All valves were mounted vertically and in line, and valve caps were actuated directly from the cams. Cylinder head and block were iron castings, and the nine-bearing crankshaft was a steel forging. Crank throws were arranged in 2-4-2 formation as pioneered by Packard, and not in the 4-4 arrangement favored by Duesenberg.

The AA had a three-speed transmission and two worm drive axles were listed, with 4.75:1 and 5.00:1 reduction. Front and rear axles were long, flat, low-rate semi-elliptical leaf springs, with Watson shock absorbers. The wheelbase was 131 inches, and standard coachwork was designed by and produced under Brewster supervision.

It had four-wheel hydraulic brakes of a primitive type, made by Timken, using a water-alcohol mixture. Wheel cylinders consisted of small rubber bellows that expanded against the shoe ends. This system was replaced by a Lockheed system in 1928.

Model AA was advertised as the Safety Stutz (Fig. 5-2). Moscovics had reasoned that Stutz needed a new image, with less emphasis on stark performance, and more on tough engineering, reliability, and safety. List price for the five-passenger sedan was $2,995.

In 1927 the engine was bored out to 298 cubic inches and compression raised to 5.0:1, which resulted in an additional 3 hp. With the arrival of the Model BB in 1928, however, power output was 115 hp at 3,600 rpm. This car could go from 10-to-50 mph in top gear in less than 15 seconds and had a top speed of more than 75 mph. The engine was bored out again in 1929, to 322 cubic inches for installation in the M-type (and MA) of 1930.

By this time Crawford was no longer with the company, having left in 1928 to join General Motors. He was sent to Germany in 1930 to run Opel's engineering department, but fell ill in 1934 and died in Indianapolis in 1935.

Fred Moscovics left Stutz in 1929 and went to New York where he served as president of something called "Improved Products Corporation." In 1931 he went to Marmon-Herrington as chairman, and then went into retirement. He was a consultant to the U.S. Army Air Corps in World War II, and in 1944 was named consultant to A. O. Smith in Milwaukee, a title he held until his final retirement at the age of 80 in 1960. He died in Greenwich, Connecticut, in 1967.

54. WILLS SAINTE CLAIRE T-6, 1926

Great as the V-8 Wills Sainte Claire was, many owners discovered that its greatness also brought great headaches. The engine was expensive to manufacture, which was mainly the producer's problem, leading directly to a complicated parts situation, and indirectly to an engine that was difficult to service.

C. Harold Wills and his chief engineer, Fred I. Tone, discussed the problem at great length and decided to build an in-line six, on the theory that it would eliminate some problems and reduce others by half. The six was designed from the start, for instance, with a detachable cylinder head (Fig. 5-3).

The six was also designed for full interchangeability, in the sense that it could be installed in the same car that had the V-8. There was no thought of actually sharing individual parts in the two engines, but the six was deliberately designed so that its major elements could be machined on the same equipment.

The block and upper crankcase were cast as a unit, with an aluminum oil pan. The cylinder head and camshaft housing were made separately as iron castings and bolted to the block. The camshaft drive system was borrowed from the V-8, with a single, vertical shaft. Wills wanted a comparable torque from the six as he was getting from the V-8, which meant increasing the displacement of each cylinder.

But due to tooling considerations, he was locked into the same 3.25-inch bore, and therefore the stroke was lengthened—by more than one-third—5.50 inches. This was accomplished without balance or vibration problems, but it did make for a strangely tall engine. This led to unsuspected cooling problems, as the thermo-

Fig. 5-2. Stutz AA of 1926.

Fig. 5-3. Wills Sainte Claire Model T-6 of 1926.

syphon system initially adopted failed to provide sufficient circulation. The remedy was to add a water pump and thermostat.

Such problems brought Wills' undeniable genius into play, and he also adopted a gear-driven fan with automatic clutch to disengage the fan when its effect was not needed and thereby save power. He also pioneered the use of an electric fuel pump on his six-cylinder car. It delivered 66 hp at 2,500 rpm, with a peak torque of 85 pounds-feet at 1,300-1,400 rpm.

The crankshaft was a rugged, counterweighted steel forging with seven main bearings. The shaft weighed 77 pounds, and bearing area occupied nearly 35 percent of its length and a total of 82½-square inches. Connecting rods were made of Lynite aluminum alloy, and the pistons were gray-iron alloy containing a high proportion of steel. All parts were machined with the greatest precision and fitted to extremely close tolerances. Every care was taken to secure trouble-free operation and long life.

The semi-floating rear axle was driven via a dry, single-plate clutch, three-speed transmission and open, double-jointed propeller shaft. The differential gears and spiral bevel pinion and ring gear ran on roller bearings.

Transmission gears and shafts were made of forged and heat-treated molybdenum steel, and had roller bearings at all points except for a double ball bearing on the countershaft.

The 1926 model T-6 was built on a 127-inch wheelbase, and semi-elliptical leaf springs were used front and rear. They were 36 inches long in front and 58 inches long in the rear. The front axle was a molybdenum steel one-piece forging, heavily ribbed at the extremities, and all vital parts in the worm-and-gear steering system were also made of molybdenum steel.

Special disc wheels, to Wills' design, carried 33 × 6 inch tires. Hydraulic brakes with contracting bands rather than internal shoes were fitted on all four wheels, manufactured under Lockheed patents. An emergency brake acted on the transmission.

There was not much difference between T-6 and B-68 prices. The Wills catalog quotes $3,775 for a V-8 sedan in 1925, and the manufacturer's literature from 1926 is marked 'prices on request.' Not enough requests were made, however, to keep Wills afloat. The company went bankrupt again and all attempts to raise capital for a third try failed. Brokers, bankers, investors and underwriters were afraid to back a two-time loser (as Wills appeared to Wall Street's eyes), and pointed to the multitude of companies that were producing cars for the same market.

Chief engineer Fred Tone stayed with the company until its last day. When Wills Sainte Clare was liquidated, C. Harold Wills spent a year collecting his thoughts, and in 1929 became a director of New Era Motors and a member of the team that produced the front wheel drive Ruxton car. When that venture folded, Wills began to look for a secure position in a concern with a future, and joined Chrysler in 1933. Fred Tone also ended up at Chrysler, becoming a research engineer for special Dodge projects, and having charge of coordination with the purchasing and production departments for such projects. He retired at age 65 and lived quietly until 1959.

Charles Morgana, who had helped orgainze Wills Sainte Claire and served as its vice president of engineering and manufacturing, went to work for Briggs Manufacturing Company in 1930. Briggs was the main body supplier to Chrysler. Morgana was killed in a car accident in 1935.

As for C. Harold Wills, he became chief metallurgist for Chrysler Corporation, but in 1940 suffered a stroke and died in Detroit's Henry Ford Hospital.

55. McFARLAN TWIN VALVE SIX, 1926

McFarlan can almost rival Austin and Porter in terms of exclusivity, for car production in the big Connersville, Indiana, plant was never the company's bread and butter. It could afford to build cars only when it was making money on other things.

During World War I, McFarlan had a series of small but lucrative defense contracts for a variety of non-automotive products. Harry McFarlan misread the signs of what was going on in the economy as a whole, and though the road to success in car manufacturing lay with still bigger, more refined, luxurious, powerful and high-priced vehicles (Fig. 5-4).

He hired Edward McConegle as chief engineer to create a new generation of McFarlan cars, and his work resulted in the fabulous Twin Valve series which made its debut in 1921 and lived on through 1928 (Fig. 5-5).

The term Twin Valve refers to the use of two valves where normal engines have one. The McFarlan T-head six thus had two intake valves and two exhaust valves on opposite sides of each cylinder. There was one gear-driven camshaft on each side of the block, operating the valves via roller tappets. The engine design was created, as in the case of pre-war models, by Jesse Kepler of Dayton, Ohio.

It was a giant in-line six with 4½-inch bore and 6-inch stroke. That comes out to 572.5 cubic-inch displacement and a power output of 120 hp at 2,000 rpm. The engine was cast in two blocks of three cylinders, and the drop-forged crankshaft ran in four main bearings. The iron head was detachable.

The air-fuel mixture was prepared in a Rayfield carburetor from gasoline supplied by a vacuum-tank and ignited by two independent ignition systems in the most sure-fire, double-guarded setup ever heard of. Twin high-tension magnetos fired separate plugs on opposite sides of each cylinder, while a third plug located near the intake valves, was sparked by coil and battery ignition. McFarlan claimed that its engine lubrication system did not rely on splash for oil supply to any item, but relied entirely on force-feed from a gear-driven pump via drilled passages in the crankshaft.

Engine and chassis changed little during the years that McFarlan was building the Twin Valve series, but the coachwork evolved as fast as fashion itself. Some of the greatest McFarlans were produced in the final years, 1925-27, and that's why this 1926 model has been selected as a top example. No two McFarlan bodies were exactly alike, though chassis specifications were remarkably constant, right down to the 140-inch wheelbase. In 1925 the Town Car was listed at $9,000, but that was the top of the line model. Customers could order a four-passenger sport touring car for as little as $5,600, or a coupe for $6,720. The Suburban sedan had a list price of $7,300.

The frame was made up of pressed medium carbon steel, with girders up to 8 inches in depth. A sub-frame at the front end carried the engine and transmission, which was a three-speed unit of conventional design. (Rather odd, one finds, for a company with a background of daring experimentation in the transmission field.) In 1914 McFarlan began using the Gray Pneumatic Gearshift, which was another way of doing what the Cutler-Hammer system did electrically. The Gray system had a pre-selector lever on the steering wheel, and the clutch pedal made the change, with an assist from a compressed-air tank with a valve hooked into the clutch linkage.

Even more radical was the Vesta electric transmission used on some McFarlans in 1917. The Vesta unit was an advanced automatic drive system, with a two-speed planetary gearset controlled by electromagnetic couplings. It was reversible for reverse driving, and could be energized to work as a starter.

By 1921 there was no thought of reviving either type. McConegle probably preferred the conventional. At any rate, the gearbox was beautifully made, with an aluminum casing, and the shafts ran on adjustable roller bearings. The transmission carried a tire-inflation pump as standard equipment.

A full-floating, spiral-bevel type rear axle having a 3.50:1 ring gear and pinion was used in combination with McFarlan's cradle-type leaf spring suspension. The springs were 64 inches long.

The front axle was a drop-forged, one-piece I-beam with roller bearings for the hubs and steering knuckles. The front leaf springs were 40 inches long. Steering was by worm and gear when the Twin Valve series first appeared, but by about 1924 McFarlan switched to cam and lever steering—a system commonly used on trucks and buses.

Fig. 5-4. A McFarlan Twin Valve Six, 1926.

Fig. 5-5. Another fine example of the 1926 McFarlan Twin Valve.

Brakes were external-contracting on the rear wheels in 1921, with internal shoes in the same drums for the hand brake. The 1924 models became available with four-wheel hydraulic brakes (using external contracting bands).

McFarlan car sales remained slack, but the body shop benefited from important orders from Auburn in 1923, Locomobile and Marmon in 1925. In an attempt to sell more complete cars, McFarlan brought out a smaller, lower-priced car in 1924, known as the Single Valve Six. It was powered by a mass-produced Wisconsin engine delivering 75 hp, and with a 127-inch wheelbase was selling at prices from $2,600 to $3,500.

Due to Harry McFarlan's ill health, business opportunities were not always followed up on, and the losses incurred in car production only got bigger.

For 1926 McConegle had prepared another new model: a sort of intermediate, built on a 131-inch wheelbase, powered by a straight-eight Lycoming engine. Despite offering the eight-cylinder series at prices competitive with Cadillac, for instance, at $2,650 for a five-passenger touring model and $3,180 for a five-passenger sedan, it failed to bring in the orders. Production came to a halt late in 1927 or early in 1928, and bankruptcy was declared during the following summer. Auburn bought the plant, but used it mainly for storage.

Harry McFarlan retired from active participation in the business about 1925, and died in 1937.

56. DOBLE SERIES E, 1927

Outwardly, there was not much that distinguished the Doble from many of America's other great cars of its period. Built on a

150-inch wheelbase, and having a curb weight of 3,600 pounds with phaeton body (4,250 to 4,325 pounds with closed bodies), the Doble fitted in well with other mastodons of the highway in size, power, and exclusivity. But on the inside, there was a fundamental difference: The Doble was a steamer (Fig. 5-6).

It could cruise at 75 mph, with acceleration to match. And it was quieter than the most refined of cars powered by internal combustion engines—not silent, for even steam machinery generates noise, but a different kind of noise.

The Doble also stood apart from other steam cars in several ways. It was the only one to compete in the very highest price class, selling for $8,000 at a time when the Stanley was listed at $2,750; the American at $1,650; the Detroit at $1,585; and the Coats at $1,085. It was also the only one that was no more difficult to drive than an ordinary car. It was the only one that was ready to go within 45 seconds from cold (and within 10 seconds if the car had been driven earlier the same day).

Despite the fearsome size of its boiler, which, with its accessories filled all available space under the long hood, it was more fuel-efficient than one would expect, returning 15 miles to the gallon of kerosene. It used up 25 gallons of water every 1,000 to 1,200 miles, and its lubrication took about a pint of oil per 500 miles.

The four-cylinder expander was mounted horizontally and rigidly attached to the rear axle. There was, of course, no gearbox, since steam engines produce maximum torque at zero rpm and therefore had no need for torque multiplication by trading off against speed.

In steam parlance, the expander was cross-compound and double-acting, which meant that power strokes occurred in both directions and that the steam was recirculated from one pair of cylinders to the other pair. Two of the cylinders ran with low pressure and two with high pressure, the latter working the two end cranks, and the low-pressure cylinders working the center cranks. The low-pressure cylinders had a 4½-inch bore and the high-pressure cylinders had a 2.525-inch bore. All had the same 5.00-inch stroke, and the drop-forged steel crankshaft ran in four roller-bearing mains.

Two piston valves controlled the supply of steam to the expander, combining cutoff, transfer, and reversing functions in one simple device driven by a Stephenson linkage from the crankshaft.

The boiler was of the single-tube type, its outer shell a cylindrical container 25 inches in diameter and 40 inches high. The burner was mounted on the cowl, and the combustion chamber extended downward from the boiler lid. Two steam turbines, a condenser, and a set of vacuum pumps took care of spent steam exhaust and water condensation. Exhaust steam was ducted to a burner-booster turbine first, then to the condenser-fan turbine, which dumped the remaining vapor into the condenser. After it had condensed back into water, it was siphoned off by vacuum pumps which fed the boiler and replenished the water reservoir.

An auxiliary drive system was shaft-driven from the expander crankshaft and served to run the vacuum pumps, water pumps, oil pump, electric generator, and speedometer.

The Series E was built in Emeryville, California, by the Doble Steam Motors Corporation. Its inventor, Abner Doble, had been working on steam engines and steam-powered automobiles since his boyhood in San Francisco. He had built his own steam car at the age of 16, and after he entered the Massachusetts Institute of Technology in 1910, he designed and built several steam cars, each one containing some improvement over its predecessor.

In 1912 he demonstrated his newest prototype to the Stanley Brothers, who were impressed with the originality of his solutions, but shied away from any sort of collaboration or licensing agreement. After graduation in 1914, the young inventor formed the Abner Doble Motor Vehicle Company in Waltham, Massachusetts, and began small-scale production of his A-series design, a two-cylinder, single-expansion design.

He realized he needed financial backing on a large scale to start regular production, and in 1915 he took his Series B prototype to Detroit, where he convinced Claude L. Lewis of its merits. Lewis was president of the consolidated Car Company, but resigned in 1916 to form General Engineering Company and build the Doble-Detroit. With this car, which went into production in 1917, Doble went to a double-acting two-cylinder uniflow expander, electrical burner firing and automatic control. It had only 22 moving parts, and 11 of them were in the expander.

The first Doble-Detroit was a big expensive car on a 135-inch wheelbase, whose chassis included hydraulic brakes (operating on drums in the rear wheels). In 1918 General Engineering was reorganized as the Doble-Detroit Steam Motors Company, and lower-priced models were added.

In 1920 Abner Doble severed his connection with this firm, which shortly afterwards became the New Detroit Steam Motor

Fig. 5-6. Doble Series E of 1927, the last of the great steam cars.

Corporation and began to compete in the popular-price market. Doble returned to California and obtained the backing of his three brothers to start his own company.

Now came the Series D, which featured a two-cylinder double-acting compound expander mounted horizontally on the rear axle, thereby forming the vital link between Doble's earlier designs and the superb Series E which was to follow in 1923. About 30 Series E cars were built in the seven-year period up to 1930, when Abner Doble was unable to attract the new financing he needed to continue car production. People who had bought Dobles were Hollywood movie stars or moguls, foreign potentates, and other celebrities. But no one, in 1930, was going to invest in Doble Steam Motors.

Finally, the company's assets were sold to George and William Besler, sons of the chairman of New Jersey's Central Railroad, who built about a dozen cars of Doble's latest design, Series F, some equipped with V-4 engines and others using parallel-twin expanders.

Abner Doble went to Europe in 1931 and for several years worked as a consultant on steam engines for two truck manufacturers, Sentinel in Shrewsbury, England, and Henschel & Sohn in Kassel, Germany. In 1939 he left warbound Europe and returned to California. He was active for nearly 20 years as a consultant to manufacturers of non-automotive steam power equipment, and died in the summer of 1961 at the age of 71.

57. STEARNS-KNIGHT MODEL G 8-85, 1927

Specifications that include a 102-hp straight-eight engine, a 137-inch wheelbase, and advertising that proclaimed the product as America's most luxurious car, are portents of greatness. The F. B. Stearns Company of Cleveland, Ohio, was famous as a builder of great cars, but the greatest were produced in its swan-song years.

Apart from the V-8 built from 1917 to 1920, the Model G was the company's first eight. It was unveiled at the New York Automobile Show in January, 1927 and was in production for about 14 months continuing with minor changes in the guise of Model H, 8-90, through 1929.

The chassis was developed from the Models D and F, announced in September, 1926, and the engine was, to some extent, based on the Model S six-cylinder which went into production in 1922. Actually, the evolution of Stearns-Knight cars had been on a fast-ascending curve since 1920, when the company acquired a new and ambitious chief engineer in the person of William E. England (Fig. 5-7).

He was a graduate of the Drexel Institute in Philadelphia, Pennsylvania, where he completed studies in 1910. The following year found him working as a machinist with the spicer Manufacturing Company in Plainfield, New Jersey. Later in 1911, he joined the Worth Motor Car Company in Kankakee, Illinois, as machinist and draftsman.

After about a year, he moved to Wabash, Indiana, as chief draftsman for the Service Truck Company. He left Service Truck after about six months for Moline, Illinois, where he accepted a position on the engineering staff of the Midland Motor Company, then producing an interesting medium-priced car to the faultless designs of chief engineer John E. Miller, who had been killed in a car accident in 1911.

Less than a year later, England joined Moline Automobile Company in the same town, and worked on projects for the Root & Van Dervoort Engine Company and the R & V Motor Company. Thus he helped design the Moline-Knight and the R & V Knight, plus a line of proprietary sleeve valve engines for sale to the trade industry. By 1918 he was chief engineer for all Root & Van Dervoort power units, leaving Moline in May, 1920, to accept an offer from F. B. Stearns to take the place of James G. Sterling as chief engineer. Sterling had left to build his own car, the Sterling-Knight.

Frank B. Stearns had sold his interest in the company in 1918, and the new owners gave England a free hand in product planning and engineering. Production in 1920-21 was concentrated on the existing Big Four, a 248.5 cubic-inch power unit with 3.75-inch bore and 5.625-inch stroke.

With its chassis on a 121-inch wheelbase and inelegant body styling, potential customers found the Stearns-Knight overpriced, and sales dwindled from more than 4,000 in 1920 to less than one-third of that volume in 1922.

England had started work on a new six-cylinder engine the first day he came to Cleveland, and it was ready for the 1923 Model S, which inherited the old chassis and the 121-inch wheelbase.

The engine was a modern design, with all cylinders cast en bloc, and a detachable head. Valves were, naturally, of the double-sleeve type, whose following was still growing at the time. The crankshaft ran in four bearings and was drilled for forced lubrication. With 3.625 × 5.00-inch bore and stroke, displacement was 309.6 cubic inches, and actual power output 75 hp at 3,000 rpm. It gave lively performance in combination with the strange quietness associated with sleeve-valve engines, and it was a tremendous value, despite its old high chassis and clumsy body design.

For 1924 came the Model C, on a revised chassis with cantilever rear suspension. It had smoother body lines, and was powered by a smaller-bore version of the same six-cylinder engine. The idea was to provide a very roomy, comfortable car, so it was built on a 130-inch wheelbase, with six-cylinder smoothness, at a reasonable price. This is accomplished, but it was sadly lacking in performance when compared to the Model S.

To remedy the situation, England switched the Model C to the 121-inch-wheelbase chassis for 1925. Mechanical rear wheel brakes were still standard, but hydraulic four-wheel brakes were optional at extra cost. Prices were lowered to attract more customers; the five-passenger touring car being listed at $1,875 and five-passenger brougham at $2,475.

The Big Four was still in production in 1925-26, on a 119-inch wheelbase. The 130-inch wheelbase chassis was used for a new Model S that went into production towards the end of 1924. This new 6-95 series had a 3½-inch bore and the usual 5-inch stroke, giving 288.6 cubic-inch displacement, and delivered 82 hp at 3,000 rpm. The naked chassis cost $2,195 complete. A sports sedan was listed at $3,250, the brougham at $2,750 and the seven-passenger sedan at $3,350.

Styling for the new Model S was much improved, though Stearns-Knight tended to build high frames and bodies (in the way of Cadillac and Lincoln) rather than following the trend towards lower lines as exemplified by Packard, Stutz, and others.

Control of the F. B. Stearns Company passed to a consortium led by John N. Willys at the end of 1925. Willys-Overland in Toledo was the world's biggest makers of cars with Knight sleeve-valve engines, having introduced the Willys-Knight in 1914. They led the way in making this high-cost engine available in medium-priced cars. John N. Willys also wanted to have a prestige car in his stable, and that attracted him to the Stearns-Knight.

Willys installed H. J. Leonard as president of F. B. Stearns, a competent administrator who had formerly been general manager of Stephens Motor Works in Freeport, Illinois. He spurred England to move farther and faster towards the top end of the market, and from the Willys organization, he obtained designs for

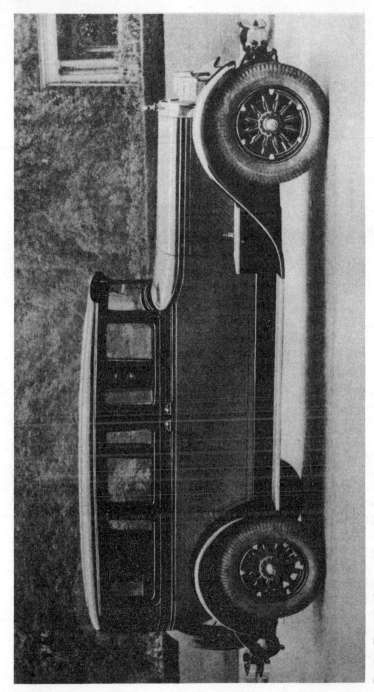

Fig. 5-7. The 1927 Stearns-Knight Model 8-85.

new low-profile bodies. England went to smaller-diameter wheels with 32 × 6.75-inch balloon tires, which lowered the whole chassis, and adopted worm drive, which lowered the drive line (and therefore the floor-level, since drive-line pumps were out of the question in those days).

Leonard ordered production of the Models C and S stopped in the summer of 1926, to be replaced by the 6-85 series Model D. With a 130-inch wheelbase its chassis was a new design with four wheel brakes (mechanically operated) as standard, the cantilever rear suspension being discarded in favor of semi-ellipitical leaf springs.

Model D gave way to Model F in 1926, carrying the same 6-85 serial identification. The most noteworthy technical advance was the adoption of a seven-bearing crankshaft. England was now designing an eight-cylinder engine, choosing the same bore and stroke (for manufacturing reasons), which gave a displacement of 385 cubic inches and raised output to 102 hp at 2,600 rpm. It went into the Model G 8-85, which was built on a 137-inch wheelbase. It was not just a stretched Model F frame, but a redesigned version with longer semi-elliptical springs all around, giving lower ride rates, and Houdaille hydraulic shock absorbers at each wheel.

Model G was available as chassis only for custom bodies, and standard bodies were produced by the Ohio Body Company in seven styles. The five-passenger touring car was listed at $3,850 and the seven-passenger limousine at $4,650. About 640 Model G cars had been produced when it was replaced by Model H in 1928.

The eight-cylinder engine was developed to deliver 112 hp, which raised the top speed from 85 to 90 mph. Correspondingly, the series identification was changed to 8-90 for Model H. The 130-inch wheelbase was retained, but model H bodies moved ahead on the styling front. Model J also had the same engine, but was built on a 145-inch wheelbase.

Six-cylinder models formed the mainstay of Stearns-Knight production, with Model M replacing Model F in 1928. The engine dimensions were reduced to 3.375-inches for the bore and 4.75 inches for the stroke, which gave a displacement of 255 cubic inches and an output of 70 hp. Model M was built on a 126-inch wheelbase and its companion, Model N, with the same power train, had a 134-inch wheelbase.

All were high-quality cars, and Stearns-Knight deserved to succeed. The end, however, followed so immediately upon the stock-market crash in 1929 that it is difficult to ignore this indication of a primary cause. Actually, John N. Willys had sold his Stearns-Knight holdings during the preceding summer, which meant that the company's main credit line had been cut off. And without continued subsidies, Stearns-Knight could not carry on in the market segment that Leonard and Willys had chosen for it. In 1930 the stockholders voted to liquidate the business.

William E. England was signed as chief experimental engineer of Auburn, where he stayed until 1934. He served for two years as chief engineer of the Ohio Rubber Company, and in 1938 was working as consulting engineer with Bantam in Butler, Pennsylvania, which was then taking the first steps towards the creation of a light military vehicle that became the basis for the wartime Jeep.

58. LA SALLE V-8, 1927

Locomobile had its Junior Eight; Marmon had its Roosevelt; Moon had its Diana; and many lower-priced makes undercut themselves with new brand names on cars built in their own plants and sold through the same organizations. When the management at Cadillac, headed by Lawrence P. Fisher, became attracted to the idea of selling a lower-priced car under a different name so as not to detract from the prestige of the real Cadillac, the La Salle was just a short step away (Fig. 5-8).

La Salle was more than a baby Cadillac, for both technically and in styling, it was ahead of the Cadillac of the same year. Built on a 125-inch wheelbase, it was not even a baby anything, but a high-class car built to an intelligent set of dimensions and engineered for a sound mixture of elegance and performance. Yes, it was even available with a 134-inch wheelbase for a seven-passenger sedan and so-called Imperial bodies with five or seven seats.

The standard bodies, which came in the form of coupe, convertible coupe, roadster, phaeton and dual-cowl phaeton, victoria, sedan, and town sedan, were all built on the regular 125-inch wheelbase. (Cadillac chassis for 1927 had wheelbases of 132 and 138 inches). La Salle prices started at $2,525 when the lowest-priced Cadillac was listed at $2,995.

The La Salle frame was not just a shortened Cadillac frame, but a lighter structure with less massive girders and cross members. Front suspension was similar, almost a scaled-down design, with a reversed-Elliott axle and worm-and-sector steering gear with a fairly quick 17.5:1 ratio. Rear suspension for the La

Salle was the first version of a new concept that was under study for the 1928 Cadillac, adopting torque tube drive instead of the separate torque arm that was still in use alongside the open propeller shaft of the 1927 Cadillac.

Semi-elliptical leaf springs were used for both axles, the rear ones being 60 inches long. The number of leaves was determined by the body style, so ride rates would correspond to the actual weight.

La Salle's engine was also a step ahead, for it was a smaller version not of the old series 314-A Cadillac V-8, but of the new Series 341 due for production in the 1928 models.

This engine had been in the design stage since W. R. Strickland had put a two-plane crankshaft in the old V-8 back in 1923. Strickland directed the work, assisted by Frank Johnson. Johnson had been a Cadillac engineer back in the days of the McCall-designed V-8, but had gone to Lincoln with the Lelands, returning to Cadillac in 1921. The new V-8 became his main responsibility, and when the design was pretty well finalized one fine day in 1926, he resigned from Cadillac and went back to Lincoln.

The Cadillac version had 341 cubic-inch displacement; the La Salle only 303 cubic inches. Both had the same basic construction, with two four-cylinder blocks mounted at 90 degrees above a common crankcase. Both had the same 4.94-inch stroke, but the La Salle had a smaller bore: 3.125 inches vs. 3.625 inches for the Cadillac. The difference was so small that both were able to use the same size valves, which meant that valve area on the La Salle faced a greater proportion of the piston area. And that, in turn, promised better cylinder filling and therefore higher efficiency. On the new three-bearing crankshaft, rods rode side by side on the crankpins, while in 1927 the Cadillac engine still had fork-and-blade mounted connecting rods. The crankshaft was counterweighted and carried a harmonic vibration damper.

Two Morse chains were driven from the nose of the crankshaft. One drove only the single, central camshaft; the other turned the water pump and generator.

Cylinder heads were detachable (as on the older Cadillac engine) and their top surfaces had cooling ribs (which Cadillac did not use, even on the 1928-model engines). The L-head valve arrangement was changed only in detail. Cadillac built its own carburetor, which was carried centrally, between the manifolds. A

Fig. 5-8. The La Salle of 1927.

new type of Delco ignition was used, with a dual-point distributor having centrifugal spark advance.

A three-speed transmission was fitted on the La Salle. It was made to the same basic design as Cadillac's gearbox, but used thinner gears with lower friction and less weight. The full-floating rear axle had spiral bevel final drive with a 3.50:1 ratio. Tires were 32 × 6 on wire wheels.

La Salle bodies were a real styling exercise. Going outside the ranks of Fisher body designers, Lawrence P. Fisher invited Harley J. Earl to work with him on new projects. Earl was a young Californian who was then designing custom bodies for Don Lee in Los Angeles, and Fisher had seen and admired some of his work. The job he did for La Salle put styling on the map as a valid, industrial function, separate from body engineering, with which it had always been associated.

The La Salle was greeted with much enthusiasm, inside General Motors first, and then by the general public, that it resulted in a full-time job for Harley Earl, as head of a new department called the "Art and Color Section." In this position he came to direct the styling for all GM divisions.

His inspiration for the La Salle front was the Hispano-Suiza, which then rivaled the Rolls-Royce as Europe's top make of car. But there was also a tribute to traditional American proportions and what we might call automotive fashion in the La Salle. Incontestably, it was the best-looking thing on wheels then built in the U.S.A.

The La Salle was also a fast car. A stock roadsters straight off the assembly line, was given a quick break-in, and then ran 951 in 10 hours at the GM Proving Grounds. That comes to an average speed of 95.1 mph.

You don't change a winning formula, and Cadillac left the La Salle practically unchanged for the 1928 model year. The 1929 model had the engine bored out to 328 cubic inches, and maximum output rose from 75 to 86 hp. The transmission was fitted with synchromesh, and a new four-wheel brake system with shoes inside the drums replaced the earlier type, which had contracting bands around the drums. Chassis for closed bodies had the 134-inch wheelbase, while open cars were built on chassis with the 125-inch wheelbase (which was discontinued in 1930).

By 1932, despite successive increases in engine size and power, the impact of the La Salle had worn off. The market had deserted it, for after its initial success, the sales curve took a dive.

Production in the first year was nearly 27,000 cars, and by 1932, was less than 3,500.

Other projects took precedence over La Salle at Cadillac, as will be shown in an upcoming chapter.

59. CHRYSLER IMPERIAL L-80, 1928

Imperial was the name Walter P. Chrysler chose for the car he launched to compete against the Cadillac and Lincoln. It was a name that denoted grandeur, possessions, omnipotence. Whether one associated the name with Napoleon's, the Roman, or the British Empire, the word outranked everything in worldly power, including royalty.

In concept and technical execution, the car that Chrysler first endowed with this exalted title was not so far removed from the solid citizen's car that made the Chrysler's reputation and which was competing successfully against the Buick and others in the professional man's price class (Fig. 5-9). All the more credit and recognition is due to the first Chrysler Six that served as the base for the Imperial. The main difference was just one of scale. Everything was bigger, more expensive, and more luxurious.

The first Imperial was announced in December, 1925, and was known as the Imperial 80. The number was played up, for it meant that the maker guaranteed the car to go 80 miles per hour. The number also had a comparative value, for it quantified the difference between the Imperial and the regular Chrysler 60 and 70 from which it was derived. The 1927 Imperial 80 Cabriolet had a list price of $3,495, or nearly three times the price of the least expensive six-cylinder Chrysler.

The Imperial was assigned a special role: It was not a mass-produced car, and making profit on its sales was not the major objective . . . it was there to lend prestige to the Chrysler name and to promote lesser vehicles carrying the same badge. From an initial single car line, Chrysler's model lineup had swelled to a full range. The profits were made on the mass-produced cars, mostly on the sixes, but also on the light four-cylinder Chrysler cars which were really not much more than renamed Maxwells.

Zeder, Breer and Skelton did a masterly job of keeping the proportions right. Fred M. Zeder, who had laid out the original Chrysler engine, now served as overall director of engineering and occupied himself with everything from forward planning on one hand to new test methods, equipment and facilities on the other. Carl Breer devoted most of his time to the engine lab and new engine design; while Owen R. Skelton took charge of chassis and body engineering.

Body design at that time was still done by Oliver Clark, the body engineer who had previously been with Studebaker and now worked closely with Skelton. Together they developed the idea of widening the track from the standard 56-inches to 57.75, which brought engineering advantages in terms of stance and stability and kept the car from looking tall as well.

Three wheelbases were available: 120, 127 and 130 inches, to suit different types of bodywork. The roadster was built on the 120-inch wheelbase, and the seven-passenger models on the 130-inch wheelbase. Tires were 32 × 6.20 all around, for Chrysler was a leader in the trend towards smaller wheels that lowered the whole chassis.

The engine for the Imperial was a redesigned L-head Chrysler six, with 3.50-inch bore and 5-inch stroke, giving 288.7 cubic-inch displacement. It became the first Chrysler engine to use Lynite aluminum pistons, and it was suspended in a new support system with rubber blocks.

With a 4.7:1 compression ratio, it delivered 92 hp at 3,000 rpm. A final drive ratio of 4.6:1 gave tremendous top-gear flexibility, as the engine generated its peak torque at 1,000 rpm. Its top-gear acceleration from very low speeds became famous.

Tire size was further reduced to 30 × 6.75 for 1927, and the axle ratio adjusted to 4.3:1. The engine breathed through a single Stromberg carburetor fed from a vacuum tank and carried Remy electrical equipment.

Block and head were made of cast iron, and the seven-bearing crankshaft, with its 12 counterweights, was fully machined. The camshaft was chain-driven and equipped with a skew gear driving

Fig. 5-9. 1928 Chrysler Imperial L-80; stiff competition for Cadillac and Lincoln.

the distributor shaft that also turned the oil pump. The centrifugal water pump was driven from an extension of the belt-driven fan shaft. The three-speed transmission had chrome-steel gears, with a roller-bearing countershaft.

Such was the power train which the L-80 inherited from the first Imperial (code-named E-80). It was bored out to 309.3 cubic inch displacement and embodied some other changes of greater interest. Under Breer's direction, the engine lab had done a lot of work on Ricardo's high-turbulence L-head configuration, and the compression ratio for the L-80 was raised to an unparalleled 6:1. This gave a healthy power boost to 112 hp at 3,200 rpm. The L-80 was a 1928 model, announced in November of 1927.

The chassis continued with Hotchkiss drive and semi-elliptical leaf springs on front and rear axles. Springs were made of chrome-vanadium steel and wrapped in fabric covers. The semi-floating rear axle had spiral bevel gears with ratios of either 4.63 or 4.27:1, and the front axle was a chrome-molybdenum I-beam with Elliott yokes. Front springs were 47.5 inches long, and the rear ones had a length of 58 inches.

All L-80's were built on a 136-inch wheelbase, and the frame had channel-section side girders of 7-inches depth. The five-passenger sedan weighed 4,105 pounds, which was remarkably light for a car its size.

The brake system was developed from the Lockheed hydraulic four-wheel system used on the 1925 model, still in combination with external-contracting bands on all four drums. Cam and lever steering gear was used, with a rear-mounted track rod.

Engineering supervision and coordination, from the moment Zeder, Breer and Skelton had signed their approval, was the responsibility of the corporation's assistant chief engineer, Howard F. Maynard. Every detail of every model crossed his desk. With his assistant, Charles E. Davy, he did much to protect the quality of the Chrysler product. Maynard had graduated from the Worcester Polytechnic Insititute with a degree in electrical engineering, and after nine years in non-automotive work came to the U.S. Motor Co. in 1910; served as chief engineer of the Lion Motor Car Co in Adrian, Michigan; and in 1913 was named chief production engineer at Maxwell. Davy was much younger and had been a machine shop foreman at Ford before he was given engineering posts with Denby Motor Truck, Universal Products, and Paige-Detroit. He joined Maxwell in 1922.

Production at Chrysler was directed by K. T. Keller, who had worked with Chrysler at Buick, when Chrysler was head of Buick and Keller master mechanic. Keller came from Mount Joy, Pennsylvania, and had worked many years for the Westinghouse Machine Company before joining the auto industry. After stints with Metzger, Hudson, and Maxwell, he joined General Motors in 1911. He worked wonders at Buick, and then served as vice president of manufacturing at Chevrolet for three years. He was with GM of Canada when Chrysler called him in 1926 to say he needed him.

After the L-80 came the L-series Imperial for 1929. It retained the L-80 drive train, but received a new, lower frame and fully restyled body. Semi-custom bodies had been introduced for the L-80 during the 1928 model year, such as a convertible sedan by Le Baron, or a Locke Touralette. This concept was further developed in 1929 and 1930.

The 80 series Imperial went to 7.00-18 tires for 1929, making it one of the most modern-looking cars on the road. In imitation of General Motors, Chrysler set up its own Art & Color Section in 1928, with Herbert V. Henderson as director. He was not a car man, but an industrial designer, and his department was subordinate to Oliver Clark's (body engineering). The L-series six-cylinder Imperial lived through 1930, when it was replaced by a startling new design, which will be examined in detail later on.

60. LINCOLN SERIES L, 1928

Lincoln was a great car from its start in 1919. If there is any element of surprise in its evolution, it must surely be that it rose to new heights of greatness after Henry Ford bought the company in 1922, when it might have been expected that Ford methods would cheapen the product. In fact, Ford never introduced mass-production methods in the Lincoln plant, and did not try to save money by using standard Ford parts anywhere in the Lincoln (Fig. 5-10).

Ford's intention was to help Henry M. Leland continue to build a high-quality car with Ford's resources and sales organization. And Edsel Ford, whose official title was president of the Ford Motor Company, took a particular interest in the Lincoln. It became a symbol for Edsel's personal view of greatness in a car.

Model L originated in 1922 and was a pure Leland design. But by mid-1923, the Lelands, father and son, had left the company. There were disagreements with Ford, but mainly over money matters and little over the product. If Henry Ford was stubborn, Henry M. Leland was headstrong. A rupture was inevitable. When the Lelands departed, Henry Ford named his son-in-law, Ernest C. Kanzler, general manager of Lincoln.

At the product end, things progressed smoothly, since Ford retained Leland's chief engineer, Thomas J. Litle Jr. Litle was an electrical engineer who had graduated from the University of Pennsylvania. He joined the Welsbach Company soon after leaving school, and became its chief engineer.

In 1917 he left Welsbach to join Cadillac, but the following year he decided his chances were greater with Leland than with General Motors, and by 1920 was chief engineer of Lincoln. He directed actual design and development work for the Series L.

Litle left the engine and drive train alone to a large extent, since neither was a source of trouble, and everything worked smoothly and with low noise despite the impressive power. As time went on, he was able to introduce improvements that not only reduced engine noise and vibration, but also enabled him to lighten the engine.

He had concentrated on chassis engineering from the start, and made some notable contributions. He developed his own theories of suspension design, and preferred springs made up of large numbers of thin leaves with tapered ends, at a time when most chassis designers were striving for a minimum number of thick leaves with uniform width from end to end.

His Model L was built on a 136-inch wheelbase with 32 × 5-inch tires all around. It had a three-speed transmission and a

Fig. 5-10. Lincoln Series L, 1929.

spiral-bevel rear axle with a 4.6:1 ratio. Brakes were mechanical, contracting and expanding against drums in the rear wheels.

Four wheel brakes were tried in 1924 and made available for police models in 1925. By that time, the standard tires were 23 × 6 with 21 × 7 balloon tires optional. Not until 1927 did the Lincoln come with four wheel brakes as standard. All four wheels carried drums with internal shoes, and rear wheel drums also had external brake bands.

That was the last Lincoln developed under Litle, who left the company early in 1926. After six months as vice president of Copeland Products, he was signed up in November of that year as chief engineer of Marmon, where he stayed until October, 1929. His later career was spent with Holley Carburetor, Evans Products, Easy Washing Machine Co., and Bendix Home Appliances.

After the loss of Litle, Ford was able to lure Frank Johnson back from Cadillac. His first task was to make the engine more powerful, and he solved it by the simple expedient of boring out the cylinders to 3½ inches, which raised the displacement to 385 cubic inches. Output was boosted from 81 hp at 2,600 rpm to 90 hp at 2,800.

A new counterweighted crankshaft was adopted to prevent vibration due to the bigger pistons. The fork-and-blade connecting rod arrangement was retained, however, as were the roller-type cam followers.

The enlarged 60-degree Lincoln V-8 remained in production through 1931, its latest version delivering 120 hp at 2,900 rpm. This power increase was made possible by going to a higher compression ratio, manifolds with less restriction, and a Stromberg dual-body downdraft carburetor.

While the standard wheelbase remained at 136 inches for the duration of the Series L's production life, a 150-inch wheelbase chassis had become optional in 1927. Both were chosen by a number of coachbuilders for their masterpieces. It will be remembered that Leland's original Lincoln plant had no body shop, all chassis being sent outside for their bodies. Under Leland, Brunn bodies were standard for the Lincoln, but after 1925, Brunn's capacity was no longer sufficient for Lincoln's needs.

Ford began to build custom-bodies for the Lincoln in its own factory, and chassis were sent to other coachbuilders around the country, including Fleetwood, Murphy, Judkins, Derham, Locke,

Le Baron, Willoughby, Dietrich, Murray, Rollston, and Waterhouse.

The standard five-passenger 1928 sedan weighed 5,030 pounds and carried a list price of $4,800. Among catalogued models there was a Le Baron Cabriolet at $7,100; a Dietrich convertible sedan at $6,600; and a Brunn Brougham at $7,000.

The Lincoln Chassis was perhaps the toughest of any American car of its period, with its robust frame and torque tube drive. Despite its huge size and weight, it steered and handled well. And above it, it had the Lincoln quality that Leland had always insisted on.

61. DU PONT MODEL G, 1929

The du Pont car came into being because of E. Paul du Pont's enthusiasm for automobiles. A member of the du Pont dynasty of Wilmington, Delaware, he was a successful businessman, a junior executive of the Bull Grain Explosive Co. which was a du Pont subsidiary. But he was not satisfied to let his career run its normal course in the explosive business. He wanted to build cars. Great cars.

He formed a company in 1913 which produced marine engines during the war. In 1919 he was ready to take the step into car production, choosing his collaborators with great care.

He was president of the company, and as vice president he hired Arthur M. Maris, who had formerly been an executive of the firm that made the Biddle car in Philadelphia. Sales manager William A. Smith had a fine reputation after serving for years as general manager of Mercer Motors. His first chief engineer, R.R. Zimmer, formerly with Crane and Crane-Simplex, had been associated with auto engineering since 1904.

The first du Pont car appeared in the New York automobile show of 1919. Named the Model A, it had a four-cylinder L-head engine manufactured by du Pont in the Wilmington plant. The chassis was assembled in a plant located in Moore, Pennsylvania, and bodies were manufactured in Springfield, Massachusetts.

Du Pont's main concern was quality. The cars were built with extreme care, and none was released until it had been thoroughly tested and brought to a high degree of perfection.

After the Model B of 1921 Model C followed in July, 1923. By this time, E. Paul wanted a six-cylinder model, but his factory was not equipped to make them. He discontinued engine manufacture and purchased six-cylinder engines from Herschell-Spillman. The power unit used in the Model C was a high-grade L-head design.

For Model D of 1924, du Pont chose a new six-cylinder Wisconsin engine. This car had four wheel hydraulic brakes and modern chassis lubrication (with grease nipples at all points).

About this time, the Moore, Pennsylvania plant was sold and car assembly transferred to the Wilmington factory. More or less simultaneously, Zimmer left and was succeeded as chief engineer by John A. Pierson, who had formerly worked for the Wright-Martin Aircraft Corporation. He was familiar with supercharging from his work on aircraft engines and experimented with supercharging on the Wisconsin engine selected for the Model E. But it never got past the test stage, and the Model E was produced from 1927 to 1930 with a normal engine.

Later in 1927 du Pont introduced its Model F, which was basically a stretched Model E built on a 136-inch wheelbase. It was the Model G that was not only du Pont's most successful car, but its greatest one (Fig. 5-11). It was in production from July, 1928, to January, 1932. John A. Pierson left the company shortly before its introduction, and general manager, L.F. Hosley, also assumed the title of chief engineer.

In keeping with the trends of the time, Model G was a new eight-cylinder car, powered by a 322 cubic-inch Continental engine. Delivering 125 hp at 3,200 rpm, it gave the 4,400-pound touring car a level of performance that could make Stutz and Chrysler owners blanch.

According to du Pont literature, the Model G was available in 12 body styles. A roadster was listed at $4,360; and the town car at $5,750. The roadster was built on a 135-inch wheelbase, while five- and seven-passenger models were built on a 141-inch wheelbase.

For good ride comfort, the leaf springs were made extra-long and fitted with hydraulic shock absorbers. With its 32 × 6.5 tires and 58½-inch track, the car had a wide stance and looked more stable than Fort Knox. Four-wheel hydraulic brakes were standard on the du Pont, when the only mass-producer to have taken that step was Chrysler. The cowl section on Model G, with its instrument panel, was a giant aluminum casting. The frame had channel-section side girders up to 8 inches in depth, with six rigid cross members. Bodies were built up on a wooden framework with aluminum panels. Bodies were produced by Merrimac, Derham or Waterhouse.

After the Model G, there was a Model H. Frames were bought from Stearns-Knight, engines from Continental, transmissions from Warner, and axles from Timken. But it could not replace the Model G, which lasted until the company went under in 1932 and E. Paul du Pont returned to the world of chemicals and explosives.

62. KISSEL WHITE EAGLE, 1929

The car that Kissel called the White Eagle vis-a-vis the outside world was actually designated Model 126 internally. And it was a series with many different bodies of remarkable styling. The seven-passenger sedan looked like a precursor of the big Marmons and Studebakers of 1930-31, and the Tourster (that's what Kissel called the five-passenger, four-door convertible) may have set the theme for the 1931 Cadillac. What Kissel called a coupe-roadster was a solid-top town coupe, very similar to the contemporary La Salle. And the Speedster even had the revived Stutz Blackhawk beat for distinctive styling, with its cut-down doors and base hinges for the soft-top frame anchored just above running-board height (Fig. 5-12).

They were big cars and they were fast cars. With wheelbases of 126 to 137 inches, their curb weights ranged from 3,900 to 4,700 pounds. Prices were very competitive covering the full $2,000 to $3,000 spread. But like many other great cars, the White Eagle came too late to save the company that built them.

The name White Eagle had first been used for a limited edition of 100 deluxe cars in 1928, powered by Lycoming L-head straight-eight engines. Kissel produced its own six-cylinder engines up to mid-1928, but after that date used Lycoming engines with six or eight cylinders in all models.

Although a pioneer engine manufacturer in Wisconsin, Kissel had a small foundry and limited machining capacity, and had a long record of using proprietary engines to supplement those it produced itself in Hartford. This began in 1913, when Kissel opened a branch factory in Milwaukee to assemble a new model known as the 6-48 powered by a Wisconsin six-cylinder engine.

Kissel's Double-Six of 1917-18 was powered by a V-12 Weidley engine, but less than 1,000 of these were built.

After building trucks powered by Kissel-made engines during World War I, the company went back to making its pre-war six-cylinder Hundred Point Six, installed in newly designed cars and advertised as the Custom-Built Six.

The engine was an L-head design by Herman Palmer, cast en bloc, with detachable head and a three-bearing crankshaft. With a

Fig. 5-11. The DuPont Model G of 1929.

bore and stroke of 3.31 × 5.125 inches, its displacement was only 265 cubic inches and power output was 61 hp at 2,500 rpm.

The 6-45 chassis served for the Kissel speedsters that earned the nickname "Gold Bug" for their all-yellow paint job, including frame, springs and axles. A smaller-engined and lower-priced series called the 6-55 was introduced in 1923. The engine was essentially a short-stroke version of the 6-45, but had notable differences, such as a timing chain instead of gear drive to the camshaft. The following year, the 6-45 was phased out, the 6-55 then becoming the single line, with a 121-inch standard wheelbase, and a 132-inch wheelbase for seven-passenger closed bodies.

Four-wheel hydraulic brakes became standard in 1925, Kissel having adopted the Lockheed system with contracting bands on all four drums. A mechanical hand brake actuated a contracting band on a propeller shaft drum.

During 1924 Herman Palmer had been busy testing a new chassis with an eight-cylinder engine. It went into production in 1925 as the 8-75, built on a 137-inch wheelbase and available in a variety of body styles, from phaeton and victoria to brougham sedan and Deluxe Enclosed Speedster. Prices started at a remarkably low $2,095. This design became the basis for the later White Eagle. Both axles were carried by semi-elliptical leaf springs, and wheels were shod with 33 × 6 balloon tires.

The engine was part Lycoming, part Kissel. Lycoming delivered the block, and Kissel added its own aluminum cylinder head, finned aluminum oil pan and aluminum pistons. With its

210

3. 19-inch bore and 4½-inch stroke, this engine displaced 287 cubic inches and delivered 75 hp at 2,750 rpm. It was quiet, reliable, simple to service, and extremely hard-wearing. It had reasonable fuel consumption and gave excellent performance.

An Economy Eight powered by an 8-65 all-Lycoming engine followed in 1927, while the 6-55 continued with the Kissel engine until the start of the 1928 model year when a Lycoming six was substituted, the car then being renamed 6-70. The 8-75 was upgraded to 8-90 designation, with higher-compression engine and lower prices, while the "Economy" 8-65 changed character and became the 8-80.

Kissel advertisements claimed 115 hp and 100 mph for the White Eagle, which had a bored-out version of the 8-90 engine, displacing 298 cubic inches. White Eagle grew into a general name for all 1929-model Kissels, including the sixes. But it is Model 126, using the biggest engine, that comes to mind when that name is mentioned.

Despite attractive prices, great styling by Fritz Werner and outstanding quality, the Kissel continued to lose favor in the market place. Less than 1,100 cars were completed in 1929, and by the end of 1930 Kissel had made the decision to close the auto plant. The Kissel family had dominated the business life of Hartford for generations. From farming they went to farm implements, next to general and electrical engineering, banking and automobiles. Cars became the main activity at the expense of other business affairs, and now it was time to reverse the process.

Kissel stopped car production early in 1931 and the business was reorganized as Kissel Industries. Herman Palmer continued as its engineering director, being responsible for the design and production of a line of outboard motors for small boats.

It was taken over by West Bend in 1944 and Palmer stayed on until he reached retirement age in 1950. George A. Kissel died in 1942, Otto P. Kissel lived to the age of 87 (1960) and William L. Kissel died at 93 in 1972.

63. DUESENBERG MODEL J, 1929

America almost lost the Duesenberg, one of its greatest cars, before it became famous. The company fell into receivership in 1924, and could have gone under but the management of Chester S. Ricker saved it until a wealthy backer could be found. Chet Ricker had been in charge of timing and scoring at the Indianapolis Speedway since 1913, and was a well-known consulting engineer.

The Brougham Sedan

Fig. 5-12. Kissel White Eagle of 1929, known also as Model 126.

He was named co-receiver with W.T. Rasmussen. In 1926 they were able to sell the company to Errett L. Cord, the 32-year-old president of Auburn Automoble Company.

Cord had started his meteoric career as a salesman for Moon in 1921; became a partner in the Moon dealership in Chicago; and sold out for a fortune. He joined Auburn in 1925 to boost its sagging sales and ended up owning the company. He also got control of Lycoming Motors in Williamsport, Pennsylvania.

It was Cord's ambition to make a new Duesenberg that would be recognized as the mightiest of all cars, a dream car come true. Fred S. Duesenberg continued as vice president and chief engineer and had no difficulty understanding what Cord wanted.

The outcome was the Model J, which went into production in December, 1928. The detail design had been carried out by chief draftsman William R. Beckman, and Pearl Watson was the factory manager who planned and supervised production in the small plant on West Washington Street in Indianapolis.

Everything about the Model J was superlative. The chassis was built on two wheelbases, 142.4 and 153.5 inches. It had to be long, for the hood took up almost half the wheelbase. The engine was not only long but a masterpiece of engineering.

Just imagine, eight cylinders in line, each with four overhead valves operated by twin overhead camshafts. It was pure racing heritage. The cylinders were not very big, with a 3.75-inch bore and 4.75-inch stroke, giving a total displacement of 420 cubic inches. Compression ratio was a brave 5.25:1, and while the claimed output of 265 hp at 4,200 rpm is inflated, it was a tremendously powerful car.

Its real output was 208 hp at 3,800 rpm with a maximum torque of 375 lb. ft. at 2,000 rpm. The five-bearing crankshaft was counterweighted and carried a torsional vibration damper, with chain drive to the camshafts. Pistons were aluminum, of course. And the chrome-plated low-restriction exhaust manifold led to a 54-inch long muffler. The carburetor was a two-barrel updraft Schebler, capable of passing more cubic feet per minute of air than anything short of aircraft carburetors.

This engine was built by Lycoming, but the design was Duesenberg's and Beckman's. It was matched with a long clutch of twin-plate type and a three-speed transmission. The rear axle was a hypoid bevel type, with final drive ratios of 3.78, 4.00, 4.30 and 4.70:1 according to the customer's needs.

The frame was too long to be entirely rigid, even with its 8½-inch deep side members and six tubular steel cross-members. Suspension was by means of semi-ellipticals all around, with Delco-Remy hydraulic shock absorbers. The chassis alone was priced at $8,500.

Duesenberg built chassis only. Bodies were made by noted coachbuilders such as Brunn, Derham, Rollston, Brester, Locke, and others. Many went to Europe, and were fitted with bodies by Barker, Gurney Nutting, d'Ieteren and Van den Plas, Figoni, Letourneur & Marchand, Saoutchik, Castagna, Graber, Kellner, Hibbard & Darrin.

The speedometer read to 150 mph, but the real top speed was 112 to 116 mph, depending on body type. Acceleration figures were also impressive, such as zero-to-60 mph in the 13-seconds range, especially when you keep in mind the weight of the car, which was usually 5,000 to 5,500 pounds depending on body design and construction. Of course, at 60 mph the car was still in second gear. It was said to reach 89 mph in second. At the same time, it was highly flexible, and could be driven in top gear down to 6.5 mph (with the shortest axle ratio). The factory claimed top-gear acceleration from 10 to 80 mph in 22 seconds. Moving this highway locomotive down the road took some amount of fuel. It would give about 9 mpg in general use, and up to 12 mpg in highway cruising at modest speed.

Naturally, the Duesenberg was not made for the silky smoothness of a Packard, the velvety luxury of a Pierce-Arrow, or the deceptively quiet punch of a Stutz. The Duesenberg's racing ancestry was apparent in the noise of its engine and drive train, and the chassis was compromised with regard to both ride and handling. Still, it was not a difficult car to drive. It was not hard to steer for instance, and the vacuum-assisted four-wheel hydraulic brakes made stopping from any speed possible in normal distances. Power brakes were not used on the first production models, but when owners complained, it took Duesenberg just a few months to find a solution and get it into production.

Wire wheels with 19-inch rims were standard, usually shod with 6.00 or 6.20-inch wide tires. The frame was so low that the car did not look narrow on its standard 56-inch tread, and the best coachbuilders in the world did all they could to make Duesenberg look low, wide and handsome.

The car stands as a monument to the ideals of E.L. Cord, which were its inspiration. And we must not let our admiration for Fred and Augie Duesenberg grow so large that we are made to forget that it was Cord who made it all possible. He set the design goals, financed the business, and even had the wisdom to keep away and not interfere in areas beyond his qualifications.

Chapter 6

Lean Years—Cars of the Early Thirties

The car was named, of course, for E. L. Cord, the same man who rescued the Duesenberg and brought it to new heights of greatness (Fig. 6-1). And it was not a disguised Auburn but a completely new creation. Cord was sitting on top of the world in 1929, and it's no wonder he wanted his name on a car—a great car. But he had the personal integrity to let the Duesenberg remain a Duesenberg, and no doubt the Auburn was not exactly the kind of car he wanted. E. L. Cord was the owner, not only of those two car companies, but also of Lycoming Motors, which produced engines for outside customers as well. He even held control of Checker Cab and Columbia Axle Company. He held no railroad interests, but spread into sea and air transport by ownership of Stinson Aircraft; Airplane Development Corporation; Aviation Manufacturing Corporation; and the New York Shipbuilding Corporation.

He wanted the Cord car to have front wheel drive like the Millers which then dominated racing at Indianapolis Speedway. He knew he had the manufacturing capacity available in the Auburn plant to build it, but he needed a whole new engineering team to design it.

Cord went about his plan by first purchasing the rights to the Miller front wheel drive patents in 1927 and retaining Harry Miller as a consultant. He discussed the project with a good friend, racing driver Leon Duray, who suggested that Cord get in touch with an engineer named Van Ranst. Duray knew Cornelius Van Ranst as the designer of a front wheel drive racing car called the Detroit Special in 1926. Cord engaged him to create the Cord automobile.

It was a wise choice. Van Ranst was then 35 years old and though he had no formal training as an engineer, he had a formidable background in car engineering; starting as a teenager by working parttime in the drafting department of H. H. Franklin in Syracuse, New York. He worked as a tester with Chase Motor Truck, and in various posts with U. S. Motors. He joined Duesenberg in 1915 but left two years later to work on his own inventions. In 1920 he met Louis Chevrolet and designed his Frontenac and Monroe racing cars. He was an engine designer with Paige for two years and then started a company to make electric fuel pumps.

The first Cord prototype was built in the Miller shop in Los Angeles, under Van Ranst's direction. It had a Lycoming straight eight engine turned around to put the flywheel in front, and modified to get the water pump and fan drive at the front also. Miller-type front suspension was used, with reversed de Dion tube and quarter-elliptical leaf springs.

The Miller transaxle, with the gearbox on the output side of the final drive unit, was unacceptable for a production car because it made it hard to shift gears. Van Ranst adopted the same layout he had used on the Detroit Special, wiht a standard three-speed transmission—turned on its side—between the flywheel and the hypoid bevel final drive. This was not as compact as Miller's solution, and caused the engine to be moved farther back in the chassis, but this was not regarded as a problem in the kind of car the Cord was destined to be.

The prototype served to establish the feasibility of the design. Van Ranst knew both its strong points and its weaknesses. Cord installed him in the Duesenberg drawing office in Indianapolis to design the production model, with assitance from the Auburn engineering staff. Herbert C. Snow of Auburn designed the Cord's cross-braced frame; and the body design was done by John Oswald, Auburn's body engineer.

Van Ranst took full advantage of the front wheel drive to give the car a low center of gravity. The low frame made for a low floor, and the production-model Cord was only 64 inches high overall, at a time when most cars stood 75 inches tall.

With a 137.5-inch wheelbase, its great length emphasized the low build even further. At the front end a Miller-type suspension was retained, with a de Dion tube and double quarter-elliptical springs on each side. Front brake drums were mounted inboard, to avoid complications around the outer universal joints, and to

Fig. 6-1. E.L. Cord's dream car, the 1930 Cord L-29.

reduce the unsprung weight. At the rear, Van Ranst used a dropped I-beam axle-carried on semi-elliptical leaf springs. For reasons that are not clear, the rear track, at 60 inches, was two inches wider than the front track. Worm and roller steering gear was used, with a 20:1 ratio . . . quite acceptable for the 46-feet turning circle. Dayton wire wheels carried 7.00-18 tires, assuring a very modern look.

The Cord engine was a substantial redesign from the L-head Lycoming Eight then used by Auburn. Changes had to be made in the head castings because of the reversed coolant flow, and the revised engine mounting system necessitated a different crankcase. The Cord version also had a different crankshaft and a different camshaft.

Displacement was 298.6 cubic inches (3.25 × 4.50 inches bore and stroke). The carburetor was a two-barrel updraft Schebler, smaller than the Duesenberg's, but the compression ratio was the same (5.25:1). Output was 115 hp which gave the Cord adequate rather than startling performance. Its advantage on the road lay in its ability to go through the curves faster.

With its 4,710 pounds curb weight, the Cord needed 26 seconds to go from standstill to 50 mph with the normal 4.18:1 final drive ratio (4.42 and 4.82:1 were optional). Maximum speed was 77 mph.

The L-29 had a list price of $3,095 as sedan or brougham and $3,295 as a convertible or phaeton. Special bodies cost considerably more, and many Cord chassis received bodies by Murphy, Rollston, Union City, Freestone & Webb, and Weymann. The engine was bored out to 3.375 inches for 1932, raising power output to 125 hp, and although it had some effect on performance, it meant little in the market place.

There was little demand for a car like the Cord in 1932. It had been sensational in 1929, but it was not everyman's transportation. It was a prestige car, but its mechanical reliability failed to live up to its promise. Outer universal joints, for instance, needed constant maintenance, and even with the best attention, frequent expensive replacement was necessary.

The Cord went out of production after about 5,300 had been made. E. L. Cord concentrated on the Auburn during the depths of the depression, and it came through in better fashion than some bigger competitors.

Cornelius Van Ranst left Cord in 1930 to join Packard, where he created a front wheel drive prototype with a V-12 engine. He worked as chief development engineer at Packard until 1936, when he left to open his own engineering office. Ford engaged him in 1940 as chief of aircraft engine design, and he did a big V-12 which was redesigned as a V-8 tank engine. During the Fifties and Sixties, he designed and developed new marine engines for outside clients. He died in 1972, having been awarded 150 patents during his lifetime.

65. PIERCE ARROW SERIES B, 1930

During the 1920's the great cars from Buffalo were eclipsed by their leading rivals from Detroit and it was not until 1930 that a real comeback was made. It was as if Pierce-Arrow had suddenly found itself again. It wasn't just new management and a new engineering team, for the company had gone through waves of high-level changes for a decade, and the preceding upheavals had been disruptive rather than productive.

One misfortune after another befell the company. Taken singly none was perhaps very serious, but the cumulative effect was adverse with regard to the evolution of the product as well as the fortunes of the firm.

Charles Clifton assumed the title of chairman in 1919, but ownership of the company fell into the hands of George W. Goethals, constructor of the Panama Canal, who had served as head of Wright-Martin Aircraft during WWI. He installed his lieutenant, John C. Jay, Jr. as president of Pierce-Arrow. Jay and Clifton embarked on an ambitious scheme to expand production. New land was bought and ground broken for new factory buildings. A small fortune was spent on ordering new production equipment and tooling. This move coincided with a severe slump in the luxury car market.

In 1920 the chief engineer, David Fergusson, resigned. Two years later he held the same title at the James Cunningham & Sons Company. He was replaced by the young and brilliant Delmar G. Roos from Locomobile. There was a constant battle between the engineering department and the Goethals managers. Jay went back to New York in 1920, giving the presidency to his longtime henchman, George W. Mixter. By the end of 1921, the Goethals management came to an end and Myron E. Forbes was named president.

Forbes was an accountant from Jarvisburg, North Carolina, who had come to Pierce-Arrow as treasurer in 1919. He had been with John Deere since 1910, and was a friend of Mixter's. However, he was not the man Barney Roos wanted to work for, so

Barney returned to Locomobile. It took Forbes quite a while to find a new chief engineer. He chose an older, more pliable man in Charles Sheppy.

Under Sheppy, the cars were slowly modernized, but also cheapened. Under instructions from Forbes, Sheppy designed a medium-priced Pierce-Arrow Series 80 to sell as low as $2,895. Consulting engineer Otto M. Burkhardt led the design of a new L-head six for this car, rather than the old and expensive T-head units with four valves per cylinder. The L-head six for the Series 80 was a 288.6 cubic-inch unit rated at 70 hp—quiet, reliable, but lazy.

Sheppy died in 1927, and Charles Clifton retired, dying the following year. Forbes named John C. Talcott, chief experimental engineer since 1919, to the top technical post. Talcott was a fine engineer who had graduated from Cornell in 1909, joined Pierce Arrow, and was to spend his whole career there. The four-valve T-head design came from him. Talcott was then working on a new L-head straight-eight which was to replace the sixes across the board in 1929. But he did not live long enough to see it go into production, leaving the chief engineer's office empty again.

On the business end, Myron Forbes was disturbed at his inability to make the company profitable. The plant was inefficiently run and output was far below capacity. He welcomed a proposal from Albert R. Erskine, president of Studebaker, to merge the companies and exploit Pierce-Arrow's surplus capacity to mutual advantage. But as the majority stock-holder, Erskine held the power to make decisions and Forbes knew he had made a mistake. He resigned in 1929 and Erskine was named president of Pierce-Arrow.

Before he left, Forbes had appointed a new chief engineer in the person of Karl M. Wise, who had been executive engineer of Studebaker. Wise had an engineering degree from the University of Michigan and had been involved with cars since 1907 when he left his post as a draftsman with the Federal Manufacturing Co. in Cleveland to work on the engineering staff of the Wayne Automobile Company in Detroit.

He developed into a skilled metallurgist, held jobs with several motor vehicle manufacturers, and worked for some time with the Crucible Steel Company of America. He became assistant chief engineer of Chalmers, and later held the same position with Oldsmobile in Lansing. From there he went to Studebaker, and in 1928 he moved to Buffalo.

Together with C. Pleuthner he directed engineering and development of the 1930 models. The Series B received the

Talcott-designed straight-eight in its original size: 366 cubic inches (3.50 × 4.75 inches bore and stroke). It had a nine-bearing crankshaft and delivered 125 hp at 3,200 rpm. Maximum torque was a massive 250 pounds-feet at 1,200 to 1,300 rpm. It was an incredibly smooth engine, with a strong pull throughout its speed range.

A smaller version of the same engine with 339.6 cubic-inch displacement was installed in Series C which replaced the low-priced Series 81. The C engine had the same stroke as the Series B but a smaller bore of 3.375 inches, while Series A, the giant in the family, had the B's 3½-inch bore with a longer stroke of a full 5 inches, giving 385 cubic-inch displacement.

Cylinder blocks were cast in South Bend, but the design, which antedated the merger, was totally different from Studebaker's L-head straight-eight. The only relationship was a tenuous one in that the Studebaker engine was laid out by that company's new chief engineer, a former Pierce-Arrow man, Barney Roos, who had left Locomobile in 1926, served a brief guest performance at Marmon, and then went to South Bend.

Some Pierce-Arrow bodies were also produced in Studebaker's coachwork section. Many were built in Buffalo and many chassis were sent to the nation's best independent coachbuilders for special bodies (Fig. 6-2).

The series B chassis had a 138-inch wheelbase. Enormous, yes, but compared with the 147-inch wheelbase of the Series A, it could certainly be called an intermediate. Series C continued the 130-inch wheelbase of the former 80 and 81 lines.

The drive line was essentially the same in all three series. A three-speed transmission featured free-wheeling on second and top, easily engaged by pushing a button on top of the shift lever knob, and the rear axle had hypoid bevel gears. The driving thrust was not taken up by the long leaf springs but transmitted to the frame via a sturdy torque arm.

Four-wheel mechanical brakes were used, Wise preferring the Bendix duo-servo type with its lighter pedal pressures to any system with separate power assist or external-contracting bands. Drums were 16 inches in outside diameter, mounted on the hubs of disc or wire wheels carrying 6.00-18 tires.

Pierce-Arrow sold 7,000 cars in 1930, which was more than Lincoln or Peerless, but a long way behind Packard or Cadillac. Pierce-Arrow's plan, approved by A. R. Erskine and enthusiastically carried out by Karl M. Wise, was to create new products that would outstrip all competitors in terms of prestige and thereby build the kind of reputation that would assure the future of the make. We shall read about the results in an upcoming chapter.

66. MARMON SIXTEEN, 1931

The same straight-eight vogue that Pierce-Arrow was caught up in also affected Marmon. Marmon's last six was the "75" of 1926. The company then standardized an eight-cylinder engine for all models.

At the same time, Howard Marmon began working on a V-16—not at Marmon's engineering office but in a separate shop masquerading as the Midwest Aviation Company in Indianapolis. Nearly five years later, the V-16 went into a 1931-model (Fig. 6-3).

After a whole generation of sixes and eights with cast-iron blocks, Howard Marmon returned to his early love of aluminum for the V-16. The block, including both banks of cylinders and the upper crankcase, was a single aluminum casting, with nickel-molybdenum steel dry liners. The cylinder heads, with pushrod-operated overhead valves, were also made of aluminum. Aluminum was also used for the oil sump, clutch housing, pistons, and intake manifold. Banks were disposed at an ideal 45-degree included angle.

Howard Marmon's initial concept for the V-16 was to combine two Little Eights (an engine designed by Barney Roos and used in the Marmon Roosevelt) on a common crankcase. This would bring the advantage of interchangeable parts but it turned out that two Little Eights did not produce the power that Howard Marmon had set as the target for the Sixteen.

Consequently the cylinders were bored out from 2.75 to 3.875 inches, with retention of the 4-inch stroke, which resulted in a displacement of 490 cubic inches. It was the biggest engine ever produced by Marmon and the most powerful. Yet its complete weight, including all essential equipment such as carburetor and air cleaner, oil filter, starter and clutch, was no more than 930 pounds.

It delivered 200 hp at 3,400 rpm on a compression ratio of 6.0:1, which gave it the best power-to-weight ratio in the industry.

Connecting rods were paired on the crankpins in a fork-and-blade arrangement, and the 2-4-2-crankshaft ran in five main bearings. It carried no counterweights, which brought a further weight saving with the crankshaft weighing only 81.5 pounds. Each piston weighed only 12 ounces.

The camshaft was centrally located right above the crankshaft and driven by triple roller chain. Valves were mounted in line with

Fig. 6-2. The Pierce-Arrow Series B of 1930.

Fig. 6-3. The 1931 Marmon V-16 had the best power-to-weight ratio in the industry at the time.

the cylinder axis, with head diameters of 1.4 inches for the intake and 1.2 inches for the exhaust. Combustion chambers were domed and fully machined.

Full pressure lubrication was a matter of course, Marmon having been a pioneer in this area. The gear-type oil pump was driven by roller chain from the crankshaft. A dual water pump setup fed coolant to each bank from separate chambers, and the dual-coil ignition system relied on a single Delco-Remy distributor and a single spark plug for each cylinder.

Howard Marmon was concerned with providing the most uniform air-fuel mixture to all sixteen and adopted a Stromberg Duplex carburetor, an early version of the two-barrel principle. Exhaust manifolds were mounted on the outsides of the block, with gentle curves and wide, unrestricted passages.

This magnificent engine was matched with a twin-plate air-cooled Tower clutch and a three-speed transmission. Second-speed gears had helical teeth for quiet running, and synchromesh on second and top made for faster, easier shifting.

The rest of the vehicle was designed under the direction of George H. Freers, who had succeeded Thomas J. Litle, Jr. as chief engineer of Marmon in October, 1929. Freers was a graduate of Rose Polytechnic Institute and began his career with the Holcomb & Hoke Company. He entered the auto industry as a truck engineer with Alden-Sampson, and served briefly on Packard's engineering staff under Russell Huff. From there he went to United States Motors, and after its collapse in 1912, joined Inter-State in Muncie, Indiana. He came to Stutz after Harry Stutz left, and then linked up with Marmon, where he began as chief draftsman, going up the ladder to the post of chassis engineer, assistant chief engineer, and finally, chief engineer.

The chassis for the Marmon Sixteen had frame rails made of 7.5-inch channel-section steel, and both front and rear axles were carried on semi-elliptical leaf springs, damped by Gabriel triple-acting shock absorbers. Front springs were 42 inches long, and the rear ones 60 inches long. The front axle was of the reversed-Elliott type, and the rear axle had hypoid final drive gears with a 3.69:1 ratio.

With a 145-inch wheelbase, the Sixteen weighed about 5,000 pounds with one of the three standard bodies—coupe, five-passenger convertible, and seven-passenger limousine. They were built from designs by Walter Dorwin Teague, Jr., then a student at Massachusetts Institute of Technology, who did the drawings in his spare time and gave them to his father's industrial-design office. Naked chassis were supplied to independent coachbuilders, resulting in cars with curb weights in the 6,000 pound range.

Marmon produced only 390 Sixteens, which sold at remarkably reasonable prices; from $5,200 to $5,700. The bulk of the company's output from 1931 to 1933 was the eight-cylinder Series 70 and 88, but the depression wiped out the market even for those. From a total output of 5,768 cars in 1931, production fell to a mere 86 cars in 1933. The Marmon assets were liquidated in 1934.

Howard C. Marmon retired to Pineola, North Carolina, and died in Fort Lauderdale in 1943. George H. Freers linked up with an offshoot of the company, Marmon-Herrington, specialists in four-wheel-drive trucks, where he spent the rest of his career. He died in 1964 at the age of 78.

67. REO ROYALE, 1932

A few blocks down from the Oldsmobile plant in Lansing, Michigan, Reo had been producing modest numbers of low- and medium-priced cars for many years. Reo was indeed an unpredictable source for one of America's greatest cars. Reo had a historical link, as well as a geographical one, with Oldsmobile since both were founded by the same man, Ransom E. Olds. When he left the Olds Motor Works in 1904, he created a new trade mark from his initials and began building Reo cars (Fig. 6-4).

R. E. Olds was not an engineer. He could better be described as a mechanic turned entrepreneur. His choice of a chief engineer

Fig. 6-4. The Reo Royale, 1932.

was a happy one, for the great Royal of the Thirties was created by the same man who designed the first Reo in 1904. Horace T. Thomas was the man. He graduated with an engineering degree from Michigan Agricultural College in 1901 and had been working part-time with the Olds Motor Works since the year before. He left Olds in 1902 and worked for over two years with Columbia in Hartford, Connecticut. He returned to Lansing when R. E. Olds invited him to become chief engineer for Reo.

The first Reo cars were single-cylinder 8-hp runabouts with underfloor engines and dummy hoods, planetary transmissions and chain drive. A 16-hp twin followed in 1905, and a short-lived four appeared in 1906. Reo concentrated on its primitive but popular one- and two-cylinder models up to 1909. In those days, Reo was regularly out-producing Oldsmobile, which had moved up into higher price brackets.

Olds and Thomas understood that they had to update their product when they saw the success for Ford's Model T, and had their answer ready by 1911. It was called Reo the Fifth, and was powered by a 226-cubic-inch F-head four-cylinder engine (overhead intake and side exhaust valves).

Selling at $1,055 as a four-passenger touring car on a 115-inch wheelbase Reo the Fifth was a great success. In 1913 it was joined by a six-cylinder version on a 122-inch wheelbase, listed at $1,385. These F-head models carried Reo handsomely through 1918, and then the six temporarily disappeared.

The original six was cast in two blocks of three (the fours had cylinders cast in pairs). For 1920, the four was discontinued, and a new F-head cast-en-bloc six was standarized for the Model T, a rugged family car built on a 120-inch wheelbase, priced at $2,750 as a five-passenger sedan. The T-6 touring car was listed at $1,850.

By 1924, it evolved into the G-series. Its F-head engine now delivered 50 hp, and the price of the five-passenger sedan came down below $2,000. In the early Twenties, Reo had made heavy investments to expand plant capacity, and its products continued to sell well and bring good profits.

R. E. Olds had relinquished the title of president in 1923 assuming that of chairman, while Richard H. Scott took over as chief executive. Scott had been general manager and vice president of Reo since 1914. H. T. Thomas was preparing all-new cars which went into production in 1927. The new chassis featured four-wheel hydraulic brakes and modern, lower-cost L-head sixes replaced the F-head engines.

Graceful new bodies were designed and produced under the direction of George W. Kerr, who had joined Reo as body engineer in 1924. Kerr was the man who had set up the coachbuilding department for Knox in 1903 and created the elegant Stevens-Duryea bodies of 1910-15. He worked with Reo from 1915 to 1918, but was transferred to Racine, Wisconsin, on a war-production scheme. In 1920 he was works manager of the H & M Body Corporation, and in 1922/23 was in charge of coachbuilding for Rolls-Royce of America in Springfield, Massachusetts.

The low-priced Wolverine, powered by a Continental Six, was not a commercial success, but the Flying Cloud series, equipped with Reo's own engine, did extremely well in the marketplace. Flying Cloud bodies were produced by the Murray Corporation to designs by Fabio Segardi, former chief engineer of Oldsmobile.

In 1928 Reo had its best-ever year with an output of 29,000 cars, more than double the previous years's figure, and entirely due to the Flying Cloud. Richard H. Scott took this as a sign that the product line should be expanded further, reaching into higher price brackets. The Wolverine was discontinued in 1929 and a new eight-cylinder engine was developed. It was first used in the 1931 Flying Cloud.

Reo's Eight was basically the L-head with two extra cylinders. The developmental work was done by Frank Pearson, who had left Oldsmobile in 1929 to join Reo. He had graduated from the Massachusetts Institute of Technology in 1920 and was a full-fledged motor engineer by this time.

Reo's greatest car, the Royale, was mechanically a Flying Cloud Eight with special coachwork. The bodies were built by Murray, as were those for the Flying Cloud, but to new designs by Murray's chief engineer, Amos E. Northup, and a young stylist with an interest in aerodynamics, Julio Andrade.

Horace Thomas outdid himself in the engineering of the Flying Cloud Eight and Royale. The chassis had a 125-inch wheelbase and the car's overall length was 200 inches. The Royale body was wider than the Flying Cloud's, though both had the same wide stance, with a 60-inch reartrack and a 59-inch front track.

The four-wheel hydraulic brakes had internal-expanding shoes working in 15-inch drums, and the wire wheels carried 6.50 × 18 tires. Farval automatic chassis lubrication was standard. For 1933, Thomas adopted vacuum-boosted power brakes and a free-wheel device was added to the three-speed transmission (which had the refinement of herringbone gears).

The Royale engine had a displacement of 358 cubic inches (3.375 × 5.00-inch bore and stroke). The cast iron block was a one-piece casting with a detachable L-head. The crankshaft ran in nine main bearings. The Schebler updraft carburetor was a two-barrel design, and the fuel feed was assured by an AC mechanical pump. With a 5.3:1 compression ratio, the engine delivered 125 hp at 3,300 rpm.

The first Flying Cloud Eight had spiral bevel final drive, but for 1932 Reo adopted the hypoid bevel, with a 3.77:1 axle ratio. Hotchkiss drive was used, as on the six-cylinder models. The front axle was also carried by semi-elliptical leaf springs, and the front wheels were steered by Ross cam and lever.

By 1933 it was becoming clear that Scott had misjudged the market. It was the new general manager, William R. Wilson, and the six-cylinder models that pulled the company through the worst of the depression years. Wilson had been manufacturing manager with Studebaker in 1911 and worked with Dodge from 1914 to 1919. He was president of Maxwell until Walter P. Chrysler took it over. Later he reorganized the Murray Corporation, where he worked closely with Reo, and made the move to Lansing in 1930.

Scott resigned from the presidency of Reo in 1934 and was replaced by D. E. Bates. By 1936 he had led Reo out of the car business to concentrate on production of the Reo Speed Wagon trucks.

Horace Thomas gave up the post as chief engineer in 1933 and was made chief research engineer. He had developed a two-speed automatic transmission which became optional that year. The new chief engineer was R. J. Fitness, who had formerly worked for Cadillac, Packard, Studebaker, Dodge, Continental Motors, Marmon, and Handley-Knight.

In March, 1935 a tired Thomas, in ill health, left Reo and retired to Florida. Ransom E. Olds had retired from any active role in the management of Reo in 1930, but was brought back as chairman of the board in 1934, supervising the transition into truck production only and finally retiring in 1937. He lived on till 1950 when he died at the age of 86.

68. HUDSON EIGHT, 1932

Hudson was late in getting caught up in the straight-eight wave, introducing its first eight simultaneously with Buick in 1930. Hudson had prospered with its Super Six throughout the Twenties, steadily improving chassis and body construction while leaving the 288.6 cubic-inch engine basically unchanged from its 1916 specifications and with a modest output of 75 hp at 2,450 rpm (Fig. 6-5).

The Hudson Eight was created under the direction of Stuart G. Baits, who had become chief engineer of Hudson in June, 1928. Howard D. Coffin had played an increasingly nominal role as director of engineering since 1920, developing his interest in industrial standardization, good roads, and aviation, while spend-

Fig. 6-5. Stuart G. Baits' creation, the 1932 Hudson Eight.

ing less and less time working on the Hudson car. He resigned from Hudson in 1930 and moved to Georgia where he became interested in the cotton industry and real estate developments. He was seemingly busy in his new career until he was found dead one day in his summer home on Sapelo Island, an apparent suicide.

Stuart G. Baits was born in Dowagiac, Michigan in 1891, and had come to Hudson as a draftsman in 1915. That was his first job, for he had graduated from the University of Michigan in 1914 and stayed on for postgraduate work until a promising opportunity appeared. He worked in posts of growing importance under such chief engineers as Stephen I. Fekete and G. G. Behn, building up his qualifications for a top technical job.

Because of the coincidence in timing, comparison is invited between the Hudson and Buick eights but there were profound differences. The Buick was a new design with overhead valves (as Buick had always used since the start in 1903), while the Hudson was an L-head unit, based on the Essex six, with two additional cylinders. Moreover, Buick's eight completely replaced the six, while Hudson brought back its sixes as the mainstay of its production after two years of making eights exclusively.

The Hudson Eight was part of a less ambitious plan than Buick's, and the engine was not launched as a rival for the nation's most powerful, but as a smooth, reliable power unit with unusual fuel economy. Despite the modesty of its design objectives, the cars it powered include some of indisputable greatness.

With a maximum output of 80 hp at 3,400 rpm, the Hudson eight gave excellent performance, to a great extent because the cars it was installed in were light. Displacement was only 214 cubic inches (2.75-inch bore and 4.50-inch stroke). The eight was made with two cylinder heads, each covering four cylinders; while the six had a one-piece head. Like the earlier sixes, the eight had a balanced crankshaft with integral counterweights, and relied on splash lubrication. And Baits retained the wet-type cork clutch.

For 1931 the engine was bored out to 2.975 inches, raising its displacement to 233.7 cubic inches and maximum output to 87 hp at 3,600 rpm. The following year, bore size was increased to a full 3.00 inches, giving 254.1 cubic-inch displacement. Maximum output climbed to a creditable 101 hp at 3,600 rpm.

The 1930 Hudson Eight was 585 pounds lighter than the 1929 Super Six it replaced. Wheelbase had been shortened 3.5 inches, frame and suspension systems were lighter, and weight also had been saved in body construction. It seemed like a guaranteed success at Hudson's low prices: the 1931-model seven-passenger sedan was listed at only $1,295. But sales dropped, and production of Hudson cars was cut back from 113,000 cars to 17,000.

Attractive prices were intended to secure Hudson's popularity even in 1932, when the Super Six was brought back and the Eight split into three series: Standard Eight on a 119-inch wheelbase; Sterling Eight on a 126-inch wheelbase; and Major Eight on a 132-inch wheelbase. Weight of the Standard was trimmed to 3,115 pounds, down from 3,200 pounds in the 1931 model. All were extremely good-looking cars. Style, trim levels, and finish approached the Packard class.

The styling came from the drawing board of Frank S. Spring, former chief designer of the Murphy Body Company. Spring was an engineer, having served his early years with the Courier Car Co. in Sandusky, Ohio, and later studied engineering in France. He joined Murphy in 1920 and became its general manager in 1924. Murphy created several innovative body designs for Hudson and finally left Murphy for a position with the Detroit auto maker in 1931.

Roy D. Chapin held no office at Hudson in this period, serving as Secretary of Commerce in the Hoover administration. Former president and co-founder Roscoe B. Jackson died in 1929, and William J. McAneeny, who had joined Hudson as a purchasing agent in 1909, succeeded to the presidency. Instead of recovering when the 1932 models went on sale, Hudson fell deeper into the red ink.

The Hudson Eight was not to blame. It had been developed to a high stage of mechanical perfection.

Three-point rubber engine mounting reinforced the idea of smoothness and absence of vibration from the drive train. Baits added a free-wheel device on the three-speed transmission, which had synchromesh on second and top gears. The propeller shaft was enclosed in a torque tube which took up the driving thrust and minimized torque reactions in the rear axle, which had spiral bevel (not hypoid, yet) final drive.

Some parts of the specification were archaic, such as the cable-operated four-wheel brakes, and the vacuum-tank fuel feed. But the Marvel "Startix" carburetor was an innovation, as was the optional vacuum-operated clutch (the first step on Baits's way to the Electric Hand gearshift—a Bendix system adopted in 1935).

Among other refinements in the Hudson Eight were the adjustable steering wheel, dash-mounted starter button, adjustable seats front and rear, and Ditzler lacquer exterior finish.

The company, however, was in serious trouble. It declared a loss of two and a quarter million dollars in 1933, and Roy D. Chapin rushed back to take charge of things, kicking McAneeny upstairs as chairman of the board with no executive duties. He left the following year to become head of Hupmobile.

A. Edward Barit, McAneeny's understudy from the purchasing department, was named general manager and Baits was named assistant general manager while retaining his responsibilities as chief engineer.

The 1934-model Hudson Eight had its wheelbase cut from 119 inches to 116, and curb weight was pared to 2,905 pounds. Engine power was increased to 108 hp at 3,800 rpm, with a further raise to 113 hp in 1935 and 125 hp (with new high-compression heads) in 1936. The smaller, livelier cars saved the company. But for greatness, Hudson hit its apex with the Major Eight in 1932.

69. STUTZ DV 32, 1932

Since the debut of the Vertical-Eight "Safety Stutz" in 1926, every Stutz was a great car. The line was to culminate with the penultimate model produced, the fabulous DV-32 (Fig. 6-6).

It was soon joined by one designated SV-16, which is helpful in explaining the meaning of their names. All were derived from the Vertical Eight designed by Charles R. "Pops" Greuter, an in-line design with a single overhead camshaft, first used in the AA series. Power units of similar layout also powered the BB of 1928, the series L of 1929, the series M from 1929/30, and the MA and MB from 1931.

In 1930 Greuter redesigned the engine with twin overhead camshafts and splayed valves above hemispherical combustion chambers. The four-valve version came first, and its identification code DV-32 stands for Dual Valve, 32 in all. A slightly less performance oriented SV-16 meant simply Single Valve, 16 in all.

The 322 cubic-inch engine, with 3.375-inch bore and 4.5-inch stroke, used in the BB series was carried over in the L and M-series. In contrast with the 299-cubic-inch AA, which had two valves per cylinder, the BB had a three-valve combustion chamber for better breathing.

The three-speed BB transmission gave way to new four-speed ones on the L and M series introduced in 1929. Stutz did not make its own transmissions, but had its gearboxes built to order by specialist manufacturers. The four-speed unit was produced by Warner Gear, and included a 'no-back' device—a sprag that blocked reverse rotation in the output shaft and there-by prevented the car from rolling backwards when restarting on a hill.

Engines for the L and M series had dual coil ignition with two plugs per cylinder and breathed through Zenith carburetors fed from a vacuum tank.

Series L was the smaller car, built on a 127.5-inch wheelbase, while the M series was available in two wheelbases, 134.5 and 145 inches.

Both had worm-drive rear axles and four-wheel hydraulic brakes with vacuum power assist. Semi-elliptical leaf springs were used all around, damped by Lovejoy hydraulic shock absorbers. Automatic chassis lubrication by Bijur was standard.

The MA of 1931 had a top speed of 80 mph in stock form. The strength of the Stutz was not, surprisingly for an Indianapolis product, acceleration and top speed, but rather high cruising speeds, with excellent roadholding and a comfortable ride. Fuel consumption averaged 12-13 miles per gallon.

The animator of Stutz's recovery while in Charles M. Schwab's ownership, and instigator of its new-found greatness, Fred Moscovics, resigned from the Stutz presidency in 1929. The following year we find him as president of a firm called Improved Products Company. He retired from business in 1932, but volunteered his services to the military as an advisor on aircraft to

Fig. 6-6. Stutz DV-32 of 1932, with a total of 32 dual valves.

assist in the war effort in 1942. He was active with the A. O. Smith company in Milwaukee after the war, long after normal retirement age, and died at the age of 87 in 1967.

Charles M. Schwab replaced Moscovics with a former Marmon executive, Edgar S. Gorrell. Schwab no longer cared to keep his seat as chairman of the board, and named Edwin B. Jackson to replace him in that capacity. Jackson had formerly been associated with Packard, Willys, Wills Sainte Claire, and Locomobile. This was the management team that enabled Greuter to design and produce the twin-cam engine.

The DV-32 borrowed some of its principles from the Duesenberg J-Type engine, but it was not a copy of it. Greuter also knew there were other twin-cam engines he could copy if he wanted to, but the fact is he designed his own, or rather, converted his own single-overhead-camshaft head to twin-cam operation.

Some differences from the Duesenberg are pertinent. Valve guides sat lower down in the Stutz head, and its tappets were bigger. Stutz used single coil springs on the valves, while Duesenberg had double coils. The combustion chambers were shaped differently, the Stutz design being flatter.

The DV 32 was first seen outside the factory in January 1931 when a chassis was exhibited at the New York Automobile Show. It went into production the following April, with the lowest-priced model, a five-passenger coupe, listed at $4,895.

Due to the abundance of valves, one spark plug had to be omitted. A new Schebler carburetor fed by an AC mechanical fuel pump replaced the former Zenith setup. With a 5.5:1 compression ratio, the DV-32 pumped out 161 hp at 4,000 rpm. With closed bodywork, it could reach 90 mph with the standard 4.1:1 axle ratio.

The chassis was inherited from the MA, with a choice of two wheelbases: 134.5 and 145 inches. The Super Bearcat roadster with the DV-32 engine was built on a 116-inch wheelbase.

Bodies for the DV 32 were produced by such famous American Coachbuilders as Brunn, Derham, Locke, Rollston, and Waterhouse. Carrosserie Weymann of Paris also chose the Stutz chassis for some of its creations, (Stutz held the U.S. rights for the Weymann-patented light-weight body construction).

The original Stutz DV-32 had 4-speed Warner gearbox, but in 1932 Stutz switched to a 3-speed Muncie gearbox with widely spaced ratios. This was not done simply to save money, but because first gear was uselessly low and second gear was used for starting except in emergencies. At the same time, tire size was coming down from 6.20 × 20 to 6.50 × 18, which also affected the gearing.

Production of the DV-32 ended in 1932, the SV-16 being continued for another two years. Then 'Pops' Greuter went into retirement. The company was failing, having lost $315,000 in 1932 and $450,000 in 1933. It struggled on, manufacturing a line of Pak-Age-Car delivery vans in 1936-37, but to no avail. Stutz assets went on the auction block in the summer of 1938.

70. CADILLAC V-12 AND V-16, 1932

As president of Cadillac, Lawrence P. Fisher was not going to stake its traditional claim to leadership on an improved V-8 at a time when the company's worst rivals were preparing twelve- and sixteen-cylinder engines. Fisher instructed chief engineer Ernest W. Seaholm to look into both types of multicylinder engine, and to lay out new cars that would use them. Seaholm put Owen Nacker in charge of these engine projects and worked closely with Maurice Olley, an English engineer recently recruited from Rolls Royce, as chassis engineer. The aging W. R. Strickland retired in 1930.

Owen Nacker was a fast worker and got the V-16 ready for production by the end of 1929. It was introduced in January 1930, installed in a chassis stretched to a 148-inch wheelbase, the complete car with Fleetwood limousine body weighing some 6,300 pounds.

In contrast with the L-head Cadillac V-8, the V-16 had pushrod-operated overhead valves. In an effort to keep the valve gear quiet, Nacker used roller cam followers and an automatic zero-lash adjustment mechanism with hydraulic control on the input side of the pushrod.

The engine was designed as two straight-eights mounted on a common crankcase, with two individual cast iron blocks mounted at an included angle of 45 degrees. The crankcase was a giant, silicon-aluminum casting, but the complete engine ended up weighing more than 1,000 pounds. The forged carbon-steel crankshaft alone weighed 130 pounds, including its counter-weights. It ran in five main bearings and carried a harmonic vibration damper at the front end.

Connecting rods were molybdenum-steel drop forgings, mounted in side-by-side fashion, and the pistons, oddly, were nickel-iron castings. The reason Nacker did not use aluminum pistons was that the engine had to be super-quiet. Therefore he worked to avoid piston slap, and chose to make pistons from the same material as the cylinder walls. This gave them the same coefficient of thermal expansion, and pistons could run reliably, and without risk of scuffing, with extremely fine tolerances.

Externally, the engine was a work of art, something that Faberge could have admired despite its lack of color. Every bolt and pipe was chrome-plated. For contrast, the exhaust manifold was black porcelain. Finned rocker covers were polished aluminum with black enamel. All wiring was concealed, reinforcing the showpiece image.

Cadillac was less scientific in the engine mounting system. True, Chrysler had not yet invented "Floating Power," and all car makers were experimenting wildly with intricate systems. Cadillac settled on a five-point mounting with rubber blocks.

With a bore and stroke of 3.00 × 4.00 inches, the V-16 had a displacement of 452 cubic inches, and delivered 175 hp at 3,400 rpm with a 5.5:1 compression ratio.

Maximum torque was an incredible 360 pounds-feet at 1,800 rpm, which meant that the car could be set in motion in top gear—the same top gear that gave it a top speed of close to 90 mph. It was normal driving procedure to start in second, and shift into top at about 10 mph. Zero-to-sixty mph acceleration would be accomplished in less than 20 seconds using first gear up to 30 mph and second to over 50. The V-16 was decidedly not designed for fuel economy, however, and returned 5 to 7 miles to the gallon, depending on body type, load, and conditions.

One of the things that made the car so heavy was the chassis frame, with side members up to 9 inches in depth. Also, Olley and Seaholm decided that the engine torque necessitated a torque tube (as was in fact used on the latest V-8 Cadillac then in production) and the axle and torque tube assembly naturally was very heavy.

Both front and rear axles were carried on semi-elliptical leaf springs, those in the back being quite stiff and giving a firm ride. The left front spring was shackled at both ends, the front shackle floating between preloaded coil springs. This was a device to prevent shimmy, and Cadillac called it a steering modulator.

Cadillac's chief body engineer, C. O. Richards worked closely with Harley Earl and his staff at the Art & Color Section as well as with the Fisher body engineers and craftsmen who built the standard bodies for Cadillac. Richards had first joined Cadillac in 1909, and progressed from foundry work, pattern making and tool-making to tool engineering. He left in 1921 to go with R. H. Collins, Ben Anibal, and other Cadillac men who were unhappy

Fig. 6-7. Cadillac's 1932 V-12.

237

with Durant's rule. But after three years with Peerless in Cleveland, he returned to Cadillac as assistant body engineer, and was named body engineer in 1930 (Fig. 6-7).

Cadillac built 3,251 V-16 cars in a two-year period, and then discontinued the series (Fig. 6-8). Its companion, the V-12, introduced in September, 1930, was kept in production up to 1936.

Nacker had designed the two concurrently, with a maximum of parts interchangeability and shared dimensions and angles. Thus, the V-12 came to have the strange angle of 45 degrees between banks. This gave highly uneven firing intervals, but with scientific counterweighting of the crankshaft, the V-12 nevertheless ran with acceptable smoothness.

The V-12 had the same 4-inch stroke, but a bigger bore of 3.125 inches, which resulted in a displacement of 368 cubic inches. The crankshaft ran in four main bearings, with the connecting rods mounted side by side on the crankpins. The V-12 delivered 135 hp at 3,400 rpm and generated a peak torque of 284 pounds-feet at 1,200 rpm. Thus it had the same ability to start in top gear that the V-16 was famous for, and almost the same top speed.

The three-speed transmission, torque tube, and rear axle were shared with the V-16. Cadillac transmissions had used synchromesh since 1929, and now the 1932 models received redesigned units with constant-mesh helical gears for all forward speeds and ball bearings instead of rollers.

Both the V-12 and V-16 became available with a free-wheel device in 1932. It was actually a vacuum-operated clutch that disengaged the drive on command, and made it possible to shift gears without declutching on the overrun.

The four-wheel mechanical brakes were, if anything, the Achilles heel of Cadillac's mastodons. The rear wheel brakes were operated by rods, the front ones by cable. Fortunately, vacuum power assist was standard.

The V-12 had a standard wheelbase of 134 inches and an optional 140-inch long wheelbase. The Fisher-bodied 1932 model V-12 touring car weighed 5,190 pounds, the sedan about 5,600. Prices ranged from $3,495, to $4,195 for models with body by Fisher. Cadillac also catalogued some Fleetwood bodied V-12 models, with prices up to $4,945.

Throughout the V-12 and V-16 years, the L-head Cadillac V-8 remained in production and accounted for the bulk of the company's production and sales. The multicylinder experience may have been a great prestige-builder vis-a-vis the public, and something of a

Fig. 6-8. The 1932 Cadillac V-16.

morale-builder internally, but it was an experience that was bought at a high price.

Times were changing fast, and Cadillac's concept of future greatness was formed along totally different lines. The results were to come forth in just a few years.

71. CHRYSLER IMPERIAL CUSTOM 8, 1932

At the height of his career, Walter P. Chrysler, the nation's third biggest auto maker, (having swallowed up Dodge and challenged Ford and Chevrolet with his Plymouth) chose the 1932-model Chrysler Imperial Custom Landau as his personal car (Fig. 6-9).

This machine was to him what the most expensive Lincoln was to Henry Ford and the hottest, costliest Cadillac was to William S. "Big Bill" Knudsen of General Motors.

The chassis had evolved from an earlier generation of Imperials and a new styling theme had been found, with narrow

Fig. 6-9. Chrysler Imperial Custom Eight of 1932.

V-profile radiator shells and front fenders with very long skirts, accentuating the length of the hood covering the straight-eight engine.

Chrysler introduced its first eight-cylinder engine in 1931, replacing the former six in the Imperial. It had a displacement of 384.8 cubic inches and delivered 125 hp at 3,200 rpm with the standard compression ratio of 5.2:1. Maximum torque was 260 pounds-feet at 1,200 rpm. Basically, it was designed as the classic Chrysler L-head six with two additional cylinders. The 5-inch stroke was retained, and the bore cut back to the original E-80 dimension of 3.5 inches (from 3.625 in the L-series).

A new nine-bearing crankshaft was developed with larger-diameter main bearings and greater crankpin overlap. It drove a side camshaft via silent chain, and the camshaft was geared to a slanted shaft that drove the oil pump and ignition distributor, just as on the six-cylinder Chrysler.

Chrysler led the industry in going to a downdraft carburetor in 1931. It was a new Stromberg product with two large-diameter throats arranged to open in sequence, so as to maintain air flow velocity under light load and assure good low-end torque, while providing a tremendous increase in flow mass on wide-open throttle.

The Imperial chassis with its 145-inch wheelbase was as modern as could be, with revised hydraulic four-wheel brakes, low-friction steering gear, and various suspension improvements.

Bigger changes still were slated for 1932. First, the Floating Power three-point engine suspension system first used on the low-priced Plymouth was adopted on the Imperial. Fred Zeder had worked it out in theory, and arranged the mounting points so that the engine's torque-reaction axis coincided with its center of gravity. The result was that rocking and vibration were not transferred to the frame and body, but were absorbed in the rubber mounts.

A free-wheel unit and an automatic clutch were added to the drive line. The automatic clutch was controlled by manifold vacuum, disengaging whenever the engine was freed of load, enabling the driver to shift gears by merely backing off the throttle and moving the lever. The free-wheel was a cam and roller device, which the driver put in or out of action by a button on the gear lever.

Next, the Imperial frame was redesigned, as a double-drop bridge-type which lowered the floor of the passenger compartment and therefore the whole body. A central cross-bracing added torsional stiffness that the straight cross-members could not provide.

Wheelbase was stretched one inch to 146, and a new I-beam front axle replaced the former tubular one. A kick shackle with a rubber buffer against the frame was added on the left front spring to counteract shimmy. Oilite discs were inserted between all leaves in the springs, front and rear, to control interleaf friction and assure consistent springing characteristics.

Hotchkiss drive was retained, the rear springs having proved capable of withstanding the drive thrust without too much bending. Tire size was changed to 7.50 × 17 from 6.50 × 18, aiding ride comfort as well as improving handling. The Chrysler Imperial of 1932 was fully comparable with Packard in both areas, and certainly ahead of other rivals.

The new styling adopted by Chrysler was undoubtedly inspired by the Cord L-29. The V-profile grille, tapering towards the lower end, and the wide, sweeping fender lines, first appeared in the sketches made by a young designer on Herbert Henderson's Art & Color staff, Herbert Weissinger. Henderson asked him to develop the theme for a car of the Imperial's proportions. The results were immediately approved by Oliver Clark, body engineer, and Walter P. Chrysler was also enthusiastic about the new design.

New chassis were developed to fit the new-style bodies, in a complete reversal of former procedures at Chrysler. Until the 1931-models were created, the chassis was finished before the body designers and engineers were invited to dress it. Zeder, Breer and Skelton, who were responsible for all technical decisions at Chrysler, were sufficiently interested in styling to have taken the initiative in making procedural changes. It made sense to them that the car's appearance should be part of any new car project since its inception, and this enlightened attitude enabled engineers and designers to work together as a team rather than oppose each other.

Chrysler bodies were manufactured by Briggs in Detroit, and that included the Imperial. Briggs also built the Le Baron bodies which adorned a number of Imperials. Many Imperial chassis were also outfitted with special bodies by such famous coachbuilders as Derham, Locke, Murphy, and Waterhouse.

All remained faithful to Herb Weissinger's theme, and the cars invariably looked extremely powerful and speedy. They did in fact possess the performance to live up to their looks. The 1932 Imperial Custom 8 had a top speed of 96 mph, and could accelerate from stand-still to 60 mph in under 20 seconds.

For 1933 the official title of the car was changed from Imperial Custom Eight to Custom Imperial, but the car was practically unchanged technically, though the styling continued to evolve.

Compression ratio was increased to 5.8:1, which raised output to 135 hp at 3,200 rpm, and increased maximum torque to 280 pounds-feet at 1,200 rpm. The low-compression engine remained available as an option.

A short-chassis Imperial (not Custom) on a 135-inch wheelbase had been added in 1932, using the same 125 hp engine as the senior models. For 1933 the Imperial Eight received a smaller engine of 298.7 cubic-inch displacement, obtained by reducing the bore to 3.25 inches and the stroke to 4½ inches. The car was made substantially lighter by reducing its wheelbase to 125 inches.

The year 1933 was the last for the classic Imperial, for the following year all Imperials were built with Carl Breer's Airflow bodies. When the Imperial and Custom Imperial were brought out of their Airflow phase for 1937, they shared the massproduced (by Briggs) sheet metal with the regular Chrysler models, and the magic was gone.

72. STUDEBAKER PRESIDENT EIGHT, 1933

Studebaker's rise to greatness was not gradual, as in the case of most other cars, but rather abrupt. For ages, Studebaker cars had been dull, low- and medium-priced transportation. Then, suddenly, great cars began pouring out of the big factories in South Bend, Indiana. The reason can be traced to the arrival of one man with a strong will, a dream, and the ability to carry it out. That man was Delmar G. "Barney" Roos, who took over as chief engineer of Studebaker in 1928.

Studebaker had been in the car business since 1904, but not as manufacturers. From 1904 to 1908, the cars sold by Studebaker were produced by Garford in Elyria, Ohio. From 1908 to 1911, Studebaker handled the EMF (Everitt-Metzger-Flanders) built in Detroit to designs by William Kelly.

That year Studebaker bought the EMF company and hired Don M. Ferguson as chief car engineer. The South Bend works were still producing horse drawn wagons, and the cars were built in Detroit. Ferguson designed a four on a 108-inch wheelbase and a six on a 121-inch wheelbase that went into production in 1913.

In 1914, Ferguson was replaced by Fred M. Zeder as chief engineer, while James G. Heaslet served as vice president for both engineering and production. Zeder created new cars for 1916, a Special Six and a Big Six, while the four continued with minor changes. Under a new president, Albert R. Erskine, who replaced Federick S. Fish in 1915, more and more of the car production tasks were transferred to South Bend and though Studebaker built its last wagons in 1919, it was not until 1925 that all phases of car production had been consolidated in South Bend.

Zeder left in 1920, after finishing a new Light Six to replace the four-cylinder series, and Guy P. Henry took over as chief engineer. He had been on Studebaker's engineering staff since 1911, but it was Vincent Link, who had joined Studebaker as a consultant on truck engineering in 1917, who led the product development in the early Twenties. The Light Six grew into the Standard Six, and new Special Six and Big Six models were developed. Barney Roos joined the company as assistant chief engineer in 1926 and was moved into the chief engineer's chair when Guy Henry resigned two years later to take over a Studebaker dealership in North Carolina.

The 1928-model President Eight was Roos's first dramatic contribution to Studebaker. The engine was an L-head design with a five-bearing crankshaft, gear-driven camshaft and one-piece cylinder head. With a bore and stroke of 3.375 × 4.375 inches, it had a displacement of 312.5 cubic inches and delivered 100 hp at 2,600 rpm.

This was not sufficient to meet performance goals Roos had for the President Eight, which was built on a 131 inch wheelbase and had a curb weight of 4,000 pounds. So in mid-year 1928, engine size was increased to 337 cubic inches (3.50 × 4.375 inches bore and stroke). Output was pushed to 115 hp at 3,200 rpm, and a short-wheel-base (121 inches) President was added. As a five-seater sedan, good for a genuine 80 mph, the President Eight had an attractive price of $1,985. The President name had first been used in 1927 as a replacement for the trite Big Six label.

For 1929, the President Eight came with wheelbases of 125 and 135 inches. John Warner was head of chassis experimental engineering and had perfected the Hotchkiss drive to take the torque of the eight-cylinder engine. He had also adapted Houdaille hydraulic shock absorbers and four-wheel mechanical brakes to the new chassis with its double-drop frame. Warner was an engineering graduate from Worcester Polytechnic Institute who had worked for the U.S. Bureau of Standards before joining Studebaker.

It was in engine development that Barney Roos concentrated his interest. The 1929 President Eight was equipped with dual coil ignition, AC mechanical fuel pump, and a two-barrel Stromberg carburetor with automatic choke. The following year he added vacuum-controlled spark advance (which Chrysler adopted in 1932).

Body design had long been a weak point in Studebaker cars (remember, the Studebaker brothers had been wagon builders, not carriage makers), with a general lack of distinction and often a poor eye for proportions. That began to change in 1931 when James V. Hughes was named body engineer. As the chassis became lower and the wheels smaller, body lines were sharpened to emphasize the new low and wide look. Headlamps were used as decorations for the chrome-plated radiator shell, and twin spare wheels in the front fenders made the hood seem longer.

The standard 125-inch wheelbase was retained for 1931, and the long-chassis wheelbase stretched to 136 inches. The engine had been redesigned with nine main bearings in June, 1930, and the crankshaft was equipped with a Lanchester-type vibration damper having a centrifugal governor continuously resetting damper tension according to engine speed. At the same time, light alloy pistons were adopted.

All 8-cylinder Studebaker cars for 1931 were equipped with a free-wheel unit which allowed coasting in second and third. A lockout knob on top of the gear lever made for easy engagement at any speed. Wire wheels were adopted, with tire size coming down from 21 to 20 inches. The brake system was still mechanical, but 15-inch drums were adopted, with the Bendix duo-servo shoe arrangement. All springs were fitted with gaiters, and the spring shackles were equipped with ball bearings.

For 1932 the three-speed transmission was given synchromesh on second and top gears, while a downdraft carburetor and higher compression ratio raised engine output to 122 hp at 3,200 rpm. Tire size was changed to 6.50-18, which improved both ride and handling.

The President Eight for 1933 had entirely new styling, with a rakish slope on the radiator shell and filled-in fender skirts, starting a trend that was to be widely copied. Tire size went to 7 × 17, emphasizing the wide stance of the car (Fig. 6-10).

Fig. 6-10. Another Roos' masterpiece, the 1933 Studebaker President Eight.

The engine was remarkably flexible as well as willing to run endlessly at full speed. The car could reach 75 mph in top gear, and would do 50 in second. At the same time, it was willing to pull top gear from 4 or 5 mph upwards, quietly and without snatching in the drive line, gaining speed as smoothly as the new diesel-electric locomotives then coming into use. It would go from 5 to 55 mph in top gear in 30 seconds. Fuel mileage was about 12-14 miles per gallon, which must be regarded as quite reasonable for a machine of that size and weight.

That year Studebaker fell into receivership. A. R. Erskine committed suicide, and it was the concerted action of Harold S. Vance, the production boss, and Paul G. Hoffman, sales director, that pulled the company through the crisis.

The Studebaker product evolved in tune with the needs of the depression market, and the 1934 President was given a smaller version of the eight-cylinder engine with 256 cubic-inch displacement (shared with the Commander series). Studebaker kept the President label alive until 1942. As for Barney Roos, he left South Bend in 1936 and spent two years in England, modernizing the Humber and Hillman cars for the Rootes brothers, returning to the U. S. in 1938 as vice president of engineering for Willys-Overland in Toledo. He retired in 1953 and died in a Philadelphia hospital during the winter of 1960.

73. PACKARD TWELVE, 1933

Seeing V-12 and V-16 engines appearing from several other car companies in 1930-31 led Packard's engineering director, Jesse G. Vincent, to dream of reviving the Twin-Six. For Packard to maintain its reputation for advanced engineering in those days, something with more than eight cylinders was needed (Fig. 6-11). The aim was not to get even with Cadillac, Marmon, Peerless, Lincoln, or Pierce-Arrow. It was, quite simply, to outdo them.

For this valiant attempt, Vincent chose a chassis with a 147-inch wheelbase. He designed a frame with side members up to 8 inches in depth and hefty cross-bracing, and semi-elliptical springs for both front and rear axles. Wide-rim wire wheels were shod with 7.5 × 17 balloon type whitewall tires. Into this chassis Vincent dropped his new V-12 engine and its three-speed transmission. The naked chassis weighed 3,965 pounds, so that complete cars weighed between 5,500 and 6,500 pounds, according to body style and construction (Fig. 6-12).

Fig. 6-11. The 1931 Packard Eight, forerunner of the Twelve.

The engine was built up as two six-cylinder cast iron blocks mounted on an aluminum crankcase. The cylinder heads were also made of aluminum. Despite such generous use of light alloys, the engine-and-transmission assembly weighed a massive 1,346 pounds.

That's a lot, even for an output of 160 hp. The cylinders had a 3.44-inch bore and a 4-inch stroke, which gave a displacement of 445.5 cubic inches. It was, in fact, a low power-to-weight ratio, about half of Duesenberg's and inferior to Chrysler's, for instance. Vincent chose to understress the engine in the interest of long life and reliability, but with the Twelve he opted for needlessly wide safety margins.

Maximum power was delivered at 3,000 rpm, and its torque curve was highest—348 pounds-feet—between 1,200 and 1,400 rpm.

The Twelve was marketed as the Twin-Six in 1932, its first year, to commemorate Packard's successful V-12 from 1915-23. But when the 1933 models were announced, they bore the "Twelve" designation.

Fig. 6-12. The 1933 Packard Twelve.

At the same time, engine displacement was increased to 473 cubic inches by adding a quarter-inch to the stroke and the compression ratio was raised from 6.0:1 to 6.4:1. This raised maximum output to 175 hp at 3,400 rpm, and boosted peak torque to 366 pounds-feet in the same 1,200 to 1,400 rpm band.

Vincent had chosen several unusual solutions in the design of this engine. It was an L-head in principle, but an L-head with a difference, for the valves were about 20 degrees from horizontal, between cylinder banks angled at 67 degrees to each other. A single central camshaft was used, driven by chain from the crankshaft. Roller followers riding against the cams were mounted on bell-crank rocker arms with separate rocker shafts for each bank. The valve-stem end of the rocker arms carried automatic zero-lash adjusters with hydraulic control, which made for extremely silent valve operation.

Ideally, a V-12 should have an included angle of 60 degrees between the banks to give perfectly even firing intervals. But the valve gear could not be accommodated inside that narrow space, so Vincent bent the V outwards to 67 degrees, accepting the loss of even power pulses. He had a secondary purpose in deviating from the ideal angle. Perhaps it was not so ideal from a vibration view-point? Even firing could set up harmonic torsional vibrations in the crankshaft, which could be broken up by alternating between firing intervals of 67 and 53 degrees.

The result was an extremely smooth engine, whether it was due to the 67-degree angle, or in spite of it. The crankshaft was a chrome-steel forging, which ran in four main bearings, with connecting rods mounted side by side on crankpins.

The Bohnalite pistons were of a full-skirted conetopped design, taking advantage of the valve angle to make a more compact combustion chamber. The spark plugs were inserted vertically and did not reach the center of the combustion chamber, but only the corner farthest from the piston. Packard built its own two-barrel downdraft carburetor for the first of the Twelves, mounted high on top of the intake manifold. The exhaust manifold straddled the intake manifold like an octopus, its squared-off cast iron contrasting with the round-shaped bright aluminum of the intake manifold. Later models were equipped with Stromberg carburetors.

At the start of production, the Twelve had a 4.69:1 axle ratio, which was so short-geared that it rendered the 2.45:1 first gear useless. Even after the axle was changed to a 4.41:1 ratio, second-gear starts were normal, and the car could of course, be moved off the line in top gear. It would even climb a 10-percent gradient in top gear at a steady 5 mph! That same top gear, with the 4.41 axle, was good for a top speed of 75 mph. Acceleration was reasonably quick in top gear, and quite impressive through the gears. But gasoline mileage was necessarily poor, averaging 7 to 9 miles to the gallon in all-around use.

Along with Henry Ford, Vincent resisted the coming switch to hydraulic brakes, and put Bendix four-wheel mechanical brakes on the Twelve. He added a unique refinement by adding vacuum power assist with selective control. The driver had a four-position handle on the instrument panel for setting the amount of power assist he wanted.

The Twelve had slow-geared worm and roller steering, which needed a lot of muscle for parking despite the 18-inch diameter steering wheel. At speed, however, the steering was light, pleasant and accurate.

The engine was mounted in a four-point suspension system well back in the frame, giving even weight distribution between front and rear. This was important for proper balance and good roadholding. The Twelve was not as nimble as the Eight of the same era, but high average speeds on country roads were still possible without loss of ride comfort.

Packard gave up building its own shock absorbers in 1930 and switched to Delco hydraulic ones with manual adjustment from the driver's seat to give the right amount of damping for varied road conditions.

A four-speed transmission became available on the 1934 models. It used straight-cut gears and was noticeable for a certain whine that was absent in the three-speed units.

Standard bodies were designed by Edward Macauley, son of Packard's president Alvan Macauley, together with Werner Gubitz, who had been active as a body engineer and designer at Packard since the Twenties. Catalogued custom bodies were made by Dietrich and Le Baron. Prices for standard-bodied models started at $3,820 and stopped at $6,435. Models bodied by Le Baron reached up into the $7,200-$7,500 bracket.

Packard produced about 2,500 Twelves from the start in 1932 through 1934. E. F. Roberts was vice president in charge of manufacturing, but retired in 1935, having come to Packard as a toolmaker in 1903. The V-12 remained in production through the 1939 model year and a total of 5,744 Twelves were built. They were high-quality cars to the end, but belonged to an era that was past before the design was completed.

74. PIERCE ARROW V-12, 1933

All makers of prestigue cars were striving for a multicylinder engine in 1930, and Pierce-Arrow was no exception. Sixes had been replaced by eights in 1928, and now the engineering staff was busy designing a V-12. Chief engineer Karl M. Wise actually laid it out towards the end of 1929, and it went into production in November, 1931, as a 1932 model. The V-12 was an addition to the line and did not replace the straight-eight (Fig. 6-13).

It was originally built in two sizes, one having a displacement of 398 cubic inches, and the other 429. Both had the same 4-inch stroke, the difference being in the bore: 3.25 inches on the smaller engine, and 3.375 inches on the bigger one. They developed 140 hp and 150 hp respectively, with a compression ratio of 5.05:1 at 3,400 rpm. Maximum torque was 355 and 375 pounds-feet at 1,250 rpm.

The smaller V-12 did not get much use, for Pierce-Arrow test drivers discovered that the eight-cylinder models, with lighter chassis and coachwork powered by the 385 cubic-inch engine rated at 135 hp were just as fast. Only the 429 cubic-inch V-12 survived the first year of production.

The V-12 layout was interesting, for Wise chose an 80-degree included angle between the cylinder banks. It was chosen partly for better breathing, partly for better accessibility to the valve gear (for adjustment), and to some extent, as a means of breaking up harmonic vibrations periods that might occur at certain speeds in V-12's with the ideal 60-degree angle between banks.

Cylinder heads were one-piece iron castings with machined combustion chambers. An L-head design, with the valves were housed in the block, line up in parallel with the cylinder axes on the insides of the V so that both intake and exhaust manifolds came down through the center.

The two blocks were of cast iron, bolted to an aluminum crankcase with an enormous flywheel housing. The blocks were offset relative to each other to permit side-by-side mounting of the connecting rods on the same crankpins. The seven-bearing crankshaft had twelve integrally forged counterweights.

Engines were assembled with the greatest precision. Pistons, rings, wrist pins and connecting rods were carefully balanced to the finest tolerances, and classed so that all sets destined for the same engine matched each other exactly in weight. The fit of the pistons in the bore was meticulously checked by ribbon-gauge measurement. All engines were not only bench-tested but received a basic break-in equivalent to about 900 miles of highway driving.

For 1933 the engine received hydraulic valve lifters, patented by a young engineer in the Pierce-Arrow drawing office, Carl Voorhies. He later went to Wilcox-Rich and ended up at Eaton as a valve and valve-gear specialist.

Russell T. Howe was chief development engineer for engines and worked steadily to improve the power units. Compression ratio was increased to 6.0:1, which raised the output of the 429 cubic-inch engine to 160 hp at 3,400 rpm. An optional V-12, bored out to 3½ inches and 462 cubic-inch displacement, was added. It delivered 175 hp, with a maximum torque of 377 pounds-feet.

Louis R. Jones was in charge of chassis engineering, reporting to C. Pleuthner, who was head of the car engineering office. Other key technical men were Maurice A. Thorne, S. Mills, and O. C. Kreis, the latter being responsible for coordination with Studebaker.

The 1933 Pierce-Arrow V-12 chassis came in two lengths, one with a 142-inch wheelbase, the other with a 147-inch wheelbase. Frame design was based on the 137-inch wheelbase eight-cylinder models, carrying the same suspension systems and steering gear. An engine suspension system with no less than 8 mounts served to hold the power unit in its place, but also revealed a basic lack of understanding of the problems involved on the part of Wise and his crew.

Mechanical four-wheel brakes were standard on all Pierce Arrows, but in 1933 the vacuum power brakes were replaced by a Stewart-Warner mechanical power assist, which was used until 1935 when the vacuum type was brought back.

Free-wheeling had been adopted for the Eight in 1931, and was standard on the V-12's since 1932. The three-speed transmission incorporated the latest developments from Cadillac, such as helical second-speed gears, and synchromesh on second and third.

A pushbutton starter broght the engine to life, and another dash-mounted control lever served to adjust the shock absorber valving for softer or stiffer damping.

Body styling reached new heights as Pierce-Arrow in the early Thirties under the influence of Lincoln, Packard, and fashionable custom-built bodies stealing the limelight at automobile shows everywhere. Pierce-Arrow remained faithful to the fender-mounted headlamps, and adopted new, imposing radiator shells as hoods grew longer. The cars also became lower as wheel diameters were reduced without ever losing their dignity and balance. The 1933 Pierce-Arrow was a true masterpiece of design.

Prices were sensationally low, having been reduced year by year since 1930. The lowest-priced V-12 in 1933 was a Club Brougham listed at $2,785, and prices for the Eight started at $2,385.

But instead of flocking to Pierce-Arrow showrooms, the public postponed car-buying plans or took their trade elsewhere. During 1933, Pierce-Arrow sold only 2,152 cars and the company was headed for bankruptcy. Under Studebaker ownership since 1928, Pierce-Arrow now shared the troubles of Studebaker's over-expansion as well as its own basic problems of low productivity and poor merchandising.

Studebaker boss Albert R. Erskine gave up the presidency of Pierce-Arrow in 1932, but installed a Studebaker executive, Arthur J. Chanter in that office. When Studebaker fell into receivership in 1933, it new managers, Vance and Hoffman, gladly accepted an offer from a group of Buffalo businessmen to buy back Pierce-Arrow for a paltry sum of $1 million plus some other considerations.

Chanter was reelected president, and told stockholders that the company could break even on an annual output of 3,000 cars and make a million-dollars profit if 4,000 cars could be sold in a year. Both targets proved far beyond reach, however. The company struggled on till 1938, adding a line of Travelodge trailers to keep the plant busy and meet the payroll, but it still ended in liquidation.

The 1935 to 1938 models were developed under the direction of Leroy Maurer, for Karl M. Wise had left Buffalo in 1934 to go to work for Bendix Aviation as a special advisor. In 1938 he was named director of engineering for Bendix Products Division, where he worked together with F. W. Davis, former truck engineer of Pierce-Arrow, to perfect a hydraulic power steering system. He retired from Bendix in 1945.

75. LINCOLN MODEL KB, 1933

Bodies by Judkins, Willoughby, Murphy, Brunn, Murray, and Waterhouse graced the car that was perhaps the greatest Lincoln of all time, the fabulous KB of 1933 (Fig. 6-14). Prices ranged from $4,300 to $7,400, and curb weights often exceeded 6,000 pounds. Still, the KB was known for its tremendous acceleration, with a time of 33 seconds going from zero to 80 mph. Top speed was 95-96

Fig. 6-13. Another great Pierce-Arrow of the Thirties: the V-12 of 1933.

Fig. 6-14. Lincoln KB of 1933, Le Baron convertible roadster.

and it was capable of cruising at 80 as long as road conditions would allow.

Its 150-hp V-12 engine was combined with a three-speed transmission, and experts got the fastest acceleration by shifting out of first at 15 mph, and from second to third at about 30 mph.

The immediate pedigree for the KB starts with Model K of 1931. It was a replacement for the aging Model L, and the K engine was a 60-degree V-8, which can be described as a Ford redesign—by Frank Johnson—of Leland's original Lincoln engine. No change was made in the crank arrangement with fork and blade connecting rods, bore and stroke, or material specifications. The two blocks and separate crankcase were similar iron castings.

Among detail improvements in Model K was the replacement of the Delco starter/generator of the Model L by separate generator and starter units by AutoLite. A new downdraft carburetor was adopted, with freer-breathing manifolds.

The chassis was a totally new creation, with a 145-inch wheelbase and 7 × 9 tires. The frame had side members up to 9 inches in depth, with a multitude of cross members to provide a suitable base for a variety of standard and custom bodies.

Both front and rear axles were carried by semi-elliptical leaf springs, and the full-floating rear axle was bolted to a rugged torque tube. Houdaille hydraulic shock absorbers were used, and cable-operated Bendix duoserve brakes replaced the Lockheed system used on Model L. Gemmer worm and roller steering gear was adopted in place of the earlier worm and sector type.

The KB inherited this chassis in 1932, but had a totally new V-12 engine. This combination led to a chassis weight of 4,350 pounds! It was an original Frank Johnson design, with banks laid out at 65 degrees, L-heads, and fork-and-blade connecting rods. The fully counter-balanced crankshaft was supported by seven main bearings of uncommonly large size. Bore and stroke were 3.25 × 4.50 inches, giving a displacement of 448 cubic inches. Maximum output, probably underestimated at 150 hp, was delivered at 3,400 rpm.

The V-8 was kept in production during 1932, but installed in a shortened Model K chassis with 136-inch wheelbase. This combination was labeled Model KA.

The following year, Model KA went to a V-12 engine without altering its name. The KA V-12 was not a smaller version of the KB engine, but a different design with the banks disposed at a 67-degree included angle.

Power output from the KA V-12 was 125 hp at 3,400 rpm from its 381.7 cubic-inch displacement. It had the same 4½-inch stroke as the KB but a smaller 3-inch bore. Keeping identical strokes could have enabled Johnson to use the same crankshaft in both engines, but that was not the case. The KA went to a lighter crankshaft with only four main bearings. As another major difference from the KB design, connecting rods were mounted side by side (and the blocks offset correspondingly).

Curiously, the KA engine was suspended in a four-point mounting system whereas the KB engine had three point mounting. The KB continued into 1933 with few engineering changes, the major items being a redesigned frame, now with diagonal cross-bracing, and manual adjustment of the power-brake assist. New and elegant bodies were created for that season.

Body engineer Henry Crecelius worked in close liaison with approved coachbuilders making catalogued Lincoln bodies. His role was not that of a creator but a critical customer, known for his impeccable but conservative taste. A sloping V-front radiator surmounted by the leaping greyhound hood ornament was used on all 1933-model KB's.

Prices were not as astronomical as one might think on first viewing the car. The lowest priced KB was a $4,300 coupe. Of course, custom-bodied models reached far higher, the range going from $5,700 to $7,300.

Naturally, the KB was not a big seller, but Edsel Ford was distressed that only 582 had been built in 1933 and decided to eliminate it. Both the KA and KB designations disappeared at the start of the 1934 model year and all Lincolns were identified simply by the letter K. V-8 models had been discontinued at the end of 1932.

The new K continued the same chassis in both 136- and 145-inch wheelbases, but standardized a new version of the smaller V-12 (KA) engine. It was bored out from 3.00 to 3.125 inches giving 414 cubic inch displacement, raising output to 150 hp at 3,400 rpm.

At the same time an oil cooler was added and the cast iron cylinder heads were replaced by new ones made of aluminum, which lightened the engine and made for faster heat dispersion from the combustion chambers.

This engine, and the new K, remained in production through 1940, but Ford was losing money on the Lincoln every year and kept it alive mainly for reasons of pride and prestige.

There was to be another great Lincoln before WW II, created by a different team of designers and engineers, and its story is the subject of another chapter.

Chapter 7
More Great Cars
of the Depression: 1934-1939

It took nearly 15 years of auto production and close to a million cars before Nash joined the ranks of America's truly great cars. Nash had started in 1917 with a line of medium-priced cars competing against Willys-Overland, Dodge, Oakland, and Studebaker. Nash's road to greatness was long and determined, thoroughly based on quality and advanced engineering, free of whim, fashion, and frivolity. Charles W. Nash was himself a stern character not given to flights of fancy, and he ran his organization as a model of his personal mentality.

76 NASH AMBASSADOR 8, 1934

Charles W. Nash was close to normal retirement age before he felt the need to expand the Nash range upwards in price, performance, and prestige. He was 66 when the first eight-cylinder made its debut in 1930 and claimed its place in the limelight. He had been active in the auto industry since the age of 46 and had his own name on a car by the time he was 54. A self-made man if ever there was one, Nash began life as an orphaned runaway Michigan farmboy. He had a meteoric rise in the Flint Road Cart Company, whose owner, W. C. Durant, brought Nash to the presidency of Buick in 1910. Nash left General Motors in 1916 and bought the Thomas B. Jeffery Company in Kenosha, Wisconsin, which he reorganized as the Nash Motor Company.

Nash had talked the chief engineer of Oakland into going with him, and Nils Eric Wahlberg served as vice president of engineering for Nash up to 1936. He was a native of Finland who had his engineering degree from Zurich, Switzerland, graduating in 1907. Wahlberg came to America in 1909 and went to work for Maxwell-Briscoe at Tarrytown, New York. Shortly afterwards, he moved to Buffalo where E. R. Thomas had position for him; and then to Detroit, where he joined Packard's engineering staff. He went to Oakland as assistant chief engineer (under Don Ferguson) in 1911, and advanced into the top technical job two years later. Oakland was part of General Motors, and at vice presidential level, Nash got to know all the top people in all the divisions. He was particularly impressed with Wahlberg's calm competence.

Wahlberg's first design for Nash was a six with a 244 cubic-inch overhead-valve engine. Throughout the Twenties, the Nash was always a leader in its price class when it came to engineering progress.

The four-cylinder Nash from 1922 had the engine carried on rubber mounts. Nash started to drill crankshafts for pressure lubrication in 1923, and the 1924 Nash 160-series had four-wheel mechanical brakes and balloon tires. Some Nash engines used dual ignition with two spark plugs per cylinder beginning in 1927. In 1928 Nash adopted aluminum pistons with Invar struts, hollow crankpins, and a crankcase breather. The chassis received worm and roller steering, the axle springs were wrapped, and two-way shock absorbers were fitted. For 1929, torsional vibration dampers were fitted on the crankshafts and rifle-bored connecting rods followed in 1931.

Wahlberg must share a great deal of the credit for Nash's many advances with Meade F. Moore, who served many years as his closest assistant, chief experimental engineer, and later chief engineer. Moore was educated at Ohio Northern University and had worked for Overland in Toledo and Standard Steel Car Co.

An important role in assuring the quality of the great Nash was played by David M. Averill, general works manager for all the Nash plants. He had met Nash at the Durant-Dort Carriage Co. in Flint in 1898. Twelve years later, when Nash went to Buick, Averill became general manager of the Dort Motor Car Co. They linked up again in 1924 when Nash purchased the Mitchell-Lewis factory in Racine and made Averill general manager for his new Ajax subsidiary (which was quietly absorbed into Nash Motor Co. two years later).

Nash's 1930 Twin Ignition Eight was an overhead-valve design with 3.25 inch bore and 4.5-inch stroke, giving 298.6 cubic-inch displacement. The counterbalanced crankshaft ran in nine main bearings, and had chain drive to the side camshaft, with pushrods to overhead rocker arms. Fuel was fed from an AC mechanical pump to a Marvel carburetor, and the 16 spark plugs were fired from double coils. Output was 100 hp at 3,200 rpm. This engine was installed in the Series 490, built on wheelbases of 124 and 132 inches. It had Hotchkiss drive with a spiral bevel rear axle and a three-speed transmission. Bijur automatic chassis lubrication was standard, along with Lovejoy double-acting shock absorbers. Duo-serve mechanical brakes were used on all four wheels, and the wire wheels carried 6.5 × 19 tires. The car was good for 90 mph, with an average fuel economy of 12-14 miles to the gallon.

A variety of body styles were offered, with prices starting at $945 for the Series 470 Standard Eight, peaking at $2,025. The chassis continued unchanged for Series 890 of 1931, but the engine now came equipped with a downdraft two-barrel Stromberg that improved gasoline mileage as well as performance. During 1931 the Ambassador name was first used on a deluxe sedan, listed at $1,825.

It was with the arrival of the 1932 models that the Nash received recognition for greatness. New low, cross-braced frames and worm-drive rear axles were adopted, enabling the body engineers and designers to lower the floor and get overall height down to 68 inches. Striking new styling gave the Nash an appeal it had never had before. Long, sweeping fender lines, a V-front radiator shell, sloping windshield, and a new rear end called "beavertail back" put the Nash up among the trend setters.

The Nash driver that year found many new attractions, such as ride control (dash control for shock absorber adjustment), selective free-wheeling, and synchro-shift transmission.

The Advanced Eight, which replaced the 990, was built on a 133-inch wheelbase, and the Ambassador Eight on a 142-inch wheelbase. Prices in the new 1090 series ranged from $1,595 to $2,055.

By 1933 engine power had been increased to 125 hp, mainly by an increase in compression ratio, revised valve timing, improved intake manifold design, and the adoption of Bohnalite pistons and connecting rods. Exterior styling was almost unchanged, but a new instrument panel with larger dials was adopted. New metallic spring gaiters were fitted on the self-lubricating semi-ellipticals that carried the front and rear axles, and tire size was now 7.0 × 18 on the Advanced Eight.

Engines were carried over for 1934. The eight-cylinder Nash was one of the best and most modern then in production in a car of its price class. That was the last year for the 298.6 cubic-inch unit, but smaller versions remained in production through 1940.

Bodies were restyled again for 1934, with a frontal appearance that borrowed something from Cadillac. The Ambassador Eight came with spats on the rear fenders and some bodies had an integral steel trunk, with the spare wheel in a metal casing forming the tailpiece (Fig. 7-1).

Independent front suspension was offered as an option. Nash's design was nothing so advanced as the GM and Chrysler systems, but rather, a simple device known as Axleflex (also used by Hudson). The standard front axle had a piece cut out of the middle, where a parallelogram was inserted, thus eliminating many of the problems associated with a beam-type front axle. Tire size in 1934 was 7.0 × 17 for Series 1290 (Ambassador Eight).

Wahlberg retired in 1936, while Meade F. Moore stayed on with Nash-Kelvinator and American Motors till the end of 1963 when he retired to Arizona. He died in 1973. David M. Averill fell ill and retired in 1937, dying at the age of 59 the following year. Charles W. Nash left the presidency to E. H. McCarty in 1932, and then served as chairman of the board till his death in 1948.

After 1934, Nash guided its quest for new and more sensible greatness into smaller and lighter cars with better aerodynamics. Its product-image soon changed, however, and it is the 1934 models that stand as the climax of Nash's greatness.

77 LA SALLE SERIES 350, 1934

Since early times, examples have shown us that the biggest car in a manufacturer's model range was not always the greatest. Smaller ones often had advances and refinements that put them ahead of heavier, more expensive, and less modern models.

What happened to the concept of automotive design in the depression years was to have lasting effect in diverting the very image of greatness away from the kind of product that was associated with many recently bankrupted auto companies. The leaders of the surviving members of America's auto industry knew that a certain popularity and a certain production volume were necessary to make the money needed for preparing successor models.

Out of this situation came a necessity for lower prices, which in turn meant added stress on manufacturing cost. Cheaper ways to

Fig. 7-1. The 1934 Nash Ambassador Eight.

achieve comfort and quietness were searched for and found. Cars were made lighter to give improved performance despite smaller engines. And the importance of styling grew enormously, since clever designers knew how to create a look of prestige and exclusivity by making small changes and additions to a base of mass-produced body panels. A lot of lip service was given to aerodynamics, but what really mattered was making the car look streamlined to the consumer's eye at that time, while making maximum use of styling elements associated with cars representing high performance, luxury, and grandeur.

What makes the La Salle of 1934 so great is not its specifications, or its styling alone, but the way its creators succeeded in translating unenunciated theory into actual hardware, doing everything that was essential for sparking a new design trend in the evolution of the great American car (Fig. 7-2). There was something revolutionary in the new La Salle that assures it a firm place in history.

It almost did not come into being, and it was granted life strictly because of its styling. GM President Alfred P. Sloan and his executive vice president William S. Knudsen, had decided to end La Salle production at the end of the miserable 1933 model year.

But the Art & Color section never abandoned the La Salle project, which started from some dramatic sketches and scale models that Jules Agramonte had prepared. Under Harley Earl's guidance, Agramonte and his small group in the La Salle studio adapted this racing-air-craft theme to the basic Fisher body planned for the 1934 Oldsmobile. The result was a car of such striking newness and such a harmonious blend of good looks that management was persuaded to let Cadillac continue La Salle production, merely on the strength of seeing a full-scale mockup.

Jules Agramonte had been a magazine illustrator early in his career and had worked as a body designer with Hibbard & Darrin—two American styling adventurers—in Paris. From there he went to Fleetwood, and in 1929 joined GM's Art & Color section. He became head of the La Salle studio, and in 1935 took over as chief designer of the Chevrolet studio.

One condition for going ahead with the La Salle project was that it must be a low-cost car. Consequently, any sharing of major components with Cadillac was out of the question. La Salle had to share chassis and power train with one of the lower-ranking devisions. All of them had excess capacity at the time, but the choice fell on Oldsmobile.

Oldsmobile was the lowest-priced car available with the Cadillac independent front suspension system that year. It was a modern coil-spring design with short and long lateral control arms, one above the other, developed by Maurice Olley for Cadillac. Buick and Oldsmobile were allowed to share it.

The rest of the Oldsmobile chassis was fairly typical of its era. It had a strong cross-braced frame and Hotchkiss drive. It was good enough, and available in any quantity Cadillac was likely to need. It was notable for using a rear stabilizer bar and 7.0 × 16 tires.

Cadillac assembled the La Salle engine from parts supplied by Oldsmobile, along with some of its own. Olds produced the blocks, for instance, and the raw castings were machined at the Cadillac factory. Cadillac made its own cylinder head, with higher compression than Oldsmobile used. Also, Cadillac went to aluminum pistons, while Olds used cast-iron ones. Instead of the plain Olds carburetor, Cadillac equipped the La Salle with a downdraft two-barrel Stromberg.

The engine was an L-head eight-cylinder, developed under the direction of Oldsmobile chief engineer Charles L. McCuen. He was born in Stockton, California, and had quit school in fifth grade, making a living as a carpenter, locomotive maintenance man, pottery worker, paint can labeler, and machine designer, before going to the Polytechnic College of Engineering at Oakland, California. He worked briefly for Packard in 1915, then had a job

Fig. 7-2. A 1934 La Salle five passenger Club Sedan Model 350, Series 50.

263

with a refrigerator company, and signed up with Eddie Ricken-backer to help design and develop the Rickenbacker car in 1922. When that venture failed in 1926, he went to Oldsmobile. He worked on engine projects, developed the Series F and Series L units, and became chief engineer in 1930.

As used in the La Salle, the Olds engine had a bore and stroke of 3.00 × 4.25 inches, giving 240 cubic-inch displacement. It was 5 hp more powerful than the Olds engine of the same size, delivering 95 hp at 3,700 rpm, on a 6.5:1 compression ratio. It was carried in a six-mount rubber-block suspension. A single, dry plate clutch was used, along with the same three-speed transmission Oldsmobile had. The rear axle was semi-floating, with spiral bevel gears, and had a 4.78:1 reduction ratio.

La Salle was ahead of Cadillac, in the brakes department, for the 1934 model had Bendix four-wheel hydraulic brakes (shared with Oldsmobile). The car was built on a 119-inch wheelbase and weighed 4,210 pounds. Top speed was 84 mph, and fuel consumption was excellent for its time, at 14.9 miles to the gallon at 50 mph.

The La Salle was not assembled in the Cadillac plant, but by Fleetwood, which had excess capacity due to the small demand for its special coachwork on Cadillac and other chassis. Thus, the La Salle came to have a genuine Fleetwood body.

That happy situation came to an end the following year when the La Salle had to share the Fisher B-body with Olds and Buick. At the same time, the engine had its stroke stretched to 4.375 inches, which raised displacement to 247 cubic inches.

Prices started at $1,495 for the 1934 La Salle, and that year 5,182 cars were sold. The following year, prices were lowered to $1,225, which sent sales up to 11,775 cars.

Cadillac introduced a smaller version of its L-head V-8 for the 1937 La Salle, and built the car on a shortened Cadillac chassis with a 124-inch wheelbase and hypoid bevel rear axle. That ended Cadillac's embarrassment over the Oldsmobile connection, and La Salle sales grew to 32,000 that year. Cadillac kept the La Salle in production through 1940 and then it was killed for good (except for use on a special show car in 1956).

78. FRANKLIN SERIES 17, 1934

Franklins were always good cars, right from the start in 1901. The factory in Syracuse, New York, never over-expanded and it enjoyed relative stability when other companies with more daring management had their ups and downs. Franklin never became a mass producer and the Franklin car, from the lowest-priced to the most expensive, had the same thorough quality (Fig. 7-3).

One thing above all set Franklin apart from the rest of the industry. Out of all those who started with air-cooled engines, Franklin stands alone in remaining forever faithful to air cooling. Others, such as Marmon and Knox, followed the majority and switched to water-cooled engines in the first decade of the century.

The first production-model Franklin was a four-cylinder 7 hp model with the engine mounted transversely under the seat, driving the rear wheels. Both axles were carried on full-elliptical springs. It was the design of John N. Wilkinson, a Cornell-trained engineer who began experimental work with an engine design in 1897 when still employed in the bicycle industry.

One day in 1901 he demonstrated one of his machines to a local die-casting maker, Herbert H. Franklin, and that was the beginning of the Franklin car.

When the first six-cylinder model came out in 1906, Franklin also switched from chain to shaft drive, but retained the full-elliptical springs. Sixes were only produced from 1914 through 1922.

About 1916 Wilkinson was named vice president in charge of engineering, and he hired Ralph Murphy as chief engineer. It was Murphy who designed and developed the new four-cylinder Franklin for 1923. Bigger and more impressive sixes were added, with prices reaching into the $3,000 bracket. F. J. de Causse was brought in to design better-looking bodies, which Franklin produced in its own shops. Franklin's body engineer was named William H. Emond, and the two produced big changes. Wide, straight-edged dummy radiator shells in shiny chrome replaced the former body-painted horse-collar front hood, and body lines were straightened and integrated, with well thought-out detailing. At the same time, Franklin began building semi-custom built bodies in its own shops, to designs by Derham, Locke, Willoughby, Holbrook, and Le Baron.

Murphy left in 1926 and Edward S. Marks became chief engineer. This was at the height of the straight-eight boom, but Marks decided it would be easier and better (in view of Franklin's insistence on air-cooling as well as the machine shop facilities) to go to a V-12. (Wilkinson had built a straight-eight Franklin racing car in 1905, and it had not been successful.)

Design and development work on a V-12 engine began in 1927. It was laid out by the chief experimental engineer, Carl T.

Doman, who had come to Franklin in 1922 with a degree in electrical engineering from the University of Michigan.

The twelve was made up as two rows of six individually cast cylinders disposed at a 60-degree included angle (the theoretically correct layout), on a common crankcase. At 3.25 inches, the bore was the same as in the 235.5-cubic-inch Model 130 six-cylinder, and stroke was shortened to 4.232 inches to keep the displacement within 500 cubic inches (it ended up at 498). The cylinders were chrome-nickel iron castings, bolted to the aluminum crankcase. Each bank had a one-piece aluminum cylinder head, securely bolted down.

Doman and Marks at first intended to use a single central camshaft, with pushrods and rocker arms to overhead valves, but ran into cooling problems because of the tight spacing of valve lifters, pushrods, etc., inside the V. Consequently, the valve gear was placed on the outside, which necessitated the use of two camshafts, one for each bank.

When serious engine testing began, it delivered 120 hp, and by the time it went into production, output had risen to 150 hp at 3,100 rpm. Doman had put in a wide margin for subsequent enlargement, and test engines were built to prove feasibility. The limit was seen as 544 cubic inches, with 3½-inch bore and 4.75-inch stroke, when no less than 250 hp was on tap.

The 12-cylinder Franklin engine went into production in March, 1932, in a car known as Model 17. It was advertised as a supercharged 12, but what Franklin called supercharging was merely bleeding off a little of the cooling air flow and ducting it to the carburetor, which hardly affected manifold pressure at all. The carburetor was a downdraft two-barrel Stromberg, fed by an AC mechanical fuel pump.

The 12-cylinder engine was matched up with the same drive train used in the six-cylinder Airman, Model 16. The transmission was a three-speed with synchromesh on second and top, and a free-wheel unit. An open propeller shaft drove a spiral bevel rear axle in a Hotchkiss drive arrangement.

The 1933-model was equipped with a two-speed rear axle, with shift control on the dashboard. The chassis remained unchanged, with both front and rear axles carried on semi-elliptical leaf springs, damped by double-acting Delco-Remy hydraulic shock absorbers. Four-wheel hydraulic brakes had been standard on Model 17 from the start, and the car had wire wheels shod with 7.5 × 17 tires. The wheelbase was 144 inches, and with the

Fig. 7-3. The air-cooled 1934 Franklin V-12.

standard body, the car had a list price of $3,885. Le Baron design made it a high-style car, whether built as a four-door sedan or a striking Brougham Club Coupe.

Ed Marks and Carl Doman resigned in 1933, apparently aware of the company's shaky financial situation, and formed a partnership to produce light, air-cooled engines for aircraft and industrial purposes. In 1936 they even planned to build a light car with front wheel drive, sleeve-valve engine, all-independent suspension, and a 120-inch wheelbase, calculated to run 30-plus miles on a gallon of gasoline. But the project came to naught.

Franklin produced its last cars in 1934, and H. H. Franklin, then 67 years old, went into retirement. He spent the rest of his years in his comfortable mansion in Syracuse, dying in 1956. Five years earlier, John N. Wilkinson had died at the age of 83, after retiring at about the same time.

Ed Marks resigned from Aircooled Motors in 1940 to go with Pratt & Whitney as manager of product quality. After the war, Aircooled Motors was absorbed by Republic Aircraft, who later disposed of it to the Tucker Corporation. Carl T. Doman served as its chief engineer until he signed up with Ford in 1949, becoming national service manager in 1950.

79. PONTIAC EIGHT, 1934

Prices for the 1934 Pontiac started at $695 . . . making it a great bargain, but not necessarily a great car. After having become accustomed to automotive greatness at ten times that price, it is perhaps difficult to understand how this Pontiac got on the list. It's a car that could be seen as competition for the hot new Ford V-8, or the lively Hudson Terraplane, but not in a class with Lincoln, Packard, or Cadillac (Fig. 7-4).

The Ford and the Terraplane were also great bargains. The Ford's greatness lay in the V-8 engine, introduced in 1932, and rather more in Ford's production techniques than in the end product. Ford was first with the cast-en-block V-8, and first to mass-produce cast-iron crankshafts (for this engine). The Terraplane's greatness was part performance, part appearance, and part price. It wasn't what one could call a style-leader, for its design was not innovative, merely "up-to-date." But it looked like it cost a lot more money than it did, and that worked wonders in 1933.

Then came the Pontiac. It was also a styling car, to a large extent. And in some ways, it makes an interesting parallel with the La Salle, due to the interdivisional collaboration that made it possible to produce and sell such a car at those low prices. With recognition of the Pontiac's greatness, we also begin to acknowledge the econimic realities of the world as it was in the mid-Thirties. It was a great car for its time, and certainly played a part in guiding General Motors philosophy on product evolution for many years to follow.

The Pontiac had a powerful eight-cylinder engine and one of the lowest-priced eights in the industry. After 1934, Pontiac became the world's biggest maker of straight-eights, succeeding Studebaker, which had taken the title from Hupmobile, the make that first claimed it about 1925.

Pontiac's straight-eight was not an old six with two more cylinders tacked on. It was a new design in which the chief engineer Benjamin H. Anibal, played a leading role. Anibal had been responsible for the original 1926-model Pontiac six, which he developed from designs Henry M. Crane had proposed to Alfred P. Sloan. It was America's first big-bore, short-stroke, slow-revving six, completely reversing the trend. Next to the Chrysler, it was America's most modern power unit at the time.

The straight-eight borrowed the turbulent L-head from the six, as well as the short-stroke layout. It had a bore of 3.1875 inches and a 3½-inch stroke, giving 223.4 cubic-inch displacement. It had a new cast iron block with wide cylinder spacing to make room for future enlargement (and bigger water jackets), extending about 2½-inches below the crankshaft center line. The crankshaft was supported in five main bearings, and the engine was carried in a three-point rubber mounting system.

With a Carter downdraft carburetor and a compression ratio of 6.2:1, the Pontiac Eight delivered 84 hp at 3,800 rpm. It gave the car a top speed of 83 mph and an average fuel economy of 15 miles per gallon.

The car was light with a curb weight of 3,330 pounds, which combined with a final drive ratio of 4.56:1, made for a very quick getaway. It could go from standstill to 60 mph in under 15 seconds, using first and second gears till the engine ran out of breath. It also had remarkable top gear acceleration, and could be driven off the line in top gear, with the engine idling, on level ground.

Ben Anibal was an engineer who knew power trains as well as anyone, and had experience from other builders of great cars. He served as chief engineer at Cadillac from 1918 to 1921, and after that spent three years in the equivalent position with Peerless. His earlier career had been spent mainly with Cadillac, where he went in 1911 after two years with Oldsmobile. He hailed from Linden,

Michigan, and had his engineering degree from Michigan State University.

Returning to GM in 1925, Anibal was named chief engineer of Oakland, and it was to Oakland that the Pontiac project was assigned. The original car was intended as a disguised Chevrolet with a six-cylinder engine, a marketing recipe rather than an engineering one. But the Pontiac was a technically superior car, and in 1931 the Oakland was phased out. Later the whole division was renamed Pontiac.

By 1934 there was not much in the Pontiac chassis that came from Chevrolet. The designs resembled each other, with cross-braced frames and Hotchkiss drive, but Pontiac made its own axles, for instance. Pontiac was also allowed to purchase components from Buick and Oldsmobile, which Chevrolet could not do in those days.

All GM cars for 1934 were available with independent front suspension as an option, and while Buick and Olds were able to use the Cadillac design, Chevrolet and Pontiac offered a curious system patented by a French inventor, Andre Dubonnet, with coil springs enclosed in oil-damped chambers mounted on an arm extending forwards from the wheel hub. It worked fine when new, but often ran into service problems, and was abandoned after a few years.

The 1934 Pontiac was built on a 117.25-inch wheelbase, stretched from 115 in 1933. The styling revolution had taken place with the 1933 models, and how it came about is nowhere near as dramatic as the creation of the 1934 La Salle, but an object lesson in how small changes can get big results.

Frank Hershey became chief designer of the Pontiac studio in the Art & Color section in 1931, when it was too late to make big changes in the 1933 models. He could not touch anything structural, and was locked into hundreds of unalterable key dimensions. Together with the body engineer, Roy Milner, Hershey made the most of the opportunity to redesign a few external parts. They changed basically only the radiator shell, headlamps, and front and rear fenders. In a couple of weeks, Hershey had transformed the original, which had little visual distinction from the 1932 model, into a car with brand new looks for 1933. Further changes for 1934 were small, and did not alter the overall theme.

Frank Hershey had come to GM from Hudson, where he had worked briefly after he lost his job at Murphy when that fine

Fig. 7-4. 1934 Pontiac Eight.

coachbuilder was forced to close down in 1931. He was to direct the styling of the 1935, -36 and -37 Pontiacs, and then served with Opel in Germany up to 1939. Ben Anibal and Roy Milner were to remain at Pontiac for the rest of their careers.

The Pontiac Eight was enlarged to 232.3 cubic inches for 1936, which increased its output to 87 hp. That was not enough to keep up with rising vehicle weights and the pressure of competition, so for 1937 engine size was further increased to 248.9 cubic inch displacement. The Pontiac Eight then boasted 100 hp. The engine reached its ultimate form in 1951, with a displacement of 268.4 cubic inches, and remained in production through the 1954 model year, after which it was replaced by an overhead-valve V-8.

80. AUBURN 8-120 MODEL 851, 1935

As sure as night follows day, Auburn, under E. L. Cord's ownership was going to make great cars. Not only great, but exciting cars, in a valiant attempt to find a health-giving antidote for the economic depression. The Cord had been great, and the Duesenberg was perhaps the greatest of all. There was no choice but for the Auburn to follow.

Just look at some of the features of the car that capped the Auburn's career: straight-eight L-head Lycoming engine, putting out a resounding 115 hp at 3,600 (or 150 hp at 4,000 rpm with the optional supercharger); Warner three-speed transmission and Columbia two-speed rear axle, and top speeds of 85 mph (standard) and 95-100 mph (supercharged). It had a straightforward chassis with cross-braced frame and semi-elliptical springs, Lovejoy double-acting hydraulic shock absorbers, and Lockheed hydraulic brakes on both front and rear axles. The bodies were styled with great flair and exquisite taste by Gordon Buehrig, and produced in the Auburn factory under the direction of Edwin L. Allen, body engineer who had joined Auburn in 1928 as chief body draftsman.

And all this could be purchased at low prices, the 851 list starting at $1,245. Sadly, the Auburn disappeared when Cord's empire fell apart in 1936, the make having reached greatness only in the final stages of its life.

The brothers Frank and Morris Eckhart built the first Auburn car in 1900 in the shops of the Eckhart Carriage Co. in Auburn, Indiana. It was a single cylinder model of primitive design, but it was successful enough for the Eckhart brothers to go into production with an improved car in 1902.

272

A two-cylinder model was added in 1905, and in 1909 Auburn built its first four-cylinder cars, using Rutenber engines. The twin was phased out, as the single-cylinder had been before, by 1910. A six-cylinder series was added for 1916, also powered by a Rutenber engine.

With arrival of the Auburn Beauty Six in 1920, the company switched to Continental engines. It was a good car, list-priced at under $2,000, but it failed in the marketplace. The company was headed for extinction in 1924 when E. L. Cord saved it.

James Crawford was chief engineer of Auburn in 1925, when the first Auburn Eight went into production. It was called the 8-63 and was powered by a Lycoming L-head engine.

In 1927 Crawford went to General Motors, and Auburn lured Herbert C. Snow away from his post as chief engineer of Velie Motors in Moline, Illinois, a company that went under in 1928. Herb Snow graduated from the Case Institute of Technology in 1906 and became a draftsman for Peerless. By 1910 he was chief draftsman of Peerless. From 1912 to 1914 he worked as assistant engineer with Willys-Overland, and then served as chief engineer of Winton for six years. In 1920 he set up a consulting office in Cleveland, and after three years signed up with Velie as chief engineer.

The Auburn 8-88 of 1928 was mainly a Crawford design, with a new pressed-steel frame of high torsional rigidity, hydraulic four-wheel brakes, and Bijur automatic chassis lubrication. Snow's influence began to appear in the 8-115 which followed later in 1928, using the same Lycoming engine but a new two-barrel Stromberg carburetor instead of the Schebler. It had a new chassis with a 130-inch wheelbase, developed under the direction of Louis R. Jones, featuring Lockheed hydraulic brakes on all four wheels, and Lovejoy hydraulic shock absorbers. Semi-elliptical springs carried both front and rear axles on a stiff pressed-steel frame, and Bijur chassis lubrication was standard.

For 1931 Auburn went to a one-series program with introduction of the 8-98. Sixes were discontinued entirely. The Lycoming 8-98 was an L-head engine with bore and stroke of 3.00 × 4.75 inches, giving a displacement of 268.6 cubic inches. It delivered 98 hp at 3,400 rpm, which made Auburn's reputation as a high-performance car.

An LGS free-wheel was combined with the three-speed transmission, which had synchromesh on second and top gears. Brakes were mechanical, and tire size was 5.50 × 17. The 8-98 was available on wheelbases of 127 and 138 inches, in seven body styles, at prices from $1,195 to $1,395. It developed into the 8-100 for 1932 and 8-101A in 1933, from which the 8-105 was an offshoot and an important step on the way to the Model 851.

Using the same basic double-drop, cross-braced chassis with a wheelbase of 133 inches, Auburn added a V-12—Model 12-160—in 1932. The V-12 engine was designed by George Kublin, who had been named chief engineer of Auburn in 1931, when Herb Snow was promoted to vice president in charge of engineering. And it was built by Lycoming, as the Williamsport, Pennsylvania, factory was now part of the Cord Corporation and manufactured all engines for Auburn, Cord, and Duesenberg as well as producing large numbers for outside customers.

Kublin laid out the engine with a 45-degree angle between the banks and horizontal valves operated via rocker arms from a central camshaft. Bore and stroke were 3.25 × 4.25 inches, giving 391 cubic-inch displacement, and output was 160 hp at 3,500 rpm. Hydraulic four-wheel brakes were adopted, and the two-speed axle was optional on custom models. It became the 12-161 in 1933 and 12-165 in 1934, being discontinued at the end of that year.

For 1934, Lycoming had placed in production a new straight-eight, created as an eight-cylinder version of a new L-head six Snow and Kublin had developed. It had 3.06-inch bore and a 4.75-inch stroke, resulting in a displacement of 279.2 cubic inches. It was first used in the Model 850Y of 1934, whose chassis was derived from the 8-105, and evolved into the Model 851 (Fig. 7-5).

What was new in the 851 chassis was a one-inch longer wheelbase, and a smaller fuel tank (17½ gallons instead of 20). Bodies were completely new. But the novelty which made the most noise was the optional supercharger. The installation was devised by Kurt Beier, chief engineer of Schwitzer in Indianapolis. The compressor was a centrifugal type driven by chain from the camshaft to a 1:1 bevel gear whose output shaft carried a planetary friction drive geared to run the supercharger at six times crankshaft speed. It gave a one-third boost in power output at a very reasonable cost.

For 1936, the 851 was renamed 852, which differed mainly in having a 6.50 × 16 tires and pressed-steel disc wheels.

Louis R. Jones was named chief engineer of Auburn in 1936, and Herb Snow resumed his activity as an independent engineering consultant. In 1940 he moved to Kalamazoo, Michigan, as chief engineer of Checker Cab, where he spent the rest of his career.

The later lives of Kublin, Cord and others will be related in connection with the last Cord.

81. GRAHAM SUPERCHARGED EIGHT, 1935

Graham launched its supercharged eight in the spring of 1934, identified as Model 69. It was a distinguished-looking car with a long hood, V-front grille tapering from a wide top to a shield-like point at the bottom, built on a 123-inch wheelbase, and powered by a 140-hp engine (Fig. 7-6).

The next year it evolved into a more modern shape, borrowing from both Hudson and Studebaker, while retaining the same chassis and power train. Driving it was a revelation, for the engine was quiet and unobtrusive, and yet packed a punch that would move it out in front of all but the most specialized high-performance machines. And it was reasonably priced, the Supercharged Eight sedan being listed at $1,395.

The chassis was unusual, for the side members had no kickup for the rear axle. Instead, each girder was split in the axle area, with a big vertical slot for the axle to pass through, with plenty of room for spring travel. At the front end, the girders did not have horns, but continued in a straight line, with sharply arched leaf springs below to hold the front axle. The spiral-bevel rear axle was also attached to semi-elliptical springs, these being nearly flat in profile. The Graham had Hotchkiss drive, with an open, double-jointed, splined-at-the-rear propeller shaft. This frame and chassis had been designed by Louis Thoms, Graham's chief engineer since 1927.

Fig. 7-5. 1935 Auburn 8-120, Model 851, available with optional supercharger.

275

Thoms was also responsible for the engine, an L-head straight-eight with 3.25-inch bore and 4-inch stroke, giving a displacement of 265 cubic inches. It was a bored-out version of Graham's first eight, introduced in 1931, for Model 820, also named Special Eight. The engine was advertised as the Blue Streak.

Graham claimed a maximum output of 85 hp from the 248 cubic-inch Model 820, and the 265 cubic-inch version was rated at 95 hp at 3,400 rpm. With the supercharger, the latter delivered 135 hp at 4,000 rpm. The supercharger installation was engineered by Floyd Kishline, assistant chief engineer, who inherited the top technical office when Thoms retired in 1935. Kishline was from Lincoln, Nebraska, and his first job in the auto industry had been as an experimental engineer with Saron in 1916. Kishline was a friend of Louis Schwitzer, who showed him how Duesenberg had done the job, and he adapted it to the Graham. The unit had a large-diameter centrifugal compressor mounted on a vertical shaft driven at 5.5 times crankshaft speed from a horizontal accessory shaft geared to the camshaft. Normal development work led to a gain of 5 hp for 1935.

Graham machined and assembled its own engines, but bought its cylinder blocks from Continental (with the Continental trade mark on them). Cylinder heads were aluminum castings, from another source, as Continental used cast-iron heads only. Pistons were of aluminum, and the eight-cylinder crankshaft ran in five main bearings. A Lanchester-type vibration damper was fitted, and the engine was suspended in four rubber-cushioned mounts.

Body designs for the Graham were done by Amos Northup, who had a fine reputation, mainly for his work as chief designer for the Murray Corporation. He had also been body designer for Wills Sainte Claire in 1926. After the Reo Royale and some nice styling details for Ford (under Murray contract), he created a new style small car for Willys (1933 Model 77) and made a sensational translation of a similar theme to big-car dimensions for the 1933 Graham.

The Model 69 evolved into Model 75 for 1935, the last true Graham, for in 1936 Graham adopted the Reo body shell (to cut manufacturing costs) and the unique Thoms-designed frame was discarded in favor of a conventional design from A. O. Smith.

Graham was a relatively new make, though with long traditions through its ancestry. The Graham name came from three brothers in Toledo, Ohio, who had made a fortune in glass-making.

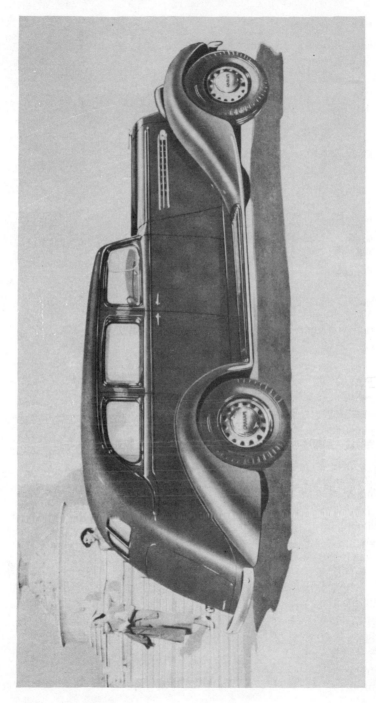

Fig. 7-6. The Graham Supercharged Eight of 1935.

277

In 1917 they began converting cars, mostly Fords, into vans and trucks, and in 1921 became associated with Dodge, serving as an unofficial truck division for five years.

They broke off with Dodge, after having added to their fortune before Chrysler took it over, and purchased Paige-Detroit Motor Co., in Detroit. Its product turned into the Graham-Paige almost overnight.

The Paige, until that time, had been a medium-priced six-cylinder family car, competing against Buick, Oldsmobile, Chandler, Hupmobile, Reo and Studebaker in the thick of an expanding market. Andrew Bachle was vice president in charge of engineering and G. C. Mather chief engineer. The Graham brothers added a Continental-powered eight to the existing sixes for 1928. The price range was expanded both downward and upward to a low of $845 and a high of $1,595, and sales tripled.

In 1930 the Paige name was dropped. Among engineering developments instituted after Thoms had taken over from Bachle and Mather were a four-speed Warner transmission on some models and Detroit carburetors replaced the earlier Johnson pump-type ones. By 1932, however, all models had three-speed transmissions and synchromesh was adopted in 1936.

Rubber bushings were fitted to the spring shackles, and tire size went from 5.50 × 19 in 1929 to 5.50 × 18 in 1930 and 6.00 × 17 in 1931. The 1934 models carried 6.00 × 16 tires, which were enlarged to 7.00 × 16 for the 1935 Supercharged Eight.

Hydraulic brakes, of the external-contracting type, had been used on Paige cars since 1926. They were phased out, model by model, in favor of the internal-expanding type between 1929 and 1932.

Much of the credit for the steady product development must go to George Delaney, who had joined Paige in 1920 as an experimental engineer and had risen to the rank of assistant chief engineer. Delaney had graduated from the University of Missouri in 1917 with a degree in electrical engineering, and spent the war years as a service technician with Savage Arms Company.

Delaney left Graham in 1934 to become electrical engineer with Pontiac, while Kishline stayed on until 1938 and then joined Willys in Toledo. He went to Nash a year later and continued a career with American Motors until retiring in 1959. He died ten years later.

Graham cars were produced up to 1940 and four years later the company was taken over by Joseph W. Frazer, former president of

Willys-Overland. The cars then being planned were called Frazer, not Graham, and the company was absorbed in the Kaiser-Frazer enterprises (whose motor vehicle business absorbed Willys-Overland in 1953 and came under control of American Motors in 1969), a strange corporate-life parallel to Kishline's story.

82. DUESENBERG SJ, 1935

A six-year-old car with a modified engine. That's one way to look at the Duesenberg SJ. In some ways it represents the ultimate for greatness of American car builders. It was unmatched for power and performance. It had worldwide prestige, and a degree of exclusivity that made a Rolls-Royce look run-of-the-mill (Fig. 7-7).

For all the admiration the SJ commands and honestly deserves, it is important to bear in mind some facts regarding its station vis-a-vis the industry. The SJ was a supercharged version of the J-type from 1929. It was not an updated J-type, but a car that had rapidly been by-passed as far as modernity goes by far cheaper and less distinguished machines.

Geography has something to do with what happened. By the early 1930's, Detroit had become the center of the nation's auto industry. There was no more car manufacturing in Pennsylvania, except for the little Bantam. It was soon to end in New York state, when Franklin in Syracuse, and then Pierce-Arrow and Stewart Truck of Buffalo closed down. The once popular cars of Connecticut and Massachusetts were no longer built. Car-making ended in Cleveland, leaving Ohio with only Toledo as the home of an auto plant. The cars of Illinois, Iowa, and Missouri died out. Only Nash remained alive in Wisconsin. Indiana was still holding on, but its main car maker was Studebaker, in South Bend, a few miles from the Michigan border, and not one of the great makes of the Indianapolis district.

As the home of the Speedway, Indianapolis had colored its cars with some of the Speedway character. It had once been important for engineering progress, but the time was coming when drawbacks began to have an effect. What drawbacks? The smooth surface, wide curves, and overall flatness of the track did not encourage development of brakes, suspension and steering in the same way that the Speedway made every little power gain tell.

Yet Duesenberg had been a pioneer in brakes, and its J and SJ were not to be faulted in that regard. As for steering and suspension, some of the most prestigious European cars of 1935 were no further advanced in their chassis engineering than

Fig. 7-7. The elegant Duesenberg SJ of 1935.

Duesenberg. It was only when viewed against Detroit (and Europe's technological leaders) that the Duesenberg was heading into an eclipse.

Detroit had developed independent front suspension systems, and had done it scientifically, not on a trial-and-error basis. Detroit had introduced synchromesh transmissions and was working on development of automatic drive systems. Detroit was beginning to grapple with aerodynamics and was testing models in wind tunnels. Detroit built technical laboratories for fundamental research, built proving grounds that could duplicate any sort of road conditions, and set up well-staffed styling studios to plan the shape of cars to come, often years ahead of time.

Duesenberg, working in the Indianapolis atmosphere, with no capacity for research or planning beyond the next day's goals, never emerged from the 1920's. The SJ looked magnificent, but in styling, it was playing a rearguard role. Its looks belonged in the past. Nor was there in 1935 anything avant-garde about the chassis or power train, which had been astounding in the daring of their execution at the time of their creation.

Well, of course, the installation of a supercharger on the 420 cubic-inch straight-eight was not without an element of daring, particularly in view of the fact that it was offered for sale and intended for use on public roads. The supercharger in itself was not new. It was used almost universally on racing and racing airplane engines since the mid-Twenties.

The type chosen for the Duesenberg was not the most common Roots-type with its twin interlocking hourglass-shaped rotors, or the Cozette or Wittig vane-type blowers, but a Schwitzer centrifugal compressor. Its shaft was driven from the crankshaft, and it ran at five times crankshaft speed. To handle higher stress loads, the SJ engine was given larger crankshaft bearings. Valve springs were stiffened to cope with higher engine speeds, and aluminum connecting rods were replaced by tubular steel rods. The first series had a single carburetor, but engines built in 1935 and 1936 carried twin carburetors. Maximum boost pressure was relatively low, about 5 psi, but that was enough to reach an output of 320 hp at 4,750 rpm.

That's a fairly realistic estimate, for calculations based on actual performance show that the engine must have delivered at least 300 hp. And its performance was nothing short of fantastic. With a lightweight roadster body, the SJ could top 100 mph in second gear!—and reach 100 mph from standstill in 17 seconds. When equipped with a long 3.00:1 rear axle, the car could get up to 130 mph.

The first of the SJ models was built in 1932, and less than 40 are believed to have been produced in all.

Chassis modifications for the SJ were few. Axle springs were beefed up and Watson Stabilators were added at the front end. The standard SJ shared the 142.5-inch wheelbase of the J. While the J was also available on a 153.5-inch wheelbase, this was not available in SJ form. However, Duesenberg did build SJ roadsters on a 125-inch wheelbase.

Bodies were built by Central Manufacturing (a Cord Corporation subsidiary) to designs by Gordon Buehrig, or supplied by Derham, Murphy, la Grande, Bohman & Schwartz, Rollston, Judkins, or Willoughby. SJ prices started at $8,000 for the chassis only in 1932, but reached $10,000 by the end. Bodies usually cost $4,000 to $5,000 extra.

Fred S. Duesenberg was killed in an accident when driving an SJ in July, 1932, and Harold T. Ames, the sales vice-president, was named president of Duesenberg. Fred's brother Augie held the title of vice president, but he had always concentrated on the racing cars and could do little to help run the company. The end of car production came in 1937, when E. L. Cord withdrew from the auto industry and let Auburn, Cord and Duesenberg go into liquidation.

83. CORD 810 AND 812, 1936-37

It was still 1935 when a completely new front-wheel-drive Cord was launched, the L-29 having disappeared in 1932. And the patent application for its totally original body design was dated May 17th, 1934, which means that its futuristic looks had been taking shape in the mind of its creator, Gordon M. Buehrig, for some time prior to that date (Fig. 7-8).

As a piece of industrial design, it was an admirable creation. But because Buehrig had understood the car's character and used the metal to illustrate it, the Cord body must also be recognized as a work of art. From an automotive point of view, it did not become trend-setting as a whole, but piecemeal, in that many of its features were adopted by other cars in later years.

Running boards were eliminated and so were exterior door hinges. It had an alligator hood, hinged at the cowl, something which soon became general practice. Front fenders were of the pontoon-type, clearly inspired by the fairings used for the wheels on high-speed aircraft before retractable landing gears came into use. Concealed headlamps were mounted in the fenders, opened and closed mechanically by a shaft and worm-gear arrangement from the dashboard. Stinson Aircraft had used something similar on planes, but for a car, it was a total innovation.

The car was called names like "coffin-nose" and "refrigerator" because of the hood and grille design, stretching the horizontal louvres of a low grille around both sides of the engine compartment, all the way back to the cowl. The Cord trademark was placed not at the top of the hood, where most cars carried their ornaments and identification badges, but down on the bulging sheet metal that concealed the mechanical parts of the front-wheel-drive.

The windshield was split in V-formation, with an airplane like slope and profile and the roofline ended in a fastback. It was only 60 inches high over-all, made possible by a step-down floor. The body was of unit construction from the cowl back, with doorsill reinforcements to provide the torsional strength a frame would otherwise have given.

Gordon Miller Buehrig was 30 years old when he sketched out the Cord. He had gone to high school in his home town of Mason City, Illinois, and then to Bradley Polytechnic in Peoria. Later, while making a living as a cab driver in Chicago, he talked with a designer at C. P. Kimball, a well-known custom-body shop, about a future as a car designer. As a result of the advice he got, he returned to Bradley and learned drafting, wood shop and metal shop modelling, and discovered he had a talent for working in clay. This experience got him a job with Gotfredson, who was then designing touring car bodies for Paige and closed cars for Wills-Sainte Claire. He worked for a couple of years under Harley Earl in the GM Art & Color section, but left to go with Duesenberg.

The patented design which became the Cord was originally intended for a baby Duesenberg, but E. L. Cord decided to revive his own name in a make of car.

The engineering of the car was handled mainly by Auburn's chief engineer, George H. Kublin, though the final responsibility rested with Herbert C. Snow. Kublin had been chief engineer of Moon since 1921, but joined Auburn in 1930.

He laid out the chassis with a 125-inch wheelbase, though custom models were available on a 132-inch wheelbase. The drive train had nothing in common with the Cord L-29, but was a totally new design with a four-speed Detroit Gear transaxle having all-indirect ratios (overdrive on top) and a 4.30:1 final drive ratio. The gearbox was mounted in front of the differential, enabling the engine to come farther forward for better weight distribution.

A Bendix electro-vacuum mechanism operated by a miniature stick shift on a stalk branching off from the steering column gave power-assisted gear changes.

Instead of the de Dion front suspension of the L-29, the 810 was given independent front suspension. Each wheel was carried on a wide-based trailing arm that was forked at the rear end to accommodate the steering swivel. A transverse leaf spring was positioned below the front sub-frame, connected to the free ends of the trailing arms via vertical rods with rubber bushings top and bottom. Brake drums were mounted outboard.

The rear end had an I-beam axle carried by semi-elliptical leaf springs. Bendix four-wheel hydraulic brakes, adapted from the Auburn, were used and a new Gemmer worm and roller steering gear installed. Tires were 6.50 × 16 on pressed-steel wheels.

The engine was a new V-8 designed and manufactured by Lycoming. The design was by Lycoming's chief engineer, Forest S. Baster, who based the combustion chambers and valve gear on Lycoming's L-head in-line engines.

Aluminum cylinder heads were used, and the counterbalanced crankshaft ran in three main bearings. With bore and stroke of 3.50 × 3.75 inches, it had a displacement of 288.6 cubic inches. The compression ratio was 6.5:1, and maximum output 125 hp at 3,500 rpm.

Fig. 7-8. 1936 Cord 810, featuring hide-away headlights.

That was enough to give the car a top speed of 92 mph, with creditable but not startling acceleration. For 1937, Lycoming was ready with a supercharged version, delivering 170 hp, and having a maximum torque of 260 pounds-feet at 2,200 rpm. Following Duesenberg and Auburn practice, the Cord (renamed 812 when powered by the supercharged engine) used a Schwitzer centrifugal compressor driven from the camshaft.

The 812 had a top speed of 112 mph, and would cover the standing-start quarter-mile in 18.2 seconds. Zero-to-sixty mph acceleration through the gears could be accomplished in 13.5 seconds, by running the engine to its limit in second gear.

The Cord had quality problems. The front wheel universal joints would give trouble if not conscientiously cared for. The transmission had an evil habit of jumping out of gear. These were things that normally would have been taken care of in the development phase, but Cord could ill afford to make thorough tests. In fact, production started before the first of the transaxles had been delivered from Detroit Gear!

In all, 3,100 Cords were built from 1935 to 1937. The four door sedan had a list price of $3,060 in 1937, when E. L. Cord sold

Cord Corporation to two groups of New York bankers and retired to Reno, Nevada, where he died in 1974 at the age of 79.

The Cord Automobile Co. closed down in 1937. Forest Baster left Lycoming to join White Motor Co. in Cleveland as assistant chief engineer for engines, later becoming chief engineer of White Trucks. George Kublin went to General Motors, where he became manager of a small engineering group based in Detroit that worked on new products for its overseas operations (Opel and Vauxhall). He went into retirement in 1956 and died ten years later.

Gorden Buehrig went to Ford and worked as body engineer on many projects, including the 1956-model Lincoln Continental Mark II. He retired from Ford in 1965.

84 BUICK CENTURY, 1936

Famous for its valve-in-head straight-eight, Buick occupied second place only to Cadillac in General Motors' ranking list. From a commercial viewpoint, Buick was far more important, producing far greater numbers of cars than Cadillac.

Buick's rise to greatness was hampered not only by the existence of Cadillac, but also by its own standing with its traditional market. The Buick was regarded as the car for professional men—doctors, lawyers, the upper middle class, and pillars of society.

Not for them any ostentatious styling, outstanding luxury, anything out of the ordinary in power and speed. All that changed when the Buick Century came along in 1936—and customers of all social layers, all walks of life, flocked to Buick (Fig. 7-9). After five or six years during which the Buick name was either disregarded, sneered at, or shunned by performance-minded drivers, the Buick suddenly became a hot car, swept to greatness on the wings of a new attitude of bravado, aided immeasurably by the basic soundness of the product, and an enlightened marketing strategy.

The Century was a new name, and the car had sparkling new looks. Buick's success, as in the case of other great GM cars of that era, was in no small measure due to styling. This one was created by Harley Earl himself and featured a convex-curved radiator shell, bulging proudly in contrast with the sunken-cheek grille designs that had recently appeared on so many of Buick's competitors.

The Fisher A-body was reskinned for 1936, so Buick got the benefit of new exterior sheet metal from stem to stern, giving an appearance of better streamlining, with longer and more bulbous fender skirts, faster windshield angles and rooflines, balanced proportions, and discreet detailing.

Earl's recipe was exactly what the market needed. Under this body stood a chassis that was one of the toughest in the business, with Buick's version of the independent front suspension that Cadillac had developed, torque tube drive with an axle carried on multi-leaf semi-elliptical springs, and for the first time, Buick had four-wheel hydraulic brakes.

The chassis had been designed and developed under the direction of Verner P. Mathews, who had joined Buick in 1927. The engine, on the other hand, was the work of the new chief engineer, Charles A. Chayne, with the assistance of John Dolza.

Chayne came to Buick in 1930 from Marmon, where he had been an engine designer. Prior to that, he had worked as an experimental engineer with Lycoming. He had an engineering degree from Massachusetts Institute of Technology, and had taught automotive engineering there for six years.

At Buick, he immediately went to work on improving the original straight-eight, which had replaced the sixes for 1931. It was made in two sizes, 220.5 and 344.3 cubic inches, to designs produced under F.A. Bower's leadership. Bower was Buick's chief engineer from 1927 to 1936, when he went into semi-retirement due to poor health. He came to Buick as assistant chief engineer in 1918, having ten years' experience from Oldsmobile and Weston-Mott Axle Co. behind him.

In the rush to get the straight-eight into production, Bower had too little time for proper testing and development of the engine. It suffered from lack of cooling capacity, and bearing dimensions were felt to be marginal. An external oil cooler was used to alleviate these short-comings, but at extra cost.

Chayne started at the low end, getting a short-stroke engine into production for the new Buick Special (Series 40) in 1934. His redesign of the big one was ready for the 1936 models. He reduced displacement to 320 cubic inches by shortening the stroke from 5.00 to 4.31 inches (and boring out the cylinders from 3.31 to 3.44 inches). Output increased from 116 to 120 hp.

Block and head were of cast iron, and the crankcase extended about 2.5 inches below the crankshaft center line. The counterbalanced crankshaft was a steel forging of tremendous strength, supported in five main bearings. The camshaft was chain-driven, and mechanical tappets worked long pushrods to rocker arms overhead. The valves were placed vertically and in line, with all ports on the left side. The combustion chamber was compact, with a slight wedge shape. Plugs were inserted almost horizontally from the right, and sparked by Delco coil and distributor ignition.

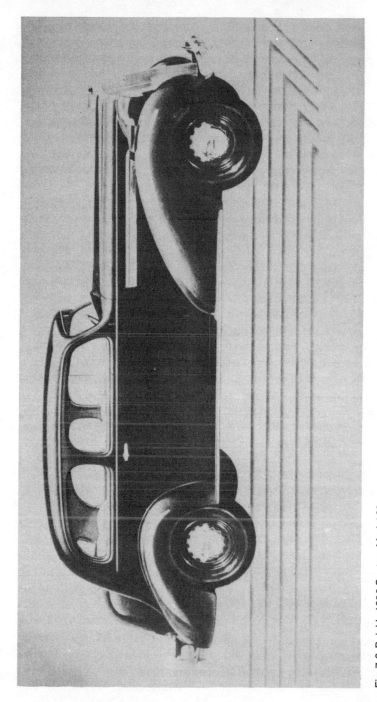

Fig. 7-9. Buick's 1936 Century Model 68.

Buick changed from updraft to downdraft carburetors in 1935. The 1936-model engines had aluminum pistons and crankshaft counterweighting was further refined. Earlier engines had relied partly on splash lubrication, but the 1936 units had full force lubrication.

This was the engine that was chosen for the Century. "The Century" was originally the name of a famous long-distance train, but Buick chose the name because of its claimed top speed of 100 mph. It was not a seriously inflated claim. Timed tests at the GM Proving grounds showed the car capable of 95 to 96 mph, which would give speedometer readings of over 100 mph.

The name was part of the bravado, and the new spirit of merchandizing that had come into the Buick organization when Harlow Curtice took over the division late in 1933. An accountant by training, he was a salesman by nature—and a fast, fearless decision-maker. In fifteen years he had worked his way up from clerk to president of AC Spark Plug just down the road from the Buick plant in Flint, Michigan.

His brilliant idea for the Century was to combine Buick's lightest vehicle with its biggest engine. The Century replaced Series 60, and was built on a 122-inch wheelbase, with curb weights of 3,960 to 4,055 pounds, according to body style.

With a three-speed synchromesh transmission and a 3.90:1 final drive ratio, this car gave acceleration figures that were remarkable, especially in the upper reaches. Lighter cars, with strong engines, could get the jump on the Century when starting from standstill, but from 25 to 75, the Buick was hard to beat. Through the gears, the Century could go from standstill to 60 mph in 16.5 seconds. And the torque of the new straight-eight, 238 pounds-feet, at 1,600 rpm, gave excellent top-gear performance, from a crawl to cruising speed.

The price range for the Century was $1,095 to $1,135, and Buick had the capacity to build enough of them to satisfy the market. Buick built just short of 180,000 cars in 1936 and nearly 45,000 of those were in the Century series.

85. CADILLAC SERIES 60, 1937

"The Spearhead of Motoring Progress" is what Cadillac's advertisements called the 1936 models. The statement is sufficiently innocuous to avoid being at odds with the facts, but totally positive in its tenor, giving the impression that Cadillac had indeed moved ahead. It was a less cynical age than ours, when few would doubt Cadillac's ability to back up its claim with solid facts (Fig. 7-10).

Of course, progress is a relative term, and it is true that in comparison with the earlier V-8 models the 1936 cars incorporated new engineering and styling with several all-new components, including the engine and transmission. Innovation is often synonymous with progress, and on that basis, one must admit that Cadillac had indeed improved its product. We cannot now close our eyes to the other side of the coin, however. Cadillac's slogan was also intended to cover up a certain loss of exclusivity by attempting to confer on a lower-cost, mass-produced car the same aura of greatness that had surrounded Cadillac's finest cars in the past.

There had been a complete reversal of policy at Cadillac in 1934, when Lawrence P. Fisher left the division and moved up to a corporate office. His place was filled by Nicholas Dreystadt, an energetic and ambitious character, who had been Cadillac's factory manager for two years. He had come into the Cadillac organization in the early Twenties, as head of the Chicago service branch. In 1926 L. P. Fisher invited him to move to Detroit and take over as national service manager. Dreystadt accepted, and later added parts managing to his responsibilities.

Extremely cost-conscious, Dreystadt introduced strict and wide-sweeping cost-control methods at Cadillac.

Rather than pursuing top quality at any price, the new Cadillac would use mass-produced components whenever "good enough." This started Cadillac on the route to sharing major elements with other GM divisions. It brought Cadillac's price range down to democratic levels, the series 60 having a base price of $1,645 in 1936. After several loss-making years, Cadillac returned to profitable operation. From a business viewpoint, Cadillac's policy change meant salvation and survival. From a product viewpoint, it was accomplished without compromising Cadillac's greatness.

Our concept and definition of greatness does take account of time and the changing priorities in the market. Thus we find that in the depths of the depression, it's the lowest-priced Cadillac, that, after profound analysis also ranks as the greatest. In view of today's necessities of economy and performance, this feeling is reinforced.

The Cadillac Series 60 gave almost double the gasoline mileage of the magnificent V-12 and V-16 models, while giving equal or better performance. It was a more modern car in every way. It was still a luxury car, but a luxury car made with common sense.

Despite being greatly reduced in dimensions and weight, it still offered reasonable passenger accommodation in terms of both space and comfort. Lighter construction resulted in better roadholding and improved braking performance. The 1936 model Series 60 sedan weighed 4,171 pounds, and the car was thus 500 to 800 pounds lighter than the various V-8-powered Cadillac models of 1935.

It shared the Fisher B-body with Buick, which provided important economics of scale. The wheelbase for the Series 60 was only 121 inches, when the 70 and 75 (also equipped with V-8 engines) were built on wheelbases of 131 or 138 inches.

The Series 60 shared the general styling theme of the bigger models, which was considerably revised from the previous year.

Usually styling trends flow from the more expensive models to the lower-ranking cars, but this year Cadillac went off in the opposite direction. There was a lot of La Salle influence in the new Cadillac and no doubt certain compromises were made to avoid costly changes in the mass-produced body panels.

Harley J. Earl personally directed the styling of the 1936 Cadillacs, and the Series 60 is a happy blend, with major emphasis on a new and modern look without losing sight of the need for continuity. The tall, narrow grille; faired-in headlamps; and split V-form windshield were all new designs, but had their roots in styling elements of the 1934 and 1935 models.

Cadillac had an all-new V-8 engine for 1936. For the first time, Cadillac made the blocks and crankcase as one single casting. It was still an L-head design, with a counterweighted crankshaft running in three main bearings.

The engine design was due to John F. Gordon, who had come to Cadillac as a laboratory technician in 1923 with a degree in mechanical engineering from the University of Michigan. By 1933 he was motor design engineer, working in direct association with Owen Nacker, who had been promoted assistant chief engineer.

Two sizes of new V-8s were made, one with 322 cubic-inch displacement and a rating of 125 hp; the other with 346 cubic-inch displacement and 135 hp. Both had the same 4½-inch stroke and shared the same crankshaft. They shared the same block, too, but the larger engine was bored out to 3½ inches, while the smaller one had a 3.375-inch bore.

The new engine was about 20 pounds heavier than the former 353 cubic-inch V-8, mainly because of the change from a cast aluminum crankcase to all-iron construction. But the new one cost

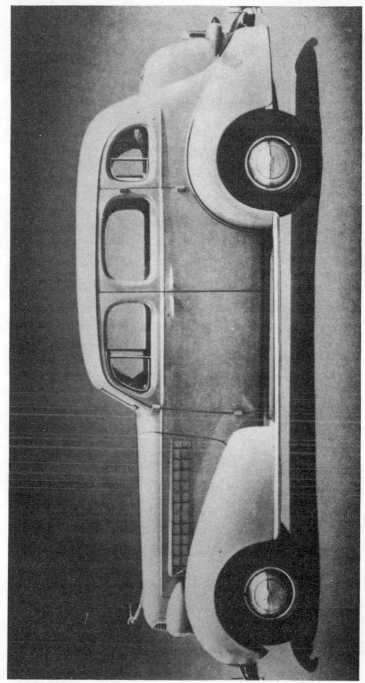

Fig. 7-10. Cadillac Series 60 of 1935.

far less to manufacture, and in Dreystadt's mind, the extra weight meant nothing when compared to the dollars saved. For 1937, the smaller engine was discontinued and the Series 60 was equipped with the 346 cubic inch engine, while its wheelbase was increased to 124 inches.

Chassis design for the Series 60 also got the benefit of mass-produced parts where applicable. That meant an inexpensive cross-braced frame, and a new hypoid-bevel rear axle. Cadillac continued its own rear suspension with semi-elliptical leaf springs and Hotchkiss drive, and also, of course, used its own coil-spring independent front suspension on the Series 60.

A new three-speed transmission with faster-acting synchromesh for quicker shifts had been developed under the direction of Earl A. Thompson, assistant chief engineer of Cadillac who was very busy at the time with automatic-transmission experiments. However, he left General Motors in 1939 to work as an independent engineering consultant.

One of the young designers then in the Cadillac studio was William L. Mitchell, who had joined Harley Earl's staff in 1936 after studies at the Carnegie Institute of Technology. He used the Series 60 as the basis for a dramatically new design which went into production in 1938 as the 60 special. It was the start of a whole new styling theme, for Mitchell really had a vision of the car as *one form*, and the 60 Special introduced a transition to the basic GM body style of 1946-48.

The 1938 60 Special was a four-door sedan with all doors hinged at the front, and a trunk designed as part of the body, not something tacked on as an afterthought. C-posts were wide and windowless, giving the steel-roofed sedan a look usually associated with convertibles. The belt-line appeared as a firm separation between the upper and lower body sections, running horizontally and unbroken from the front of the hood to the rear edge of the rear door, where it was swept down to conform with the fender line and trunk profile.

Bill Mitchell became GM's vice president of styling in 1958, the same year John F. Gordon was named president of the corporation. The Series 60 Cadillac served as an important stepping stone for both.

86. LINCOLN ZEPHYR, 1938

At the time of its birth, the Lincoln was most notable for its lack of styling. That was soon changed as Ford sent Lincoln chassis to the best coachbuilders in the country for custom bodies. It was to change even more, for in 1936 Ford began producing a Lincoln that was based entirely on a styling idea: the Zephyr (Fig. 7-11).

Its smooth lines, with faired-in headlamps and long fastback, invite comparison with Chrysler's bulbous Airflow models. Ford did not claim low air drag for the Zephyr, and it probably was no better in that regard than the Chrysler (which was poor, in spite of the maker's best intentions).

But the Lincoln had the advantage of looking modern and pretty. Carl Breer and his team at Chrysler had made important engineering studies, not just in aerodynamics but also in body construction, springing and ride, and the Airflow embodied the fruits of their thoughts and findings. The engineering that went into the Zephyr was, well, let's not say "makeshift" but rather use the term "opportunistic." There was no serious attempt to put an advanced-design chassis under the Zephyr body. What was done basically was find the simplest and most expedient solution. That's not despicable, it's a principle on which many a great car has been built. And the Zephyr was a great car despite its weaknesses. Those weaknesses were not the results of the decision to adapt mass-produced Ford parts and principles to the car, but stem from the unfortunate fact that what was available in the Ford parts bin at the time was obsolete.

Fig. 7-11. The 1936 Lincoln Zephyr.

The whole project had its start when Edsel Ford made the acquaintance of John Tjaarda in 1932. He was a pioneer aviator, aircraft designer, and auto engineer who had moved from his native Netherlands to America in 1923, and worked in succession for Locke, GM Art & Color, and Briggs.

He began designing his vision of the ideal car about 1927, and Briggs built a prototype in 1932: a low, streamliner with a Ford V-8 installed in the rear. He called the car the Sterkenburg (after his middle name). The Sterkenburg interested Edsel Ford a great deal. The Lincoln plant was almost at a standstill, and the need for a new product was desperate. Briggs wanted to use it as an entry to a Ford Contract and offered full body-engineering services for the project.

Of course, the Sterkenburg prototype was not suitable for Ford's production setup. Fundamental changes were needed. The engine could not stay in the rear—that created drive line and suspension problems that Ford was not equipped to solve. And while the V-8 would provide adequate performance, a Lincoln car must have a Lincoln engine, if only to distinguish it from a mere Ford. And that meant a V-12. Such changes were bound to affect the exterior appearance of the car, and what survived of the Sterkenburg design was mainly its styling theme. Tjaarda was paid off, and Edsel Ford put his own designer on the job of restyling it.

This designer was Eugene T. "Bob" Gregorie, who had come to Lincoln in 1931 after a couple of years with Brewster and a short stay at GM Art & Color. He was educated as a naval architect, and began his career by designing yachts. His first complete job for Ford was a smaller car for the British branch, and Edsel liked its lines so well that he ordered it scaled up for the 1934-model American Fords. Gregorie's body design for the Lincoln Zephyr was quickly approved, and Briggs went to work on the production problems of a semi-unitized structure.

In this regard, Briggs did contribute something novel to the Zephyr engineering, for the body was built up as a bridge-truss cage. It was an advance towards unit body construction of equal importance with the Airflow's interlocking frame and body, without copying it. Chrysler's structure relied heavily on stressed sheet metal, while the Lincoln put all major loads into the cage members.

The engine for the Zephyr was based on the Model K V-12, and designated Model H. It was laid out with the banks disposed at an included angle of 75 degrees. Following Ford practice, the block and crankcase were cast as one single piece. Detachable aluminum cylinder heads were used in combination with side valves operated from a single, central gear-driven camshaft. The crankshaft was fully counterbalanced and ran in four main bearings.

It shared the 3.75-inch stroke of the Ford V-8, giving a total displacement of 267.3 cubic inches. With a 6.7:1 compression ratio and a two-barrel downdraft Stromberg carburetor, it delivered 110 hp at 3,900 rpm. Maximum torque was 186 pounds-feet at 2,000 rpm. Despite the high-speed character of this engine, Ford used cast iron pistons in it, when aluminum ones would have given great advantage.

The three-speed transmission had synchromesh on second and top, and shifts were made by a long and whippy lever curving its way up from the floor. Torque tube drive was used, as on contemporary Fords, with diagonal radius arms to locate the rear axle. Suspension was also taken from the Ford, using transverse leaf springs both front and rear. Steering was by Gemmer worm and roller, and the brakes worked by mechanical linkage to all four wheels.

The wheelbase was 122 inches, and tire size was 7.00 × 16, with pressed-steel disc wheels. The Zephyr was capable of 90 mph and gave an average fuel economy of 15-16 miles to the gallon, making it the most spartan of V-12's in its appetite for gasoline. Zero-to-sixty acceleration was a matter of 15.5 seconds—remarkably quick for such a silent, luxurious car, and no doubt due to its light weight of 3,470 pounds.

Prices started at a sensationally low $1,275, and Ford sold 17,715 Zephyrs in 1936 (out of a total of 18,994 Lincolns), it had done a grand job of saving Lincoln, and was outselling the price leader models issued by other prestige car makers, such as the Packard 120 or Cadillac La Salle.

The 1937-model Zephyr had a new, twisted gear lever emerging from the console on the driver's side to permit three-abreast seating. Bigger changes were in store for 1938, when the wheelbase was increased to 125 inches and an impressive facelift put the Zephyr into the front line of fashion (Fig. 7-12). At the same time, the engine was equipped with hydraulic valve lifters, and a hypoid-bevel rear axle enabled Ford to cut 1.3 inches from the height of the floor tunnel. The instrument panel was redesigned with a giant circular speedometer mounted at the center. Hydraulic brakes were adopted for the 1939 model.

Sales volume for the Zephyr fell below 10,000 cars a year in 1938 and 1939, and Ford decided to phase it out. At the same time,

Fig. 7-12. The 1938 version of the Lincoln Zephyr.

a new medium-priced Mercury was introduced, while the Zephyr became the basis for a limited-production model called the Continental.

Of the people behind the Zephyr, the first to go was Edsel Ford, who died in 1943. John Tjaarda remained for some years with Briggs then settled in California, and after WW II, mounted a project to build a modern car he called the Cortez—but that never went beyond the planning stages. He died in 1962. "Bob" Gregorie remained styling director of Ford up to 1948, and then retired to Florida.

87. PACKARD SUPER EIGHT, 1939

The Thirties were trying times for Packard. Many of its challengers had gone under: Peerless, Pierce-Arrow, Marmon, Stutz, Stearns-Knight and Auburn were forced out of business during the depression. Only the strength of General Motors in the low-priced end of the market secured Cadillac's survival, just as it was the resources of the Ford Motor Company (and the Zephyr) that saved Lincoln. Chrysler had to abandon the prestige market, transferring the Imperial name to cars sharing bodies and engines with mass-produced models.

What could Packard do to survive? It had no presence outside the luxury car market, a market that was drying up fast. Its engineering staff had no experience with low- or even moderately-priced cars, and its dealer organization was unaccustomed to handling popular-class clientele.

Yet there was nothing else for Packard to do, as chairman Alvan Macauley saw it, than to build and sell lower-priced cars. Engineering vice president Jesse G. Vincent rose to the occasion, and in the spring of 1935 the factory began production of the Series 120, an eight-cylinder car manufactured by Packard, selling at prices starting below $1,000!

The One-Twenty was instantly identifiable as a Packard, sharing the modernized grille with the bigger models, carrying the same flutes on both sides of the hood and having hub caps with the same red-painted hexagon. Built on a 120-inch wheelbase, the One-Twenty gave 16-mpg fuel economy and an 85-mph top speed. And it saved Packard.

Proven right in its policy by its success, Packard brought out a six-cylinder version, Series 115, on a 115-inch wheelbase for 1937, reaching down into the Oldsmobile-Hudson-Dodge market.

These cars were made to make money, and they did. However, Macauley and Vincent fully realized that they were not the kind of cars on which Packard's reputation rested, and they

Fig. 7-13. A 1937 Packard Super Eight.

insisted on keeping the glorious high-priced models in production. This was costly, for they accounted for about half the operating expenses and only about ten percent of revenues.

Much of the credit for the success of the low-priced cars must go to the chief engineer responsible for their over-all soundness and quality, having shepherded them through the design and development phase and into production in record time, while keeping up steady improvement of the senior series.

This was Clyde R. Paton, who had joined Packard as an experimental engineer in 1930, becoming chief engineer two years later, at the age of 40. He was born in Almont, Michigan, and was manager of Paton Electric Service Co. until he enlisted in the U.S. Army Air Service in 1918. After the war he attended the University of Michigan, graduating in 1923. In 1925 he got his first auto industry job, as a research engineer with Studebaker. He stayed in South Bend for five years, rounding out his experience with work on all parts and systems in the car.

Another man who also comes in for a great deal of credit is George T. Christopher, who served as vice president in charge of manufacturing. He had vast experience in all aspects of production, inspection, and quality control, from 15 years at Oldsmobile and four years with Oakland/Pontiac, before joining Packard in 1934.

The last of the great classic Packards was the Super Eight of 1939 (though the Twelve was still in production, it shared the same chassis and body). Body designs were produced by Werner Bubitz and Edward Macauley, with minimal year-to-year variations after 1937, when the fenders had reached modern proportions and the grille had taken on its maximum tilt.

Independent front wheel suspension had been introduced on the original One-Twenty. It was a coil-spring system, working on the same principles as Cadillac's but not copied from the Cadillac design. A new system with different geometry, dimensioned for the greater vehicle weights, was adopted for the Eight, Super Eight, and Twelve for 1937.

Frame design was basically similar for all models, with box-section side members and cross-bracing. All models used Hotchkiss drive, with open propeller shafts, hypoid-bevel rear axles, and semi-elliptical leaf springs. Three-speed transmissions were standard, and hydraulic brakes had replaced the mechanical system in 1936 (for the 1937 models).

Packard's L-head Eight, as used in the 1939 Super Eight, was essentially a version of the Vincent-designed straight-eight from

1923. Its main features never changed much, which bears eloquent testimony to the flawlessness of the initial design.

Among its key features were a forged-steel crankshaft, fully counterweighted, running in nine main bearings. A single camshaft in the side of the cast iron block was driven by silent chain from the front of the crankshaft. Heads, too, were cast iron, until aluminum heads were adopted in 1937.

The 1939 Super Eight was powered by a 320 cubic-inch engine with 3.1875-inch bore and 5-inch stroke which was put into production in 1928 for the 1929-models 626 and 633, Light Eight and Standard Eight. The Super Eight designation was first used on the 1933-model 1003, powered by a 385 cubic-inch version of the same engine (with 3½- inch bore, in production since 1927 for Custom Eight and Deluxe Eight cars).

As compression was put up from 5.0 to 6.3:1 by 1933, output increased from 106 hp to 120 hp at 3,200 rpm. The 385 cubic-inch engine was in use through the 1936 model year, producing 150 hp at 3,200 rpm in its ultimate form. The 320 cubic inch engine was adopted for the 1937 Super Eight (while the Eight series shared the newer 282 cubic-inch engine with the One-Twenty).

By 1939, the 320 cubic-inch Super Eight delivered 130 hp and gave the car a top speed on the upper side of 100 mph. Three wheelbases were available: 127 inches for the 1703 models, 134 inches for the 1704 models and 139 inches for the 1705 limousine.

The year 1939 was the last for the ancient eight-cylinder engine, which was replaced for 1940 with a new L-head straight eight with shorter stroke, hydraulic valve lifters, and higher compression. During the war Packard built aircraft engines and other war material to its fullest capacity, and the company was in good shape when civilian production could be resumed in 1946. As for its post-war product, its description follows a few pages further on.

Chapter 8
The Cars of Post-War America: 1941-1957

Being Cadillac isn't easy, particularly when people like Harlow Curtice and Charlie Chayne are running Buick. Up in Flint, Buick had far greater production capacity and played a bigger part in assuring GM's financial health than did Cadillac down in Detroit. Since Curtice took charge of Buick in 1933, the division had gone from strength to greater strength. With Chayne as chief engineer, the Buick car had evolved into a machine with an image all its own, and an enviable reputation with the public. In the GM firmament, Buick's star often had a brighter shine than Cadillac's, and the men of Flint had no qualms about their ambition to outdo all rivals on every front.

88. BUICK SUPER, 1941

Of course, Buick's arch-rival wasn't Cadillac, but Oldsmobile. The Lansing boys, always more daring and innovative, were underselling Buick in price. Olds had a line of low-priced sixes, while Buick built valve-in-head eights exclusively.

Horsepower was Buick's game and in 1941 Buick offered the most powerful cars built in America. With an output of 165 hp from the big 320 cubic-inch eight, Buick's 1941 Roadmaster, Century, and Limited had 15 more horses than the most powerful Cadillac of that year. Oldsmobile, with its L-head eight, was far behind with a maximum of 110 hp.

Indisputably great as the 126-inch wheelbase Century and Roadmaster, and even the 139-inch Limited were, it's the Super that stands out in the 1941 Buick lineup (Fig. 8-1). The Super shared the 121-inch wheelbase with the Special Series 40-B, and had the smaller, lighter 248 cubic-inch eight-cylinder engine tuned to an impressive 125 hp, 10 hp more than in the Special.

The Super got its power from a new compound carburetion setup that consisted of twin two-barrel carburetors with a throttle linkage arranged to give sequential action (and closing off the secondaries for improved fuel economy when power was not needed).

The smaller engine weighed 672 pounds, or 122 pounds less than the big one, and with the shorter wheelbase, the Super scaled only 3,930 pounds against the Roadmaster's 4,245 pounds. Performance levels were about the same, with top speeds just above 100 mph and zero-to-60 mph times around 13 seconds. But the Super did everything more efficiently, which meant better fuel economy, and also easier handling.

The 248 cubic-inch Buick Eight originated in 1937 and was essentially a small-bore, slightly de-stroked version of the 320 cubic inch version, which dates from 1936. But the blocks were different castings, with closer cylinder spacing for the smaller one, and that's where most of the weight saving was realized.

The Super name had been used briefly for Buick's Series 50 during 1935, but then taken out of use temporarily. It was brought back for 1940, and continued for 1941-42 and after the war, from 1946 through 1958.

The 1941-model Super was also classified as Series 50, which means one step above the Special, but outranked by the Century (Series 60), Roadmaster (Series 70), and Limited (Series 90). Prices were exceedingly reasonable, starting at $1,031 and extending to $1,555 for the 1941 Super, which was built as a four-door sedan, two-door sedan club coupe, business coupe, two-door convertible, and four-door convertible.

The sheet metal was shared with the other GM divisions, which helps explain how Buick was able to keep the prices down so well. Buick's body engineer, E. F. Reynolds, did a fine job of building Buick bodies from standard Fisher Body elements, to designs by Harley Earl and the stylists in the Buick studio. George A. Jergenson created the basic theme for the 1941 models, and George Snyder was responsible for much of the detail. The Buick chassis had evolved gradually under the direction of Verner P. Mathews and J. H. Booth.

Mathews laid out the new rear suspension for 1938 models with coil springs instead of the former leaf springs, and torque tube

Fig. 8-1. Buick's 1941 Super.

drive. Booth designed the new front suspension for 1939 to replace the Cadillac design used from 1934 through 1938. Mathews had been with Buick since 1927, and was to become the division's chief engineer in 1952. Booth was a steering-and-suspension expert when he came to Buick in 1935.

There was no automatic transmission, power steering, or power brakes for the 1941 Buicks. The Buick had a reputation as a he-man type of car, and Chayne tended to be conservative in anything related to safety, preferring what was known to be reliable rather than seeking to develop new (and possibly better) systems.

The transmission was a three-speed with synchromesh on second and top, with column shift. The linkage was tough and worked with great precision. Twelve-inch brake drums were fitted on all wheels, with duo-servo action in the shoes to help keep pedal pressure low. The brake system was, of course, hydraulic, and the pedal had enough leverage to make power assist unnecessary.

Nor was there any real need for power steering. The Saginaw worm-and-nut steering gear worked with low friction, and the ratio was chosen to reduce the muscle effort, but it meant a large-diameter (18 inches) steering wheel, and four and a half turns lock to lock.

The Super was maneuverable, with excellent down-the-road stability, ample power reserves, and better-than-average brakes.

But no Buick Eight could be called an economy engine, and average fuel consumption ranged from 12.5 to 15 miles per gallon.

The men behind it went on to big things at General Motors. Harlow Curtice was named president in 1953 and served in that office until his retirement in 1958. He died five years later.

Charles A. Chayne stayed on as chief engineer of Buick until 1951, when he was named vice president in charge of the GM Engineering Staff. Under his regime, which lasted until 1963, there was a notable emphasis on engines, the part of the car he loved best. He retired to California and died at the age of 80, late in 1978.

89. PACKARD SUPER CLIPPER, 1947

Like most 1947 models from other companies, Packard's Super Clipper of 1947 was essentially a pre-war car. The industry gradually got back into civilian production during 1945-46, and in most cases there was not much opportunity to make big changes from the 1942 models. That was Packard's case, and it's noteworthy that the company was one of the first to convert its plants back into producing cars, building its first post-war car on October 19th, 1945 (Fig. 8-2).

Fortunately, Packard had a very modern car in 1941-42, which on its reappearance in 1945, looked like the future. The Packard body had smoother lines than the transition-styled GM cars and the hopelessly outdated Ford and Chrysler designs. It was far more attractive than the slabsided Kaiser-Frazer models that appeared in 1946 and probably had better aerodynamics, too.

Designed mainly by Werner Gubitz, who was assisted by Charles Yeager, the Clipper front end was a masterpiece, blending traditional styling elements with modern shapes and giving due attention to the demands of contemporary fashion.

Little details that were practically trademarks of strong Packard identification, such as the notched top of the grille frame, and the flute lines in the hood were translated into a symbolic combination which artistically and functionally contributed to the wholeness of the total design. It existed in sketch and clay-model form as early as 1939, and went into production on the 1941-model Clipper.

The Clipper was a radical departure from the Classic Packard, and there was indeed something tentative about its introduction, as if Packard half expected it to fail in the marketplace.

It was offered as one model only, a four-door sedan on a 127-inch wheelbase, and not as a series. It was priced at $1,375 for the Six and $1,420 with an eight-cylinder engine, placing it midway between the 120 and the 160, whose bodies carried on the classic style through the 1941 model year.

The original Clipper was aimed at a fairly narrow market segment, where its principal adversaries were the Cadillac 61, Chrysler New York, and Buick Roadmaster. For 1942, the Packard 160 and 180 were given the Clipper body, leaving only the lowest-priced models with the traditional Packard look.

The pre-war Clipper engines were shared with the 110 and 120 series. After the war, Packard built only Clippers, and more than 42,000 of them were produced in 1946.

Three engines were offered, the 245-cubic-inch 105-hp Six, the 282-cubic-inch 125-hp eight, and the 356-cubic-inch 165-hp eight which had first been used in the Super Eight of 1940. Clippers were built on three different wheelbases: 120 inches for the six, Standard Eight and Deluxe Eight; 127 inches for the Super Clipper and Custom Super Clipper (which came with the 165-hp engine); and 148 inches for the Custom Super Clipper limousine.

The long-wheelbase limousine was discontinued in 1946, and the most popular Packard of 1947 was the Deluxe Clipper Eight, using the old 282 cubic-inch engine in a 120-inch wheelbase chassis. It accounted for nearly half of Packard's output that year (over 51,000 cars), while the Super Clipper remained fairly exclusive.

Packard built 7,500 Custom Super Clippers and just short of 5,000 Super Clipper eights. Any 1946-47 Packard with the Super label in its title was powered by the 165-hp engine. In retrospect it may seem strange that Packard chose the in-line L-head approach to a brand-new engine, when an overhead-valve V-8 would have fitted in the car beautifully. The reasons are not hard to find however.

Jesse G. Vincent, Packard's engineering director, was not impressed with overhead valves, taking a critical view of the Chevrolet and Buick examples, which were noisy and needed frequent adjustment. Nor did he feel that the V-8 configuration was suitable for Packard. There was no prestige in having a V-8, since Ford had standardized one. Vincent did not greatly admire the Cadillac V-8, and would certainly never risk being accused of copying it. His straight-eight was smoother and quieter, with even firing intervals and better balance.

Finally there was the tooling question. Packard was equipped to machine blocks and heads of in-line eights in large numbers with

Fig. 8-2. The 1947 Packard Super Clipper.

great precision. The same with crankshafts and camshafts. Any change in this department could only have been effected at the cost of important investment spending, while the possible returns looked extremely dubious.

The new L-head in-line eight of 356 cubic inches was a lighter engine than the former 326 cubic-inch unit of the 1937-39 Super Eight. Yet it put out far more power; 165 hp at 3,600 rpm. The compression ratio was a modest 6.45:1 and the carburetor a downdraft two-barrel instrument with automatic choke.

While Vincent was as intent as ever on good low-range torque, he did make an accommodation with shorter stroke, settling for 4.625 inches. The 3½-inch bore was unchanged from the 1927 version. As before, the crankshaft ran in nine main bearings, and block and head were gray-iron castings.

Clyde Paton developed the vehicle per se, ably assisted by Forest MacFarland, a meticulous perfectionist admirably suited for Packard quality.

The 1947 Super Clipper had coil-spring independent front suspension and the usual Hotchkiss drive with a hypoid-bevel rear axle and semi-elliptical leaf springs. The transmission was three-speed column shift unit with synchromesh on second and top. It was available with Packard's Electromatic clutch, first offered in 1940, which could be put in and out of operation by a simple push-button. When in use, it would disengage on a trailing throttle (serving more or less as a free-wheel at the same time) and permit gear changes to be made without touching the clutch pedal.

The car weighed 4,090 pounds and could reach speeds of 110 mph, with zero-to-60 mph acceleration times centered around the 16-second mark. Fuel consumption was difficult to get above 13 mph in normal use. For customers to whom that mattered, there was always the short-wheelbase six-cylinder models.

Ride and handling were good in the Clipper. Bad roads and good were swallowed up in great style and comfort. Down-the-road stability was impeccable, and steering response was slow but every bit as good as in the contemporary Cadillac.

In 1948 Packard went to a new style, from a model by Edward Macauley, and the Clipper name fell into disuse (to be revived in 1953, when Packard was nearing the end of the road).

J. G. Vincent retired at the end of 1950 and was succeeded by LeRoy Spencer. He lived to the age of 82 dying in 1962.

Clyde R. Paton left Packard when Vincent's retirement approached, and went to Willys-Overland as director of engineering. In 1958 he formed his own engineering company, Spartan Design, Inc. He died at the age of 78 in Bloomfield, Michigan, in 1972.

George T. Christopher resigned from the presidency of Packard in October, 1949, and was succeeded by Hugh J. Ferry, who had joined the company in 1910 as a cost accountant. Ferry became chairman in 1952 after naming James J. Nance as his successor. Nance arranged the merger with Studebaker which spelled death for Packard. The Clipper and Super Clipper are revered as the last of the great Packards, for the future to which they pointed never came to be.

90. HUDSON COMMODORE, 1948

While Studebaker scored highly with its postwar look created by Raymond Loewy in 1947, it must be recognized that its merit was based entirely on its value as a piece of industrial design. There were no technical advances in the car.

When Hudson came along a year later, with a car that was even more dramatically new and different, it was widely assumed that its depth of innovation did not go far under the skin (Fig. 8-3).

Of course, the truth was quite different. The 1948 Hudson was the result of an engineering program that had its roots in pre-war studies and had been conducted in an organized fashion since 1943.

This was the "Step-Down" design with the Monobilt body construction, which represented fresh new thinking on (a) what a car should look like, and (b) how to build it. The basic idea was to put the frame side members where the running boards used to be and to put a low floor between them rather than on top of them, as was standard practice. The high door sills that resulted gave rise to the "Step-Down" slogan which Hudson used in its advertising.

Lowering the floor helped lower the car's center of gravity. Passengers sat lower down, too. The car was built on a 124-inch wheelbase, which placed the rear seat comfortably ahead of the rear axle and allowed the use of full-rectangular rear doors.

To our eyes, accustomed to more recent designs, the Hudson looks odd, because the belt line was not lowered in proportion, and the upper body seems sort of squashed, with its low windows. At the time of its launching, however, that was an advantage, calling immediate attention to its low build. The Hudson was only 60 inches high overall, compared with an industry average of 66 inches.

It had a wide track in front and a standard track in the rear, with coil-spring independent front suspension and a rear axle

Fig. 8-3. Hudson's finest for '48, the Commodore Eight.

carried on semi-elliptical leaf springs (Hotchkiss drive). The engine was placed well forward in the chassis, and the cowl was moved up to where it practically met the wheel arches.

This did not produce weight-distribution problems, for the structure was uniformly heavy throughout and there were other mass concentrations in the rear such as the axle, fuel tank, and spare wheel. When Hudson went into racing, it had no trouble with wheel-spin due to insufficient load on the driving wheels, or handling problems due to excessive weight on the front wheels.

Hudson's remarkable perimeter frame was welded to the main stress-carrying members in the body, forming a basic unit-construction cage, not unlike the Lincoln-Zephyr body. But the Hudson was not a copy of the Lincoln. The Hudson came about through totally independent work.

It was Frank S. Spring, Hudson's director of design, who invented the perimeter frame and the body structure it supported, and patented the design in 1941.

Others who played an important role in making it a reality were Millard H. Toncray and Carl Cenzer. Toncray was named chief engineer in 1942, after serving under Coffin, Fekete, Behn and Baits since 1918. Cenzer came to Hudson in 1939 with a background including 11 years experience in body engineering from Dodge, Graham-Paige, and Willys-Overland. With Toncray's encouragement and Spring's ideas, Cenzer forged ahead and did the body engineering for the Monobilt unit.

Among its peculiarities is the way the frame side members envelope the rear wheels. The structure was tremendously rugged, with great torsional stiffness, but it was excessively heavy, and probably 200 or 300 pounds could have been pared off if Cenzer had had access to computers and could have performed three-dimensional stress analysis.

Still the car had good performance without needing enormous engine power. The standard engine for the 1948 Commodore was a new L-head six of 262 cubic-inch displacement, delivering 121 hp at 3,600 rpm. The former six was a long-stroke 211 cubic-inch unit which originated with the 1934 Terraplane, and was judged inadequate for the job and was taken out of production.

The new six was Hudson's first engine with full pressure lubrication, right down to rifle-drilling of the connecting rods. Stuart Baits had long resisted the departure from splash lubrication, but he finally yielded. On the other hand, the old in-line eight continued without change, and was optional in the new Commodore. It was the 254 cubic-inch L-head design which had originated with the Pacemaker Eight of 1932.

Both engines gave outstanding performance and surprisingly good fuel economy. The six was designed with cylinder spacing to allow for subsequent displacement increases, going first to 270 cubic inches, and eventually to 308, in which form it put out 145 hp at 4,000 rpm (with a new aluminum cylinder head and a 7.2:1 compression ratio).

Standard transmission was a normal three-speed column shift. But Hudson was a pioneer in semi-automatic and easy-shift transmissions, having introduced the Bendix-built Electric Hand in 1935, and wasn't going to stop now, particularly since GM's use of the fully automatic Hydra-Matic drive had spread as far down the price scale as the Pontiac by 1948.

One option for the Hudson was Vacumotive Drive, which was an automatic clutch, disengaged by manifold vacuum above a certain level, allowing clutchless shifts and free-wheeling. With Drivemaster, shifts between forward gears were also automated. The driver merely engaged top gear, and the car would upshift in accordance with speed and load (and downshift on the same basis). Finally, a separate, manually controlled overdrive was offered.

In 1948 Hudson offered three bodies in the Commodore series; a four-door sedan, a club coupe, and a convertible brougham. With the six-cylinder engine, the sedan weighed 3,540 pounds and had a list price of $2,399. The eight-cylinder counterpart was 60 pounds heavier and was priced $115 higher.

The styling theme was basically Spring's, but a lot of variations were created in the studio and the final product benefited from some of the better ideas. Art Kibiger was the chief designer, and other artists like Robert F. Andrews (who did most of the 1953 Studebaker while a member of Raymond Loewy Associates) and Holden A. Koto (who was the main influence behind the 1949 Ford) made their contributions.

The unit-construction step-down body and frame was ill-suited to styling changes, without going into structural redesign. Thus it condemned Hudson to making minor changes only until the company could afford to develop a second-generation and more flexible unit.

The 1954-55 models were still basically 1948 Hudsons, with new exterior sheet metal. In 1954 Hudson was merged with Nash to form American Motors, and the 1956 Hudsons were built around the Nash body shell. The Hudson name plate disappeared in 1957.

91. OLDSMOBILE FUTURAMIC 98, 1949

Above all, what made the Ninety-Eight so great, was the high-compression Rocket V-8 engine. Oldsmobile's chassis was as up-to-date as anything else produced by General Motors at the time, but not different or more advanced in any important areas and the Fisher-built Futuramic body was a GM Styling creation, shared with Buick (Fig. 8-4).

It's true that Oldsmobile had been the prime developer of the Hydra-matic transmission, but it was no longer exclusive to Oldsmobile, for Cadillac began using it in 1946 and Pontiac in 1948.

All that was extraordinary about the Olds was the new engine. It was a very special engine, a technological trailblazer, and years ahead of anything except one in-house rival: Cadillac. Cadillac had a new overhead-valve V-8 ready for production at the same time and it was no coincidence. Both stemmed from the same research project, instigated in 1937 by Charles F. Kettering.

By 1943 GM Research was running tests with a 30 cubic-inch single-cylinder engine whose pistons and cylinder heads could be quickly changed to alter compression ratios in a number of steps between 6.2:1 and 15.0:1. Three years later, the high-compression engine was ready to emerge from the laboratory stage to the in-car test and development phase.

It was still a corporate research project, and Oldsmobile was not yet involved, but the research engineering team led by Darl F. Caris chose an Oldsmobile for their road tests. They built a six-cylinder test engine that would have comparable power output with the standard 328 cubic-inch L-head unit which had a 6.4:1 compression ratio.

To deliver that kind of power with its 12.5:1 compression ratio, the overhead-valve test engine needed no more than 181 cubic-inch displacement! Apart from the valve gear, basic design differences lay in the stroke-bore ratio and the crankshaft configuration. The L-head Olds was a long-stroke unit (3.00 × 4.25 inches bore × stroke), while the test engine had "square" cylinder dimensions of 3.375-inch bore and stroke. Its crankshaft was made with generous crankpin overlap and was supported in seven main bearings, while the Olds crankshaft had four main bearings and minimal overlap.

Both engines delivered a maximum of about 90 hp and the Kettering engine, as it was called informally, gave slightly better acceleration. The high-compression unit also gave 40 percent lower fuel consumption in city traffic. Installed in cars of equal weight and with identical gearing, the test unit returned 26.5 miles to the gallon at a steady 40 mph, compared with 18.5 mpg for the stock engine.

Spontaneously, both Oldsmobile and Cadillac decided to design and develop V-8 engines based on the Kettering principles. In Lansing, chief engineer Jack Wolfram put Gil Burrell in charge of the V-8 project.

Burrell was a native of Lansing who had graduated from the University of Michigan and joined Oldsmobile as a draftsman in 1929. By 1946 he was the division's motor engineer. He had

Fig. 8-4. The 1949 Oldsmobile 98 Futuramic Holiday Coupe.

worked on the design and development of the L-head sixes and eights in all their different versions, and embraced the overhead-valve concept with enthusiasm.

Of course, the octane rating of the gasoline available at pumps across the nation did not allow him to retain the 12.5:1 compression ratio of the research engine. He had to bring it down to 7.25:1, which was still a big jump from the L-head designs.

The production-model V-8 delivered 135 hp at 3,600 rpm and had a maximum torque of 263 foot-pounds at 1,800 rpm. Its displacement was 303 cubic inches, with bore and stroke of 3.75 × 3.44 inches.

Compared with the 257-cubic-inch L-head eight of 1948, the V-8 had 25 percent more horsepower and 24 percent stronger torque. The engine weight had increased from 614 to 671 pounds, but the weight per horsepower had been lowered by better than 11 percent.

Hydra-matic drive was standard on the Oldsmobile Futuramic 98. The automatic transmission as it then existed was composed of a hydraulic coupling—not a torque converter—and had planetary gearing to provide four forward speeds.

And it was quite efficient: combined with the high-compression V-8 it gave tremendous performance. Compared with the 1948 Olds eight-cylinder model, the 98 had higher top speed—95 mph vs. 88 mph. High-gear acceleration from 10 to 60 mph was slashed from 18 to 13.5 seconds. And fuel mileage at a constant 50 mph had been increased by exactly one mile per gallon.

Overall responsibility for the complete car rested, of course, with Jack Wolfram, who celebrated his 50th birthday the same year the Futuramic 98 went into production. Wolfram hailed from Pittsburgh, where he had been educated in public schools and taken correspondence courses in drafting, machine design, and business administration.

He worked for a railroad, a heating and ventilating equipment firm, and a tool manufacturer before he joined the auto industry in 1921 as a draftsman with Chandler in Cleveland. Seven years later he went to Lansing as experimental engineer for Oldsmobile. He became assistant chief engineer in 1940 and chief engineer in 1944.

The running gear for the Futuramic 98 was soundly conceived and strongly built. The frame was a rigid-girder structure with cross-bracing, and coil springs were used at all four wheels. The rear axle was located by a three-link system, and the front wheels were carried independently by upper and lower control arms.

Stabilizer bars were fitted both front and rear to restrict body sway, for the coil springs were quite soft, with long travel. Steering was by Saginaw worm and double roller (without power assist), and tire size was 7.60 × 15. Brake drums were 11 inches in effective diameter and had duo-servo shoe action. With its 125-inch wheelbase, the 98 had a 42-feet turn diameter. Futuramic 98 prices started at $2,290 for the Club Sedan and topped at $2,810 for the convertible coupe. The series included a sedan at $2,360 and a deluxe sedan at $2,450.

92. CHRYSLER NEW YORKER, 1951

Chrysler had been out of the running for a long time, not having come forth with any product for which claims to the title of greatness could be made since the classic Imperials of the early Thirties.

Walter P. Chrysler had died in 1940, and K. T. Keller succeeded to the presidency. The Zeder, Breer and Skelton engineering group had broken up, Fred M. Zeder retiring in 1949. Carl Breer relinquished his title of executive engineer the same year, retaining a seat on the board until 1953. Skelton was still active, also with a title of executive engineer but his retirement was approaching and he was to leave the corporation at age 63 in 1951.

James C. Zeder, Fred's younger brother, who had been head of the Chrysler Laboratories since 1933, left that post in 1946 to accept a more honorary post as head of the Chrysler Institute of Engineering.

Somehow the system that these great engineers had brought into being had taken on a veritable existence of its own, able to continue without their presence, and the product evolved in keeping with the times. That situation would have been acceptable for a limited time, as an hiatus that could be concealed if it did not stretch out too far in time. But the vision that had guided the affairs of Chrysler in years past was gone.

K. T. Keller was a great production man, and he understood all there was to know about cost accounting and productivity. Unfortunately he was not future-oriented. Sure, he saw next year, and perhaps the one beyond clearly enough, but the long-term evolution of the automobile was out of his view. He provided a healthy budget for research, but never saw the connection between what went on in the laboratories and what was coming off the production lines.

Chrysler was experimenting with front wheel drive, true-construction bodies, gas-turbine engines, and many other innovations of importance to the auto industry before WW II, and the fruits of this work were ready to be picked, to some extent, long before Chrysler's competition turned their attention to these things.

Under Keller, Chrysler was doing research almost for the sake of research alone, as an activity totally divorced from production and selling. Keller has been called conservative, which was justified in that he resisted change in the Chrysler product, but many others have been just as effective in avoiding costly changes for no other reason than the attraction of change itself. Keller's problem was more likely a kind of blindness which made him shy away from facing the challenges of the mid- and long-term future.

There was no lack of purpose at Chrysler research. The engineers and technicians were well aware of what they were doing. But the disinterest of the corporation in practical applications of their work saddened and frustrated many.

Some left Chrysler: Max Roensch, a Texan with engineering degrees from Rich Institute and University of Michigan, had joined Chrysler as a research engineer in 1926 and run the engine laboratories at Highland Park since 1937, left in 1945 to become chief engineer of a bearing company in Cleveland, and in 1957 went to Chevrolet.

Robert Janeway held out somewhat longer. He had joined Chrysler in 1931 and became head of the dynamics research department. He was the brains that put ride-and-handling into the Chrysler, saw to it that the cars steered and stopped, and were generally safe in their road behavior. He held a number of patents on chassis engineering features and designs, and was recognized throughout the industry as a leading expert in his field. It was in the spring of 1956 that he left Chrysler to form his own company.

Because of such men, however, the Chrysler product advanced, since the engineering staff working on production models could always get quick and correct answers from the research department.

The overhead-valve high-compression V-8's did not hit Chrysler like a bombshell, because research in the same area had been going on for a long time. If Chrysler's management had wanted to be first in production, its engineers would have been ready with the know-how.

James C. Zeder directed an all-encompassing study of alternative power systems as early as 1938. Chrysler's gas-turbine work also dates from that time. The high-efficiency V-8 also stems from the same project.

The Chrysler hemi-head V-8 went further in the direction of volumetric efficiency than the Olds and Cadillac examples, but not as far in combustion theory and thermal efficiency. Its principles were well-established and of proven validity, having been part of most racing car engines built between 1912 and the present time. The astonishing thing is that it got cleared for production during Keller's presidency, for it was an expensive power plant to produce.

The engine was designed and developed by two engineers, W. E. Drinkard and M. L. Carpentier, who were assigned to the project in 1946. Its early starting date shows that its creation (and the decision to produce it) was no knee-jerk reaction to the Oldsmobile and Cadillac high-compression V-8's. Drinkard had been brought in as supervisor of the engine lab in 1943 (and an understudy for Roensch), and Carpentier had been with Zeder, Breer and Skelton since their pre-Chrysler days.

They started fundamental research with a single-cylinder test engine, and initial results led them to choose the hemispherical combustion chamber as the top candidate for future development. Well worth noting that it was an oversquare cylinder, with 4-inch bore and 3.75-inch stroke, displacing 47.2 cubic inches. The hemi-head gave more power at a *lower* compression ratio than any other valve configuration, which meant less sensitivity to fuel quality and less risk of abnormal combustion in consumer use.

The production engine was somewhat less oversquare, with a bore of 3.8125 inches and a stroke of 3.625 inches, giving a displacement of 331 cubic inches. It delivered 180 hp at 4,000 rpm, with a 7.5:1 compression ratio, putting it 20 hp ahead of the Cadillac.

The Chrysler had a single central camshaft with pushrods to rocker arms above the cylinder head. There were two rocker shafts per head, with rocker arms facing in opposite directions, so as to operate valves splayed at an included angle of about 66 degrees. Double overhead camshafts had been tested in the lab, but were turned down for production because of cost, noise, reliability and maintenance problems.

The 1951 New Yorker was built on a 131.5-inch wheelbase and weighed 4,350 pounds. With a 3.73:1 final drive ratio it could go from standstill to 60 mph in 15 seconds flat and cover the standing-start quarter-mile in 20 seconds. Top speed was about 105 mph, and average fuel consumption 15 miles to the gallon.

Its appearance was still in the transitional stage, and there was nothing new in frame and body construction (Fig. 8-5). Henry King was in charge of body design. Virgil Exner had not yet arrived at Chrysler, still being tied up with Loewy and Studebaker, and the styling for the 1951 Chrysler was mainly due to Charles G. Walker.

Chassis engineering was the province of Alan Loofbourrow, who had supervised the development of a semi-automatic Fluid-Torque transmission and the adoption of the Gemmer full-time power steering system for the Chrysler.

The Chrysler hemi-head V-8 was enlarged to 354 cubic-inch displacement, but it was soon found to be impossible to recuperate its production cost. For the Dodge, De Soto, and Plymouth, the corporate engineering office developed a simpler engine with in-line overhead valves and combustion chambers that were called polyspherical.

The hemi was kept alive for stock car racing and dragstrip events, and enjoyed a revival in the muscle-car market of 1966-71, but it was phased out by 1974.

93. LINCOLN COSMOPOLITAN, 1952

Which way for the Lincoln? was a question that cropped up at Ford when the planning of postwar models began in 1943. But it was pushed in the background while the more immediate matters of Ford and Mercury were solved first.

The Zephyr was not revived, nor was there a place in the postwar market for the K-series. Consequently, only a few Continentals were produced from 1946 and into 1948.

It was a stopgap solution when one finally came in the form of a 1949 Lincoln. It was little more than a glorified Mercury with a bigger version of the same engine.

This power unit was a flat-head V-8 of 337 cubic-inch displacement, delivering 152 hp at 3,600 rpm. It was actually designed for a truck, not a car, but proved quite suitable for both tasks, though it was excessively heavy and had poor fuel economy.

The same basic Lincoln, on a 121-inch wheelbase, and its more expensive Cosmopolitan companion series on a 125-inch wheelbase, were modified in detail for 1950 and 1951, but it was not till 1952 that a modern Lincoln appeared (Fig. 8-6).

As was only to be expected, it looked like a GM car, some indefinable amalgram of Oldsmobile, Buick and Cadillac. It was to be expected, because the Ford Motor Co. was being run by former GM executives. Ernest R. Breech had come to Ford from Bendix after many years with Sloan and Knudsen in the top echelon of

General Motors' management; and Ford's new engineering vice president had come from Oldsmobile via Borg-Warner. And if that was not enough, the Lincoln engineering office was headed by a former Chevrolet man!

In 1946 Breech had persuaded Harold T. Youngren to leave Oldsmobile, where he had been chief engineer since 1933, and join him at Ford. Youngren was then 54 years old. He had begun his career as a draftsman with Allis-Chalmers and later held engineering posts with Westinghouse, Falls Motor co., and Harley-Davidson. In 1917 he helped design the Fergus car, and in 1921 he was busy on development of the Houdaille shock absorber. Later he worked on new engines and chassis design for Pierce-Arrow and became a consulting engineer to Studebaker in 1927. From there he went to Buick, but was soon transferred from Flint to Lansing.

At Ford, his responsibilities were enormous, and he not only reorganized the engineering staff and its operations, but greatly expanded it. He brought in new people from all over, and not unnaturally, some ex-GM men he knew and trusted were put in key positions.

The Lincoln was a particular headache, and Youngren wanted to find a clever and durable solution. Therefore he was pleased when he learned in the spring of 1947 that Earle S. MacPherson was unhappy at Chevrolet and might consider an invitation to work at Ford.

Now MacPherson's last project at Chevrolet was the Cadet, the small car that never made it into production. For years and years at Chevrolet MacPherson, along with Alex Taub and other

Fig. 8-5. Chrysler's 1951 New Yorker.

Fig. 8-6. The Lincoln Cosmopolitan of 1952.

automotive free-thinkers had been arguing in favor of smaller, lighter cars. Perhaps Youngren knew what he was doing, putting the Lincoln into the hands of such an engineer. Perhaps he didn't.

MacPherson was one year older than Youngren and had joined Chalmers-Detroit upon graduation from the University of Illinois in 1915. He spent much of WWI in Europe, servicing aircraft engines, and worked with Liberty from 1919 to 1922. He joined Hupmobile in 1922 and was its assistant chief engineer a few years later, but left in 1934 to accept a position in the GM central engineering office, whence he was transferred to Chevrolet in 1935.

The first thing MacPherson did was persuade Youngren, Breech, and others that the Lincoln should not be aimed at the Cadillac, but at a lower price bracket, which more or less coincided with Oldsmobile's market. This made sense from a manufacturing viewpoint, since such a product could more extensively share mass-produced Ford parts.

The Lincoln was to have its own engine, however, MacPherson and Youngren set up a new advanced-engine design office that was to plan a whole family of modern engines, starting with the 1952 Lincoln. As head of this office, they picked Victor G. Raviolo, a native of New York City who had joined Ford in 1940 but spent most of the war working on aircraft engines for Consolidated Vultee with William B. Stout. Earlier, he had worked for Chrysler and Packard, and for three years was associated with C. W. Ranst in Detroit.

318

The new Lincoln engine became an overhead-valve V-8 of 317.5 cubic-inch displacement, delivering 160 hp at 3,900 rpm. It weighed only 684 pounds, despite its deep cast-iron Y-block construction. Cylinders were oversquare (3.80 × 3.50 inches), and the compression ratio was up there with the best, at 7.5:1.

Youngren had directed the design of new chassis with coil-spring independent front suspension and Hotchkiss drive rear ends for all the 1949 models, and the same principles were carried over into the 1952 Lincoln, though all parts were new and not interchangeable.

MacPherson designed a new front suspension linkage with ball joints on the steering knuckle, thereby eliminating king-pins (something he had been working on at Chevrolet years before), and laid out a new, lighter frame.

Shortened to a 123-inch wheelbase, the 1952 Cosmopolitan was about 500 pounds lighter than the 1951 model, the four-door sedan weighing 4,060 pounds. The body was a totally new design by William M. Schmidt, breaking sharply with the old style which had germinated in Bob Gregorie's hands during the war years and undergone revisions and decorations by Tom Hibbard, who was called in to replace Gregorie in 1947.

Schmidt was a native of Detroit who had studied at Wayne State University and joined Ford during the war as a defense-product designer. He designed all the later Lincolns up to and including the 1956 Capri, and joined Studebaker in 1955, but left within two years to work on Exner's design staff at Chrysler.

The 1952 Cosmopolitan would easily top 100 mph and acceleration times from zero to sixty were in the 14.5-second range with the optional Hydra-matic transmission that was used on nearly all Lincolns. Average fuel consumption was about 15 miles to the gallon.

The real performance potential of the car became clear late in 1952 when a team of Lincolns with 1953-model engines tuned by Bill Stroppe and entered by Clay Smith won the stock car class in the Mexican Road race at an average speed of 90.96 mph. Lincoln went back and won its class handsomely in 1953 and 1954.

But a racing image was not what Ford really wanted for the Lincoln, which was advertised as a luxury car. Racing had not helped sales at all. Now Henry Ford II was beginning to take a bigger part in the decision-making, and the top executives agreed that MacPherson's positioning of the car at the Oldsmobile level had been wrong. The Lincoln was doomed to grow bigger and heavier, to justify higher prices.

MacPherson had arranged for a transfer to Ford of Britain, where he was happily revolutionizing small-car design. When Youngren retired in 1952, MacPherson was brought back to Dearborn as vice president of engineering, and he laid out the basic design for the Falcon in 1956, going into retirement two years later. He died in 1960; Youngren in 1969.

Vic Raviolo is still alive at this writing. He became Ford's director of engine design in 1954, and worked as head of engineering for Ford of Britain for four years, leaving Ford in 1966 to go with American Motors, where he stayed only two years before setting up his own consulting business.

94. CHRYSLER 300 B, 1956

The number 300 stood for horsepower, and there was something magic about it that fueled the horsepower race that had started with Chrysler's going into production with the hemi-head V-8 in 1951.

To beat the 180-hp Chrysler, Cadillac reworked its V-8 to get 190 hp in 1952 and 210 hp in 1953. Chrysler responded with a rating of 235 hp in 1954, when Cadillac had stopped at 230. Cadillac did not want to be left behind again, and raised power to 270 hp for 1955, only to find that Chrysler had gone to 300!

The 300-hp Chrysler engine was available only in a special car designated C-300, a limited production model. The C-67 Windsor series had a smaller-displacement engine rated at 188 hp, and the C-68 New Yorker had the 331 cubic-inch V-8 tuned to deliver 250 hp at 4,600 rpm.

The 300 had the same block, but special camshaft and carburetion. This engine had been developed with an eye on the lessons learned from the Indianapolis version of 1953 as well as modified engines used by Briggs Cunningham's Le Mans racers. With a compression ratio of 8.5:1 it delivered its 300 hp at 5,200 rpm, with a healty peak torque of 345 pounds-feet at 3,200 rpm.

It was destined to keep Chrysler on top in the horsepower race for several years. Displacement was increased to 354 cubic inches for 1956 by boring out the cylinders from 3.81 to 3.94 inches, retaining the short 3.63-inch stroke. That boosted maximum output to 340 hp at 5,200 rpm with 9.0:1 compression. Optional pistons giving 10:1 compression raised the output further to 355 hp at 5,200 rpm thus breaking the 1-full-hp per cubic-inch barrier.

The 1956 model was officially designated C-72-300 but marketed as the 300 B (Fig. 8-7). Body and chassis were practically unchanged from the original C-300 of 1955. It shared the 126-inch wheelbase and body shell with the Windsor series, but carried the Imperial grille.

The use of standard body and chassis components enabled Chrysler to control its production cost for the 300 very closely. Its special items were restricted mainly to the power train, beefed-up suspension, wire wheels, and interior trim. It was assembled on the Imperial line at Chrysler's East Jefferson Avenue plant in Detroit, in quite low numbers: 1,725 cars in 1955 and 1,102 in 1956.

The styling was handled by Clifford Voss who ran the Chrysler-Imperial studio under Virgil Exner's direction, and the body engineering was the responsibility of Cifford B. Doty. The inspiration for the 300 styling came from a show car Exner had designed in 1951. It was built by Carrozzeria Ghia in Torino, Italy, and named K-310. Many of its styling features were to show up on subsequent production cars.

When Voss was working on proposals for the 300, Exner decided the car should carry a minimum of chrome, to distinguish it from the New Yorker and Imperial, which were rather overloaded with what the factory workers called "gingerbread." The 300 stood out for its discreet elegance, with chrome used only for the grille and bumpers, window frames, lamp housings, wire wheels and rims, plus one straight, horizontal molding to serve as an accent line.

Engineering for the 300 came from Robert M. Rodger. In fact, it was his idea. He looked at all the performance equipment Chrysler had, and made up a proposal to use selected items to create a new kind of automobile. He got the approval of E. C. Quinn, who was then manager of the Chrysler Division, and the support of Bill Braden, the sales manager. It was more than a reply to the Chevrolet Corvette and Ford Thunderbird. It was a roomy, luxuriously equipped high-performance coupe with race-winning potential. Chrysler president L. L. 'Tex' Colbert told them to go ahead and build it.

Bob Rodger had been at Chrysler since 1939, when he began studies at the Chrysler Institute of Engineering, to follow up on his mechanical-engineering degree from Clarkson College of Technology. He was not a Detroiter by birth, but came from Hammond, New York.

Fig. 8-7. The sleekly styled Chrysler 300-B of 1956.

From 1941 to 1943 he worked in the Chrysler engine laboratory, and then spent seven years as a project engineer, rounding out his experience by working on all systems in the car and learning to regard the complete car as one entity, one basic concept. In 1951 he was promoted to assistant chief engineer and the following year he became chief engineer for the Chrysler car.

He is remembered most for the creation of the 300 and its development. Apart from the increase in displacement, engine modifications for 1956 included adoption of a case-hardened forged-steel crankshaft, special connecting rods, and bearing shells. The solid valve lifters and dual four-barrel carburetor setup was retained.

The C-300 had not been available with manual transmission; a two-speed automatic was standard. The 300 B received a new Torque-Flite three-speed automatic as standard, and customers could order a three-speed column shift if they preferred. The axle ratio was raised from 3.00:1 to 3.54:1 to improve acceleration. Gemmer power steering was standard, and stock-car racing drivers found they had to pay extra for manual steering. Power brakes were also standard.

Tire size was 8.00 × 15 and the 300 B weighed 4,145 pounds in standard trim. The suspension system, coil springs in front and semi-ellipticals on the rear axle, was set for a firm, sporty ride, and disappointed some buyers who had failed to understand the character of the car. Spring rates were almost twice the New Yorker's, and the shock absorbers had different valving. Its luxurious interior was certainly misleading of the true nature of the beast.

With the standard axle ratio, the 300 B had a theoretical road speed of 24 mph per 1,000 rpm (and nine other ratios were available for racing). Top speed was 120 to 125 mph as sold to the public, and race-tuned versions could top 140 mph. In normal use, the standard 300 B would average between 10.5 and 13.5 miles per gallon.

Although more and more horsepower was stuffed into the 300, the vehicle itself went into a decline after the B series.

The 300 C of 1957 was rated at 375 hp, engine displacement having gone to 392 cubic inches as a result of boring it out to a full four inches and stretching the stroke to 3.90 inches. The high-compression engine that year was rated at 390 hp at 5,400 rpm.

But the body was redesigned with finned rear fenders, a trapezoidal grille, and a hardtop coupe that lacked the special appeal of the older models. The 300 was becoming integrated with the rest of the line and losing its exclusive appearance.

The ride was softened for the 300 C, with a new torsion-bar front suspension, longer, more flexible rear leaf springs. At the same time, the car's weight increased to 4,350 pounds and wheel diameter was reduced to 14 inches, while tire section went up from 8.00 to 9.00 inches.

The 300 D of 1958 gained a further 150 pounds. Engine size was unchanged, but the standard unit now had a 10:1 compression ratio, raising output to 380 hp, and an optional 390-hp fuel-injected version was listed as optional.

The hemi-head V-8 was abandoned for the 300 E, which was equipped with a 413 cubic-inch engine with polyspherical combustion chambers. Despite identical horsepower ratings, it just did not give the same performance, and the 300 was falling into disrepute among the competition-oriented clientele.

The letter series went on through F, G, and H, and the 1962 Chrysler range included a new model called simply "300," but it was a tame machine, replacing the Windsor in the product lineup. The fate of the creator of the original is a sad postscript to the degeneration of the cars carrying the 300 label.

Bob Rodger added product planning to his duties as chief engineer of Chrysler in 1958, and in 1964 was transferred to the corporate product planning office under George Gibson (former chief engineer of Dodge) as Special-Car manager. He died of leukemia in February, 1971, aged only 53.

95 PONTIAC BONNEVILLE, 1957

"The Breath-Taking Bonneville," proclaimed Pontiac's sales literature. Other slogans were "Action-Styled" and "Fuel-Injection Powered." With no sense of shame or modesty, Pontiac described the Bonneville as "by far, the most spectacular sport convertible ever built."

Truth is, it was an exciting car, but it was true more because of its power than because of its appearance, which did not have much impact (Fig. 8-8). By choosing to make it only as a convertible, Pontiac was courting an image akin to Chevrolet's short-wheel-base two-seater Corvette, but the Bonneville was in fact built on a standard Super Chief chassis and shared the sheet-metal of the Star Chief convertible.

Thus it was a car created from mass-produced components, more in line with the Chrysler 300 C than with either the Corvette or the Ford Thunderbird (which became a four-seater in 1958).

The Bonneville name came from the Utah Salt Flats that had been the grounds used for setting speed records since the thirties. Pontiac had first used the name on a "dream car" built in 1954. It was created by a new general manager and a new chief engineer, shortly after their arrival at Pontiac, but relied entirely on engineering from the past regime.

The new general manager was Simon E. "Bunkie" Knudsen, and the new chief engineer was none other than Elliot M. "Pete" Estes. Knudsen was the son of Sloan's former lieutenant and GM's executive vice president, who made his own career within General Motors. After graduating from Massachusetts Institute of Technology in 1936, he held jobs with outside companies before coming to Pontiac in 1939 as a tool engineer. He worked in weapons production during the war and became master mechanic of Pontiac in 1947. He worked in a corporate process development office for three years, held production and management posts with Allison, and served for a year's time as general manager of Detroit Diesel. When he returned to Pontiac in 1956, he was the youngest general manager in the corporation.

Pete Estes had worked under Kettering at the GM Research Laboratories and been associated with a lot of unusual engineering projects. He was transferred to Oldsmobile in 1946 and became assistant chief engineer for Oldsmobile in 1954.

Fig. 8-8. The fuel-injected 1957 Pontiac Bonneville.

Knudsen and Estes realized that the Pontiac car, as it existed when they arrived, was a good product, but sadly lacking in image. Their first priority was to give it image without going into deep and costly changes. Pulling the Bonneville out of Pontiac's hat was a stroke of imagination, aided by good luck. The luck consisted mainly in the form of a sound engineering basis provided by the team from which they took over.

Pontiac's V-8 engine, for instance, had been the result of a study that started in 1946. It went into production in 1955 with a displacement of 287 cubic inches, with a 3.75-inch bore and a 3.25-inch stroke.

It was an overhead-valve design with hydraulic valve lifters and ball-stud-mounted rocker arms, the latter invented by Clayton B. Leach of Pontiac's engineering staff. Mark Frank did the overall layout of the engine, and Malcolm R. McKellar did the detailing.

In base form the engine had a compression ratio of 7.4:1 and delivered 173 hp at 4,400 rpm. A high compression version with an 8.0:1 ratio put out 180 hp at 4,600 rpm. The same basic engine was to go without major change for a 21-year production run.

For the 1957 Bonneville, the block was bored out to 370 cubic inches (after intermediate steps of 317 and 347 cubic inches), with a 4.06-inch bore and a 3.56-inch stroke.

The fuel-injection system came from Rochester, which had been working with Chevrolet on the development of Stuart Hilborn's racing car system for high-performance production cars since 1951. As it turned out, Pontiac did a better job of the adaptation, and the first Bonneville engine delivered 310 hp at 4,800 rpm, with a peak torque of 400 pounds-feet at 3,400 rpm.

Top speed was somewhere above 130 mph, and acceleration was shattering, with zero-to-50 mph times at about 5.5 seconds and zero-to-60 mph times at between 8.0 and 8.25 seconds. The standing-start quarter-mile was a matter of 18 seconds. Fuel consumption varied greatly according to use. In the Mobil Economy Run, the 1957 Bonneville did superbly well, with a 20.4 miles-per-gallon average. A magazine reported an average of 16.8 mpg for a 100-mile test run in California traffic at an average speed of 50 mph.

The car was built on a 124-inch wheelbase and had Pontiac's standard suspension, with an independent coil-spring system in front and a rear axle attached to semi-elliptical leaf springs. Curb weight was 4,285 pounds and the basic list price $4,400, which, because of tempting options, usually ended up about $1,200 to $1,500 higher.

The publicity value of the original Bonneville far exceeded its popularity. The total production was only 630 cars in 1957.

For 1958, with the new wide-track Pontiac still a year away, Knudsen decided to turn the Bonneville into a series, adding a sport coupe on the same basic body and chassis. The prices came down, and fuel injection became an extra-cost option.

The 1957-58 Bonneville bodies were low-budget specials, designed by Paul Gillan, who was head of the Pontiac studio at the time. He was severely limited by production considerations, since the Chieftain and Star Chief were restricted to the underbody and main panels of the same Fisher B-body that was used by Oldsmobile and Buick.

In overall appearance, the first Bonneville does not have immediate recognition as a Pontiac. It could easily be mistaken for an Edsel or a Mercury, or possibly an Olds or a Buick. Pontiac had a real identity crisis at the time, for Knudsen had eliminated all the familiar Pontiac features, such as the Silver Streak and the Indian head. But no new theme that could be produced within the constraints of the corporate body program suggested itself to anyone at Pontiac. The result was a rather anonymous mixture. Its greatness lay in the progressivity of its engineering and the imagery of Pontiac's publicity.

Chapter 9
America Moves Into the Future: 1963-1979

Offering customers a vehicle that purported to be "the car of the future, available today," was a hackneyed and futile approach to product planning and merchandising. During the 1950's, particularly after the presence of European imports in relatively large volume began to make itself felt, the American car buyer grew out of his former naivete. What was happening was significant enough to steer the Big Three (Chrysler, Ford and General Motors) into compact-car programs.

96. STUDEBAKER AVANTI, 1963

The Avanti was not Studebaker's compact (Fig. 9-1). Studebaker had the Lark, which was not exactly a compact, but a downsized car, treading in the footsteps of the Rambler, and preceding the Ford Falcon, Plymouth Valiant, and Chevrolet Corvair, and selling at competitive prices.

The Avanti really was a futuristic car, and totally unrelated to the main product line except for sharing mechanical components. It was to be a high-priced limited-production model, a showcase to demonstrate Studebaker's new thinking and foster the idea that here was a forerunner of a whole future generation of Studebakers. It came out of desperation, when there was very little future left for Studebaker, and all its radical departures from normal Studebaker practice were made possible by the weakness of the basic product.

The job intended for the Avanti was to be an image-remaker, and out of that realization grew a determination to make it a great car. It succeeded despite the hopeless shortage of time for proper

Fig. 9-1. The 1963 Studebaker Avanti.

development and tragically insufficient funds for ideal rather than possible choices.

The Avanti was not to be an imitation of any other American car but a new type, as if Studebaker could translate the European GT concept into American hardware. Studebaker did have European connections, for Curtiss-Wright owned a big slice of Studebaker, and had arranged for Studebaker's sales organization to handle the Mercedes-Benz car line in the U.S.A. Mercedes-Benz grilles showed up on the 1962-model Larks, but there was no real engineering cooperation between Stuttgart and South Bend. It was strictly a commercial bond that Studebaker attempted to exploit in any way possible.

The Avanti was a pure American design, more in the tradition of the Cord than influenced by Ferrari, Jaguar, Talbot or Porsche. Strangely, Porsche had actually done a prototype for Studebaker some years earlier, but it had no effect on company policy at the time or on the Avanti project.

The animator and guiding spirit of Avanti was Sherwood Egbert, who became president of Studebaker-Packard in February, 1961. He came from McCulloch, where he had started a career in purchasing in 1946, rising to vice presidential office in 1951. He had formerly worked for Boeing, served in the U.S. Marine Corps, and in the U.S. Navy Bureau of Aeronautics.

Egbert understood a great deal about why Studebaker had been losing ground, and knew that the most direct way to get his message across to the car-buying public would be through a new product. He drew up some sketches for the kind of car he had in mind, and then called in Raymond Loewy. Loewy tackled the assignment with two of his closest associates, Robert F. Andrews and John Ebstein. Drawings and scale models were shown to Egbert as early as March, 1961.

The model that was chosen had been done almost entirely by Bob Andrews. He had been with Loewy Associates for a long time, and had helped create the 1953 Studebaker.

Andrews had started drawing cars at the age of six. He was born in Monroe, Michigan. His first job was with Monroe Auto Equipment Company, designing hydraulic equipment for World War II tanks. In 1945 he went to Hudson and was one of Frank Spring's team that helped put the finishing touches on the step-down body.

The shape that resulted was notable for its unusual overall proportions, with more overhang in front than in the back, a wide front and a tapered tail, and the absence of a conventional grille. As Loewy was reported to describe it, "Avanti's front is avid, its rear end is sudden."

It was a two-door, four-seater fastback coupe with a fiberglass-reinforced plastic body and a chassis that was basically the same as the Studebaker Lark, suitably beefed-up.

On Egbert's orders, the Avanti was made a high-performance car, much closer to Corvette than anything Ford, Chrysler, or American Motors were doing. The engineering was Gene Hardig's responsibility.

Gene Hardig had been a draftsman at Studebaker as early as 1918 and had worked under Guy P. Henry, Barney Roos, Stanley Sparrow, Roy Cole, and Harold Churchill before becoming vice president of engineering in 1959. Chief development engineer for the Avanti was Michael P. de Blumenthal, who had joined Studebaker in 1935 with a degree in mechanical engineering from Purdue University.

Of course, the budget for the Avanti was in the shoestring class. It's a near miracle that the car was as good as it was. The engine was Studebaker's own 289 cubic-inch V-8, a design that had gone into production in 1952. For the Avanti, it was tuned to deliver about 240 hp, with a 10:1 compression ratio, in the R-1 version.

But that was not enough. Sherwood Egbert had brought Paxton into the Studebaker organization and a Paxton blower installation was perfected, raising power output to about 290 hp for the R-2.

The R-1 Avanti would go about 125 mph, and the R-2 could exceed 140. Acceleration in the R-1 was more than most people were ready for: 0-60 mph in 8 seconds and 0-100 mph in 21 seconds. Paxton president Andy Granatelli drove a specially tuned R-2 at Bonneville in August, 1962, setting a two-way flying-mile average of 168.5 mph and being clocked at 171.1 mph for a 2½ mile course.

The speed-tuned engine served as the basis for the R-3 option, bored out to 299.4 cubic-inch displacement with about 335 hp, of which only a few were built.

Most Avantis were equipped with a Borg-Warner three-speed automatic transmission, but a four-speed Warner T-10A manual gearbox with floorshift was available. If the Avanti was made for speed, it was also safe at speed. And it could stop. Bendix disc brakes (to Dunlop designs) were fitted on the front wheels—the first use of disc brakes as standard equipment on an American production car.

The car was assembled on its own separate line in South Bend with bodies supplied from the Molded Fiber Glass Co. in Ashtabula, Ohio. The body shell was made up of 100 contoured and 30 flat sections, the largest single piece being the floor pan. The body weighed only 400 pounds, and Studebaker engineers estimated that a similar body made of steel would have been 200 pounds heavier.

The complete Avanti, built on a 109-inch wheelbase weighed 3,375 pounds. Prices started at $4,445 for the 1963 models, and less than 5,000 Avantis were built before Studebaker closed down its operations in South Bend and moved to Canada—minus the Avanti.

Two old-time Studebaker dealers in South Bend, Nate Altman and Leo Newman, bought the rights to the Avanti and continued production, using Chevrolet chassis and engines.

Gene Hardig left Studebaker to go to work for their Avanti Motor Corporation, where he's still active. Two of his principal colleagues on the Avanti project died all too soon; Mike de Blumenthal at the age of 53 in 1964, and Sherwood Egbert five years later, only 49 years old.

97. BUICK RIVIERA, 1964

Cadillac could have had this car, but turned it down, while Buick snapped at the chance to build it. The body originated in the Advance Studio of GM Styling, after Bill Mitchell had explained some new ideas he had to Ned Nickles. They called it La Salle II and expected Cadillac to make use of it.

The type of car was not new, like the Chrysler 300 or the Avanti. This project was aimed at the Lincoln Continental and Ford Thunderbird market, a comfortable, roomy, well-appointed coupe with a style of its own. It was a sensational look in the fall of 1962, when Buick presented the Riviera. It had poise, and balanced proportions. It was modern, and aggressive. It was totally in tune with the times. It had no sheet metal in common with other Buicks, which gave the Riviera a special cachet of exclusivity.

What Buick's engineers managed to put under this body was nothing short of a masterpiece. For all its great size and weight, the Riviera was much closer to the Chevrolet Corvette in performance, ride and handling, than the T-bird or Continental.

(Readers may have noticed that no Continental is included in the selected 100. Their ill-bred road manners, poor space utilization and disregard for weight control kept them out of consideration for the period in which they were built.)

The Riviera was also far superior to the Chrysler 300 B of the previous decade, with a civilized ride and a docile engine, never betraying its fireworks until an enthusiastic driver asked for it. It was a car for the enthusiast, and a car which even consumers who could not afford it became enthusiastic about. It was a car intended not just for the enthusiast, and which produced no disappointment in the minds of people who bought it for reasons other than driving pleasure and performance.

The credit for its thorough engineering development goes to Phillip C. Bowser, whose will and determination overcame all obstacles. He had come to Buick in 1957 as head of a new section devoted to research and development. He had five years' experience of how that kind of task was being handled at Chevrolet, and prior to his time there had worked two years in the GM Research Laboratories. He came to GM straight out of Ohio State University, a native of Columbus, Ohio.

After the project was approved, the Riviera was supposed to use standard Buick components for everything except the special body. By the time production started, there were plenty of variations, but within tolerable cost limits.

The full-size Buick Electra 225 of that era was built on a 126-inch wheelbase and had a pure cruciform frame. This frame was shortened to give a 117-inch wheelbase. Front and rear suspension systems were retained, essentially as they were used for the Electra, but the track was narrowed slightly to maintain the same relationship.

All-coil suspension was used, with a three-link and track rod system to locate the rear axle, and upper and lower control arms for the front wheels. Despite its forward bias in weight distribution, the Riviera had only moderate understeer, with fast steering response and excellent handling precision. Yet it had a well-cushioned ride, with body roll restricted by a hefty stabilizer bar.

The car weighed 4,140 pounds, and was powered by the latest 401 cubic-inch V-8 which had evolved from Buick's first V-8 of 1953. It delivered 325 hp at 4,400 rpm and was coupled to a Super Turbine 400 automatic transmission. No manual gearbox was available for the Riviera.

For 1964, Buick bored out the V-8 to 425 cubic inches, and raised output to 340 hp with a single four-barrel and 360 hp with dual four-barrel carburetors. With the 340 hp engine and a 3.07:1 axle ratio, the 1964 Riviera had impressive acceleration times, going from standstill to 60 mph in 8.3 seconds and to a full 100 mph in 25.5 seconds. Top speed was 125 mph and it would cruise at 110! With the 360-hp option, the Riviera was America's highest powered production car in 1964 (Fig. 9-2).

Fuel consumption was, of course, very heavy if the car was driven hard, but in normal driving, say expressway cruising at moderate speed, the Riviera could get as high as 17 miles per gallon.

The engine was designed by Joseph D. Turlay and had started life as a pentroof job, with all valves standing vertically (not in relation to the cylinder axes, but in absolute terms). This made for a narrower engine, easier to install. From its original displacement of 322 cubic inches, it grew to 364 in 1957 and 401 in 1962, the latter receiving new pistons and combustion chamber design.

Brakes for the Riviera were taken wholesale from the heavier Electra. The system had aluminum front wheel drums with a cast-in-iron liner and external cooling ribs, certainly the ultimate in American brake designs until the arrival of disc brakes. Power assist was standard, of course. Power steering was also standard on the Riviera, and practically a marketing necessity for a car in its price class ($4,333 in 1963 and $4,408 in 1965).

The Nickles-designed Riviera body was kept in production for only three years, during which some 115,000 Rivieras were built. Ned Nickles had been chief designer of the Buick studio from 1945 to 1958, when he was invited to work in the Advanced Studio which handled projects for all divisions. He was a Wisconsin farmboy who had started to draw cars at the age of five and had come to GM Styling in 1940, working mainly on defense projects and future Chevrolet models. The Riviera remains the crowning point of his career.

Phil Bowser became chief engineer of Buick in 1968, served briefly as general manager of Delco-Moraine in 1975-76, and then was named technical assistant to George R. Elges, GM vice president and group executive in charge of the car and truck group.

For 1966 the Riviera was made to share GM's new E-body with the Oldsmobile Toronado, which lowered Buick's production costs for the car. On its new 119-inch wheelbase, the Riviera was still a great car, but it was moving in the wrong direction, getting

Fig. 9-2. 1964 Buick Riviera with 425 cu. in V-8.

heavier instead of lighter, and its character weakened to attract a wider clientele, instead of sharpening its marketing focus.

As for the Toronado, it was a daring attempt to apply front wheel drive to a full-size American car, but too many problems remained unsolved when the car went into production (steering response at the limit, insufficient braking capacity, brake fade, and front/rear braking imbalance). With all due credit to Oldsmobile for making the attempt, the Toronado does not qualify as a great car.

98. PONTIAC GRAND PRIX, 1970

For many years Buick's Riviera was the car to beat, and by extension, the car to imitate. Pontiac went after the same image and market with its Grand Prix and failed, mainly because the Grand Prix of the years 1962-68 was built on the Catalina chassis and shared the same sheet metal. It had no special appeal, and acquired no image.

In contrast, Pontiac built up a fine reputation as a maker of high-performance cars, based on the Tempest-GTO (an interesting car, both technically and from a merchandising viewpoint, but not a great car under the definition which we now apply to the mid-Sixties).

And yet there was a great deal of GTO feeling in the 1969 Grand Prix, which broke completely with past models bearing that name. It was a very personal car, in that it was made first and foremost for the driver, but had seating capacity for five.

Built on a 118-inch wheelbase, it was 210.2 inches long overall, with a curb weight of 3,715 pounds in its basic version. Such low weight made for excellent performance and roadholding, and both were strong points in the Grand Prix.

Its power unit was a V-8 of 400 cubic-inch displacement, basically similar to the engine used in the 1957 Bonneville. With a compression ratio of 10.5:1, it had a maximum output of 350 hp at 5,000 rpm (mainly as the fruits of GTO experience), fed by a single Rochester four-barrel carburetor.

It had a top speed of 121 mph, and would go from standstill to 60 mph in 9 seconds flat. Fuel consumption varied between 12.8 and 18.0 miles to the gallon. A 428-cubic inch version was listed as optional, with outputs of 370 and 390 hp.

The car was built exclusively as a two-door hardtop and the body was instantly recognizable as a Pontiac product from any angle. Aerodynamically, it was above average, with clean body sides, concealed windshield wipers, and a blunt front having the bumper integrated with the grille, and headlights mounted where they did not add to frontal area or protrude into the airstream.

From the long hood to the cockpit-type interior, the car had terrific personality, and it looked like a lot more money than its $3,866 baseline sticker price.

The new concept for the Grand Prix was due to Benjamin W. Harrison, who was in charge of special projects at Pontiac in 1967. He wrote a memo to John Z. De Lorean, the general manager, who gave it the highest priority and started a crash program to get it ready in time for the 1969 model year.

The concept was brilliant in its simplicity: Take the Le Mans frame in its long-wheelbase (four-door) version, with the rear half of the two-door version of the Fisher A-body. Therefore the extra length within the wheelbase was added ahead of the windshield base, which meant a longer hood. De Lorean wanted a much, much longer hood, and Jack Humbert and Irvin Rybicki in the Pontiac studio came up with an extremely bold front end design which added considerably to the front overhang as well. To Fisher, it became the G-body (Fig. 9-3).

The engine remained set on the front wheel axis, so that weight distribution was kept within normal bounds. The Grand Prix carried 54 percent of the weight on the front wheels, at a time

Fig. 9-3. The 1970 Pontiac Grand Prix.

when several other high performance cars went as far as 57 percent.

De Lorean was himself an engineer, gifted with great technical imagination as well as a strong sense of marketing. He had come to Pontiac in 1956 from Packard, where he was a research engineer, and worked on Pontiac's advanced projects (such as the original Tempest) before he was named chief engineer in 1961, succeeding Pete Estes as general manager four years later.

His personal attention is evident throughout the Grand Prix, and his youthful ideals are reflected in the kind of car it was. It handled like a sports car, and compared with the Riviera, ride comfort had been sacrificed in favor of improved traction and superb roadholding. The rear suspension was not free of harshness, but the joy of having such positive control over the car was more important to most of the people who bought it.

The detail engineering and development was entrusted to Stephen P. Malone, who had replaced De Lorean as chief engineer in 1965. He began his career as an electrical engineer, graduating from Ohio State University and joining Delco Products in his native Dayton in 1940. From 1942 to 1945 he was a pilot in the U.S. Air Corps, and at the end of the war he returned to Delco, where he worked as a staff engineer until he applied for transfer to Pontiac in 1956.

His first job at Pontiac was as chassis development engineer, becoming assistant chassis engineer in 1960, and assistant chief engineer in charge of body and styling in 1963.

Because the Grand Prix was made almost entirely from standard components, Pontiac easily got corporate approval for its production, and it was a great success. Sales almost doubled, from under 50,000 in 1968 to just short of 93,000 cars in 1969.

No big changes were made for 1970, the most significant being the availability of a bigger version of the V-8 engine, with a displacement of 455 cubic inches. It delivered 370 hp at 4,600 rpm with a compression ratio of 10.25:1, a single four-barrel carburetor and dual exhausts.

Though the standard transmission for the Grand Prix was a manual three-speed with column shift, most 1969 models were equipped with Turbo-Hydra-matic drive, and a console-mounted selector styled to look like a stickshift. The open double-jointed propeller shaft took the drive to the rear axle, which was located by a four-link suspension system incorporating coil springs and telescopic shock absorbers. The front suspension was taken from the GTO, with unequal-length control arms, coil springs, and stabilizer bar. Standard brakes used drums on all four wheels, but front discs were available as an extra cost option.

John De Lorean went to Chevrolet in 1969 and took the G-body concept with him, and that resulted in the arrival of the Chevelle-based Monte Carlo in 1970. Pontiac's new general manager, F. James McDonald, continued the Grand Prix with strictly minor body modifications through 1972.

For the following year, Fisher began production of a new A-body, which naturally affected the G-body's construction. The Grand Prix became wider, heavier and despite the difference in wheelbase and proportions, it was more difficult for the stylists to set it apart from the Le Mans.

Sales soared to over 144,000 units in 1973, dropped below 100,000 in 1974 and 1975, during the first wave of fuel shortages, but recovered to set new records of nearly 235,000 cars a year in 1976 and 1977.

For 1978, the Grand Prix was downscaled and made to share the standard A-body with the rest of the Le Mans series. The biggest engine was a 301 cubic-inch V-8 rated at 135 hp (140 hp with dual exhaust), giving 18 mpg in the EPA urban driving cycle and 25 mpg on the highway. A nice car in many ways, but devoid of the past greatness associated with the name Grand Prix.

99 PONTIAC GRAND AM, 1973

Another Pontiac! Whither greatness? The facts not only support this selection, but show that no other candidate can be deemed acceptable. What was it with Pontiac in these years that made its products so outstanding?

Pontiac repeatedly demonstrated a flexibility in its product planning, and a capacity for continuous readjustment to the realities of motoring life in the United States that was either lacking elsewhere, or the other car makers were far behind in responding to.

Product planning at the other GM car divisions was less inspired, abdicating more and more of their initiative to corporate groups and task forces. At Ford, the evolution was regressive, as the company's high-class cars (Lincoln, Continental, and Thunderbird) grew into grotesque caricatures.

Chrysler was hoplessly outpaced. The Cordoba, when it finally came, did not have a chance at either greatness or commercial success. The corporation could no longer afford to build a special body for the Imperial and was unable to make the standard shell look different enough from the New Yorker to assure its survival. It was dead by 1975.

There was a different spirit at Pontiac. Perhaps it came in with Bunkie Knudsen. It certainly grew under De Lorean, and it went on long after he had moved further up in the organization. Jim McDonald was not afraid of loading responsibility on young men, challenging their ability to think along new lines, and encouraging them to find better solutions in every field. In engineering, Steve Malone organized his staff to get his people involved, and to get maximum benefit from their engagement.

We shall see how this worked in the case of the Grand Am of 1973. When the top brass at GM gave the green light for new intermediates for all divisions back in 1967, new rules were laid down for the design, development and production. The whole project was controlled by a corporate task force, and each division was given responsibility for certain areas.

Buick was the expert on brakes, Chevrolet on suspension and frame-and-body structures, Oldsmobile on steering, and Pontiac on vehicle handling. Each division still made its own engines independently.

The corporate-design intermediates were originally intended for 1972, but a strike in the fall of 1970 delayed their progress for one full year, coming out as 1973 models.

One basic body shell was to be shared between the Chevelle, Le Mans, Cutlass and Century, with two wheelbases, 112 inches for all two-door cars and 116 for all four-door models (Fig. 9-4). All cars had the same frames and suspension systems, the same brakes and steering gear. The divisions could make variations only in such things as wheels, tires, spring rates, shock absorber valving, steering-gear ratios, and type of steering wheel.

The divisional styling studios had an unenviable task, for they were locked into a set of basic proportions, a fixed floor pan and the same dimensions between cowl and backlight base, the same windshield rake, the same door size, and many more items. Their freedom was restricted to front and rear ends, lights and bumpers, and to some extent, the exterior sheet metal for doors and fenders (Fig. 9-5).

Differences between the basic Le Mans and the Chevelle were therefore only skin-deep. But Pontiac added one special model within the Le Mans series which used whatever freedom existed to the fullest, all in a well-coordinated scheme that made the Grand Am a truly great car.

Fig. 9-4. The 1973 Pontiac Granc Am sedan.

It was developed by William T. Collins, who had worked briefly at Pontiac in 1954 between his graduation from Lehigh University and his entering military service. He returned to Pontiac in 1958 after two years on the engineering staff of an automotive supplier firm, and worked on the original Tempest. Later, he was assigned to advanced projects, worked in production engineering, and rose to the rank of assistant chief engineer.

Collins had always worked to make Pontiacs great road cars, and did a lot to make the GTO steer and hold the road, instead of being just another hot-rod. He designed and developed a small roadster that was rejected in favor of a Pontiac version (Firebird) of the Chevrolet Camaro, and worked hard to put some real Pontiac traits into the Firebird chassis.

Now he started a project to convert the Le Mans into a high-performance family car of distinction. He chose the biggest engine, the 455 cubic-inch V-8, with Turbo-Hydra-matic drive. Rated net output was 250 hp at 4,000 rpm, and the car, despite its 3,960-pounds curb weight, was a fantastic performer, with a rich, throaty exhaust note. The suspension had nothing in common with the GTO, for Collins left the standard coil springs in place, but completely reworked the shock damping, reinforced the front stabilizer bar, added one behind the rear axle, and fitted 70-series 15-inch tires on wide-rim light-alloy wheels. The result was a car with a superb ride in combination with cornering ability in the Riviera tradition. It was a revelation.

The Grand Am had looks to match its performance. Within the permitted framework Pontiac's styling studio, where William L. Porter was chief designer, succeeded in creating a new and unique theme. Jack Humbert had been placed in charge of coordinating the Buick, Olds, and Pontiac studios in 1968, and played a supervisory role in the shaping of the Grand Am.

Bill Porter came from the corporate advanced-design studio and had formerly worked on Chevrolet styling. He was perhaps inspired by Bob Andrews's design for the front end of the 1953-54 Studebaker, for the Grand Am had a split grille with a protruding bow-shaped center piece.

Collins was able to use the instrument panel and controls from the Grand Prix, reinforcing the performance orientation of the Grand Am. Bodies were built in both coupe and sedan versions, on standard wheelbases. The Grand Am coupe had a base price of $4,178 and the sedan was listed at $4,267.

The Grand Am continued unchanged except for superficial cosmetic touches in 1974. Then Pontiac killed it, victim of the fuel crisis. When the downsized A-body went into production in 1979, Pontiac revived the Grand Am nameplate for models powered by an economy-tuned V-six engine.

Bill Collins left Pontiac in 1974 to lead the GM task forced that developed the new B- and C-body cars for 1977, but parted from the corporation in 1976 to sign up with John De Lorean in his new venture to build the De Lorean sports car. Before long, however, Collins accepted an invitation to join American Motors and work with Roy Lunn on advanced projects.

100. BUICK RIVIERA S, 1979

No car entering the project stage after the first fuel-shock of 1973-74 can be recognized as possessing greatness if it's heavy, bigger than its intended payload can justify, or wasteful of fuel. Thus our definition of greatness again takes a turn, this time towards efficiency in all aspects of production and operation.

To reach greatness despite this reordering of priorities was something that called for drastically new solutions, and the Buick Riviera has two of them: A turbocharged engine, and front wheel drive.

The turbocharger allows the use of a small-displacement engine, with a power reserve that consumes nothing when it is not

Fig. 9-5. The 1973 Pontiac Grand Am coupe.

being tapped. It is a lightweight and fairly inexpensive method for (1) shrinking engine size and weight without loss of power, or (2) obtaining a 30 to 50 percent boost in maximum power without increasing the size and weight of the engine.

Front wheel drive works in the interest of greater efficiency by eliminating the long propeller shaft and heavy rear axle. That saves raw materials, cost, and weight. It allows a flatter floor, better seating accommodation and a roomier trunk, within reduced overall dimensions, and makes for a vehicle with a lower center of gravity. When cars are being downsized, any gain in space utilization is important, and the use of front wheel drive plays no small part in that regard.

Buick had been working on turbocharging since 1975, and General Motors was formulating plans for a major conversion to front wheel drive. The two key elements of the Riviera's greatness came together in 1979.

Cadillac and Oldsmobile had been preparing downsized versions of their front wheel drive Eldorado and Toronado since 1974. The Riviera shared the Fisher E-body with these models, and thus it made sense from a manufacturing viewpoint to switch the Riviera to front wheel drive.

Buick had built the Riviera on a 119-inch wheelbase from 1966 through 1970, and then went to a new E-body for 1971, with a new perimeter-frame chassis and a 122-inch wheelbase. A downsized Riviera appeared as an interim solution in 1978, with a 115.9-inch wheelbase. Then came the front wheel drive model on a 114-inch wheelbase for 1979 (Fig. 9-6).

The engineering of the new Riviera was directed by Lloyd Reuss, who took over as chief engineer of Buick in 1975. He was transferred from Chevrolet, where he had started as an experimental engineer, served as executive engineer for the Vega, and risen to the post of head of forward planning.

He is the sort of an engineer who really has the big overview of the industry and its situation vis-a-vis the consumer, its employees, its shareholders, and the government, and can translate his conclusions directly into product changes. The Riviera is one of several examples of what he accomplished in his three years at Buick. Before he returned to Chevrolet in 1978 as the division's director of engineering, he had turned Buick's faltering product line into a team of winners.

In contrast to the new Toronado and Eldorado, in which the standard engines were still V-8's, the Riviera was equipped with

Buick's own V-six engine in its turbocharged version, which was improved from that introduced a year earlier for the Century Turbo Coupe.

Both had the new crankshaft with individual crankpin and even firing intervals. The 1979 edition of the 231 cubic-inch 90 degree V-six had new cylinder heads, new intake manifold, new camshaft, new exhaust manifolds, and new carburetors, all of which earned it the description of a "free-breathing" engine.

All turbocharger work was led by Herb Fishel, who had joined Chevrolet in 1963 after graduating from South Carolina State University. Starting as a draftsman, he became one of Chevrolet's top men on heavy-duty engine design—Reuss brought him to Buick in 1976.

Power output for the Riviera S engine was raised to 185 hp at 4,200 rpm, which gave the 3,950-pound car a top speed in excess of 100 mph. Acceleration times from standstill were 6,8 seconds to 50 mph and 9.5 seconds to 60 mph. Getting from zero to 100 mph was a matter of 40 seconds. Fuel mileage averaged between 14.5 and 19 miles per gallon, all depending on conditions.

For its front wheel drive arrangement, the Riviera inherited the Oldsmobile solution. A Turbo-Hydramatic was split in two, carrying the torque converter in the normal position on the end of the crankshaft, and the planetary gearings alongside, reversing the shaft rotation as it took the drive forward to the differential.

Fig. 9-6. Buick's 1979 Riviera S, with turbocharging.

Four-wheel independent suspension was used, with coil springs all around, and trailing arms carrying the rear wheel hubs. Stabilizer bars were fitted at both ends to restrict body roll, and Delco automatic level control was standard. The Riviera S had stiffer springs and firmer shock absorber settings than the standard model. Power steering was standard, geared for an even three turns lock to lock, with a turn diameter of 39.2 feet.

Four-wheel disc brakes were optional with ventilated rotors both front and rear, and power assist by vacuum servo. GR70-15 tires were mounted on steel disc wheels.

The task of styling the new Riviera received the personal attention of Irvin Rybicki, who succeeded Mitchell as GM design vice president in 1978. He brought back the landau-type roof for a lot of cars, including the Riviera where it clashed violently with the overall styling theme. A full-glass hatchback would have been prettier, but would have been heavier and added to the cost.

The complete car had a base price of $10,374, which put it above the Thunderbird but well below the Continental Mark IV and face-to-face with the Chrysler Cordoba and the Oldsmobile Toronado.

Of them all, the Riviera is the one that best epitomizes current engineering trends in the luxury-car class. It provides a fitting finale for a review of 100 of America's greatest cars of all time.

Index

Index

351